SOMMAIRE

MÉTHODES

PROGRAMME : UE 12 • ANGLAIS APPLIQUÉ AUX AFFAIRES

Programme du diplôme de comptabilité et de gestion (DCG)
Décret n° 2006-1706 du 22 décembre 2006. *JO* du 29 décembre 2006 complété par l'arrêté du 8 mars 2010, *BO* du 18 mars 2010, abrogeant l'arrêté du 22 décembre 2006, *JO* du 29 décembre 2006.

Niveau L : 150 heures – 12 ECTS

1. Thèmes économiques et sociaux
Les chocs pétroliers et leurs conséquences
Les traits contemporains des échanges internationaux
La place des firmes multinationales
La globalisation des marchés
La constitution d'espaces économiques régionaux (Union européenne, ALENA)
La montée en puissance des pays asiatiques
Les technologies de l'information et de la communication
L'aménagement du temps de travail
L'évolution de la protection sociale
La concurrence et le droit
2. L'entreprise
Les formes juridiques de l'entreprise (française)
L'organisation de l'entreprise
Les grandes fonctions de l'entreprise
Les partenaires de l'entreprise (fournisseurs, clients, banques)
La création d'entreprise
La stratégie de l'entreprise
L'analyse des performances de l'entreprise
La communication interne et externe de l'entreprise

Indications complémentaires

Le candidat doit montrer une connaissance suffisante de la langue (niveau B2 du cadre commun de référence) pour :
- comprendre et commenter, en anglais, des documents de la vie des affaires tels que des textes, graphiques et tableaux tirés de revues ou d'un rapport annuel d'entreprise ;
- rédiger une note de synthèse, en français ou en anglais, à partir de documents en anglais concernant la vie des affaires ;
- rédiger, en anglais, un document commercial de base (lettre, devis, bon de commande).

MODE D'EMPLOI

Les 18 chapitres correspondent aux thèmes du programme officiel du diplôme de comptabilité et gestion (DCG) niveau L pour l'épreuve n° 12 de l'anglais appliqué aux affaires.

Chaque chapitre est organisé en trois parties.

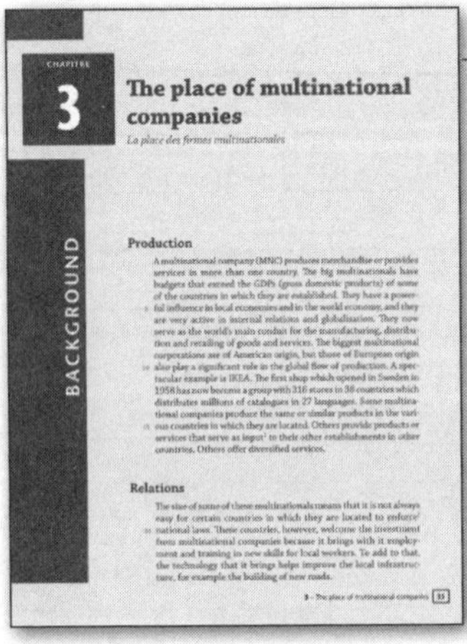

- Le texte de la partie « Background » contient des informations détaillées et du vocabulaire sur le thème du chapitre.
  Les traductions des termes peu connus et/ou importants sont données.
  Un travail de repérage des notions essentielles aboutissant sur un résumé du texte guide la compréhension approfondie et aide à la mémorisation.
  Des suggestions de recherches personnelles sur le thème du chapitre incitent à approfondir la question.

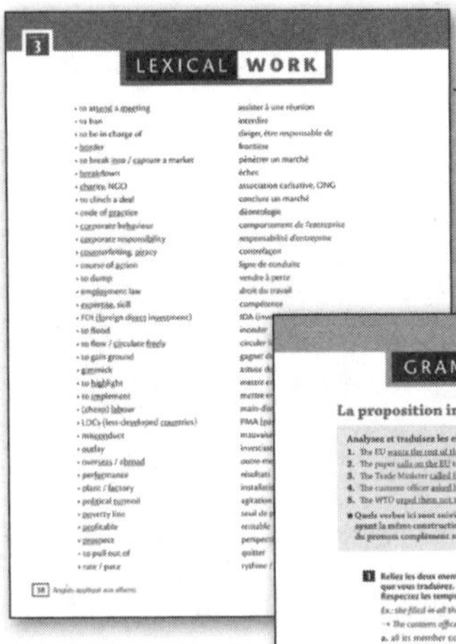

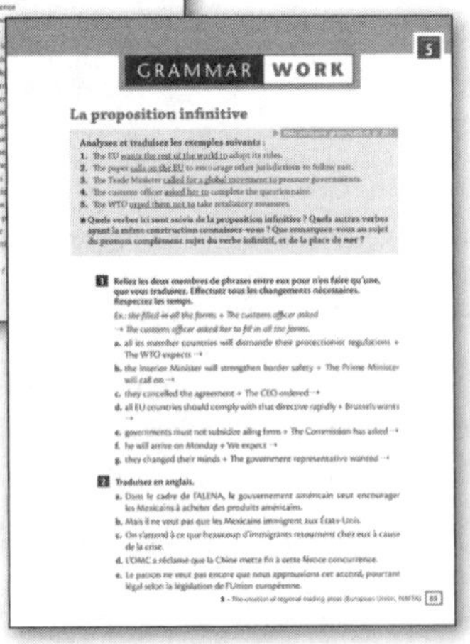

- Le travail linguistique porte sur :
  – l'enrichissement lexical, à partir d'une liste de vocabulaire et d'exercices d'application ; c'est l'objet du « Lexical work » ;
  – le perfectionnement de la maîtrise grammaticale, avec des exemples, des renvois à l'Aide-mémoire grammatical et des exercices de manipulation et de traduction ; c'est l'objet du « Grammar work ».

EXAM WORK

Trading in the European Union

La préparation à l'examen, « Exam Work », repose sur des ensembles documentaires variés, semblables à ceux qui sont proposés à l'épreuve.

Chaque document donne lieu à des questions de lecture approfondie et des questions de compréhension diverses (résumé et/ou traduction, etc.).

Chaque ensemble documentaire donne lieu à un exercice de COMPRÉHENSION, à rédiger en français ou en anglais, à une note de synthèse guidée par une ou plusieurs questions et à un ou plusieurs exercices d'EXPRESSION en anglais sur le modèle des épreuves de l'examen.

À la fin de l'ouvrage :

AIDE-MÉMOIRE GRAMMATICAL

FICHE 1 Articles

1. L'article défini : THE

2. L'article ∅

Les 24 fiches de l'**Aide-mémoire grammatical** traitent de façon claire et synthétique les principales difficultés de l'anglais des affaires et les points traités dans les chapitres.

MÉTHODES

Describing charts[1] and tables[2]

Une partie **Méthodes** apporte des conseils pour l'examen et la pratique de l'anglais des affaires, en anglais ou en français.

CHAPITRE

1

Oil crises and their consequences

Les chocs pétroliers et leurs conséquences

BACKGROUND

Oil prices vary according to the supply and demand, and depend on the type and quality of oil. Several reference prices are now used: Saudi Light, WTI (West Texas Intermediate) or Brent (from the North Sea), which creates confusion. One thing is clear: there are crises[1] when there are shortages and/or when prices increase a lot suddenly.

A brief history of the oil crises

1973: Although there had been oil and energy crises before, the first major global crisis took the world by surprise that year. The price of crude oil[2] quadrupled in just a few weeks from $4 to $12 a barrel[3], which seemed enormous at the time. The Organization of Petroleum Exporting Countries (OPEC) suddenly decided to stop shipping[4] crude to the countries that supported Israel during the Yom Kippur war, and to raise its prices in general.

1979: Second major oil crisis due to the Islamic Revolution in Iran which reduced production and raised prices.

1990: The third oil crisis, due to the Gulf War, was milder[5] and shorter. The price of oil shot up[6] to $50 a barrel.

Afterwards, there were ups and downs, but on average[7] the price of oil was down to $25 a barrel.

2007-2008: The world was hit by wild fluctuations, which led to price hikes[8] reaching $150. This sudden oil crisis was mostly due to growing demand from emerging countries like China and India, but also to manipulations.

2008-2011: Prices went on fluctuating, but less wildly, as the economy slowed down in many parts of the world. Future prices are unpredictable, thus increasing widespread confusion.

Consequences of oil crises

When oil prices fall, this is obviously good for most economies because it helps to reduce transport costs and, quite often, the prices of other commodities[9] and products too.

Between 1985 and 2007, this contributed to low inflation rates, and sometimes deflation, all over the world which, on average, enjoyed a high growth rate that reached a peak in 2006.

The downside[10] was that there was then little or no incentive[11] to reduce energy consumption or to develop alternative sources of energy. People started to squander[12] oil again, which meant pollution and the increasing production of CO_2, a by-product[13] of burning fossil fuels. The public eventually became aware[14] of the problem of greenhouse gases[15] that cause climate warming[16] with its dire[17] effects.

After 2008, most developed countries experienced economic slowdowns for various reasons, which reduced demand and contributed to the relative stability of prices.

When oil prices go up, transport costs follow suit[18], as well as[19] those of other commodities. This has an adverse effect on international trade, economic growth and people's living standards[20], at least in the short term. It can lead to speculation, recession and even food riots[21]. The sectors that mostly profit from such hikes are the OPEC countries and oil companies, which make record profits.

On the other hand, oil consumption goes down, which is good for the environment. People suddenly start remembering that oil wells and oil fields are not bottomless, even if there are still oil reserves for a certain while[22]. Oil prices may fluctuate irrationally, but are bound to go up and up[23] in the long run.

In either case, the heavy dependence of the oil consuming countries on the oil producing countries has a significant impact on world politics and economic growth. For all these reasons, research in alternative sources of energy is a must.

Solutions: alternative sources of energy

Other fossil fuels are natural gas (which is cleaner than oil, but is also in limited supply), and coal, of which some countries have huge reserves but which is dirty and highly polluting.

Nuclear energy: clean and relatively cheap, but controversial for various reasons. France has many nuclear plants. Some other countries are building more of them.

Solar energy: useful, especially for heating individual houses, and renewable. But it cannot power all transport and factories.

Wind power: renewable too, but only possible in windy areas and windy periods. It is therefore unreliable.

Geothermal energy: renewable, but it cannot be produced in many places and has a limited use.

Biofuels (made from agricultural plants, like vegetable oil, corn-starch, etc.). Fuel plants are renewable but grown to the detriment of food plants, which leads to higher prices and shortages of food in some countries.

Fuel cells[24]: car makers have been investing a lot in research, but the results have been disappointing so far.

The electric vehicle or EV has recently become a more promising and popular alternative to the petrol-driven one: it uses energy stored in rechargeable batteries. The hybrid car is fuelled by petrol/gasoline, and uses a battery to improve efficiency. But both are expensive, and consume energy, even if they are not a source of pollution or of carbon dioxide (CO_2) emissions.

Indeed, these alternative sources, even the renewable ones, are not likely to replace oil for years to come. So, the best way to try and forestall[25] – or at least delay other crises in the future – before it finally runs out[26] is to save energy. Don't forget to switch off[27] the light when you no longer need it!

1. *Crises:* pluriel de *crisis:* crise.
2. *Crude (oil):* (pétrole) brut.
3. *Barrel:* baril (159 litres).
4. *To ship:* transporter.
5. *Mild:* modéré.
6. *To shoot (shot, shot) up:* monter en flèche.
7. *On average:* en moyenne.
8. *Hike:* augmentation.
9. *Commodity:* produit de base.
10. *Downside:* inconvénient.
11. *Incentive:* encouragement.
12. *To squander:* gaspiller.
13. *By-product:* sous-produit.
14. *To become aware:* prendre conscience.
15. *Greenhouse gases:* gaz à effet de serre.
16. *Climate warming:* réchauffement climatique.
17. *Dire:* désastreux.
18. *To follow suit:* faire de même.
19. *As well as:* de même que.
20. *Living standards:* niveau de vie.
21. *Riot:* émeute.
22. *A certain while:* un certain temps.
23. *To be bound to go up and up:* aller forcément en montant.
24. *Fuel cell:* pile à combustible.
25. *To forestall :* prévenir.
26. *To run out:* s'épuiser.
27. *To switch off:* éteindre.

REPÉRER LES NOTIONS ESSENTIELLES

Answer the following questions with the help of the text.

a. What is OPEC?
b. How many big oil crises were there in the last forty years?
c. Describe several positive consequences of falling oil prices.
d. Describe several negative consequences of rising oil prices.
e. Why is oil consumption important in world politics and for growth?
f. Can you name three clean sources of energy?
g. What sources of energy are renewable?
h. What is recommended at the end of the text and why?

Résumer le texte en français

Faites un résumé de ce texte en *100 mots environ*.

Approfondir

Answer the following questions, using the Internet or other documents.

- **a.** Which countries currently belong to OPEC? Which other oil producing countries do not belong to it?
- **b.** Why is nuclear energy controversial?
- **c.** What else can be done to save energy?
- **d.** What is the current price of the barrel of oil, and what is the situation like today?
- **e.** Do you know of any other alternative source of energy: which one?

LEXICAL WORK

• to agree	se mettre d'accord
• agreement	accord
• to bottom out	atteindre son plus bas niveau
• to clinch / do a deal	conclure / passer un accord
• to cut / reduce	réduire / baisser
• deal	transaction / accord
• to diversify	diversifier / se diversifier
• to dwindle / drop / decrease	diminuer
• energy bill	facture énergétique
• energy needs	besoins énergétiques
• energy provider / supplier	fournisseur d'énergie
• to fill up	faire le plein
• fuel	carburant / combustible
• fuel efficient / economical vehicle	véhicule économique / sobre
• gas guzzler (US) / car very heavy on petrol	voiture gourmande
• gas oil / fuel oil / diesel oil	gazole
• gas pipeline	gazoduc
• to go down / fall / drop	diminuer / baisser
• heavy / light oil / petroleum	pétrole lourd / léger
• to hold reserves	détenir des réserves
• hybrid / petrol / diesel engine	moteur à essence / diesel / hybride
• hydrocarbon	hydrocarbure
• to level off	se stabiliser
• Middle East	Moyen-Orient
• mileage (of fuel)	consommation (de carburant) au kilomètre
• to negotiate	négocier
• negotiations	négociations
• nuclear waste	déchets nucléaires
• oil riches	richesses pétrolières
• oil shipment / delivery	livraison de pétrole
• oil spill	marée noire
• oil tanker	pétrolier
• oil well / field / platform	puits / champ / plate-forme pétrolière
• to peak	atteindre un sommet
• Persian Gulf	golfe Persique
• petrochemical (product)	produit pétrochimique
• pipeline	oléoduc
• power	énergie

• proven reserves	réserves confirmées / prouvées
• to push prices up	faire grimper les prix
• shale oil	schistes bitumineux
• shortage	pénurie
• sluggish / upward / downward demand	demande molle / en hausse / en baisse
• spot market / price	marché / prix au comptant
• stable / volatile prices	prix stables / instables
• supply	approvisionnement
• to supply	approvisionner
• tank	citerne
• tar	goudron
• two star petrol (GB), regular gas(oline) (US)	essence ordinaire
• windfarm	parc d'éoliennes
• windmill	éolienne

USE THE LIST

1 Fill in the gaps with words from the list, making the necessary changes, then translate the sentences:

a. At last, oil prices seem to have d...: this is good news.

b. With the latest petrol price hikes, we now have to buy f... e... cars now.

c. There is a big controversy about building a new p... across Alaska.

d. There will be dire oil s... when the p... r... bottom out in 42 years.

e. We should n... with our suppliers to get a better d... in view of all the recent changes.

f. They will have to raise their prices because of their heavier e... b... .

g. My car t... is empty: I need to f... u... at the nearest petrol station.

h. Big oil companies have recently p... u... their prices because of the u... d... from developing countries.

i. Prices have just gone up again on the s... m... in Rotterdam.

2 Choose five other words in the list which you think are important and write sentences with them, with the help of a dictionary or the Internet if necessary.

GRAMMAR WORK

L'utilisation de *the*

▶ Aide-mémoire grammatical, p. 227.

Analysez et traduisez les exemples suivants :

1. The price of crude oil.
2. The countries that supported Israel.
3. The world.
4. The economy.
5. Oil prices.
6. Climate warming.
7. The environment.

■ **Pourquoi *the* est-il tantôt présent, tantôt absent là où, en français, l'article défini est présent ?**

1 **Ajoutez si nécessaire *the* dans les phrases suivantes :**

a. ... oil is produced in many countries of ... Persian Gulf.
b. ... oil crisis of 1973 was triggered by ... Yom Kippur war between ... Israel and its neighbours such as ... Egypt.
c. ... crude (oil) produced in that country is very heavy.
d. ... oil field that has just been found in ... Brazil is bound to bring ... oil prices down.
e. Do you know ... latest price of ... Saudi light?
f. I wonder if it is possible to cut ... energy needs of ... world.
g. Unfortunately ... reserves of ... fossil fuels are limited, in varying degrees.
h. On ... other hand, ... renewable energies are inexhaustible, by definition.
i. ... chemical industry also needs ... oil to produce such things as ... fertilizers and ... plastics.
j. ... competition is growing around ... world for ... commodities and raw materials.
k. ... world economy is paying ... price of ... expensive oil.
l. In fact ... petrol today is not more expensive than in 1980.

Le présent simple ou progressif

▶ Aide-mémoire grammatical, p. 254.

Analysez et traduisez les exemples suivants :

1. They help to reduce oil consumption.

2. Other countries are building more of them.

2 **Mettez les verbes entre parenthèses au présent simple ou progressif selon le cas.**

a. SIT is an American firm which *(make)* solar-powered equipment.

b. Mr Hertz, its managing director, *(complain)* that the development of renewable energy *(depend)* on irrational political decisions.

c. However, some Californian politicians *(try)* to change that.

d. They *(want)* to subsidize the solar industry more efficiently.

e. But the problem is that now such companies *(hire)* lobbyists to get even more subsidies.

f. In fact, as the industry *(grow)* at present, politicians *(grant / give)* more and more subsidies, but they may stop it one day.

g. Mr Hertz *(believe)* that firms should make affordable and environmentally friendly products.

h. He *(say)* that is just what his company now *(do)*.

i. It *(make)* cheap, portable power sources that *(sell)* very well at the moment.

j. He *(hope)* that many potential customers will buy his products.

k. And he *(hire)* scientists to create new and more efficient products.

l. What *(count)*, he *(say)*, is to make products that people *(buy)*.

3 **Traduisez les phrases suivantes en anglais.**

a. Le prix du gaz naturel augmente aussi vite actuellement que celui du gazole.

b. Il affirme que la production mondiale de pétrole ne diminuera jamais.

c. Le pétrole joue le même rôle dans la croissance économique de nombreux pays que le charbon autrefois.

d. Lorsque la demande pour un produit augmente, cela fait monter le prix de ce produit, et également ceux d'autres produits.

e. Croyez-vous que les réserves pétrolières prouvées soient actuellement à leur maximum ?

f. Beaucoup de gens critiquent l'exploitation des schistes bitumineux car elle pourrait être extrêmement polluante.

EXAM WORK

DOCUMENT 1

Oil reserves

End 2010, billion barrels

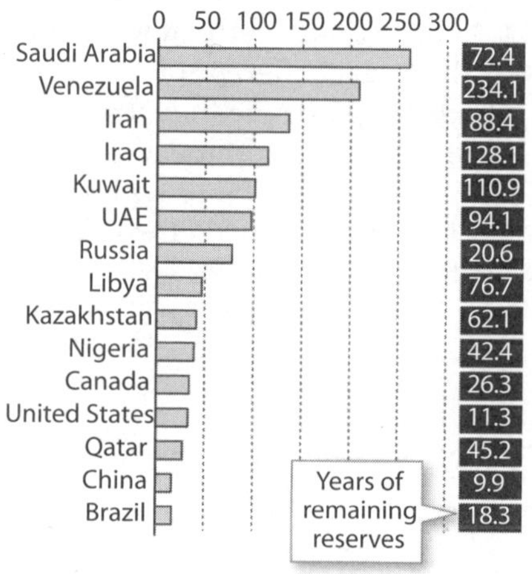

According to BP, an oil company, the world's known reserves of oil rose by 6.6 billion barrels during 2010, as increases in reserves in Brazil, India, Russia, Colombia, Uganda and Ghana outstripped[1] declines in Mexico and Norway. This brought the amount of oil that could, in theory, be extracted under existing technological and economic conditions to 1.38 trillion barrels. Over half the world's oil reserves are in the Middle East, with Saudi Arabia having just under a fifth of the global total. If China continued to pump out oil at the rate it did last year, it would exhaust[2] its reserves in under a decade. In contrast, Venezuela could keep pumping oil at its current[3] pace[4] for another two centuries and still have some left over[5].

The Economist, June 9th 2011.

1. *To outstrip:* dépasser. **2.** *To exhaust:* épuiser. **3.** *Current:* actuel. **4.** *Pace:* rythme. **5.** *Left over:* restant.

1 **Answer the following questions in English.**

a. When was this document published, and what does it show?

b. What does it say about the world's proven reserves?

c. Compare the situation between two very different countries, using them as examples.

d. In conclusion, is there reason for optimism or pessimism?

2 **COMPRÉHENSION. Après avoir observé ce graphique et son commentaire, puis répondu aux questions, rédigez une note de synthèse en *100 mots environ* sur l'ensemble du document.**

DOCUMENT 2

The key to the future of energy in the 21st century

[Tony Hayward, Group Chief Executive of British Petroleum, gave a speech at the 13th Asia Oil and Gas conference in Malaysia on June 9, 2008. This is his conclusion.]

"Ladies and gentlemen

In my view, the responsibility of addressing the issues[1] of supply and climate change lies with both the industry and governments. I guess if I had to summarize it all in one word it would be **invest**. We need to invest in new technology, to invest in new capability[2] and to invest in new forms of Alternative Energy. The best way we can do that is by working together, by creating new reciprocal relationships throughout[3] the industry, while also recognizing the importance of markets. Only through major investments in new projects and new technology can we bring on those new supplies and develop the new technologies required to tackle[4] climate change. The key to new investment is to make the market work by getting the conditions right. Our industry is 150 years old. It's been at the forefront of[5] human progress over that entire time – without it, the world would be a very different place. BP has been at the heart of the industry for 100 years. The challenges of today are as great as any we have been faced with in our history. I am confident[6] that we can provide the energy the world is going to need to sustain it for the next 100 years.

Ladies and gentlemen, thank you very much."

www.bp.com/press, June 2008.

1. *To address an issue:* aborder un problème. **2.** *Capability:* capacité. **3.** *Throughout:* partout dans. **4.** *To tackle:* s'attaquer à un problème. **5.** *At the forefront of:* à la pointe de. **6.** *Confident:* sûr, confiant.

3 **Find the expressions or words in the text that mean:**

a. to deal with something which is new and difficult

b. to sum up

c. to supply

d. the way to achieve something.

DOCUMENT 3

Rigging the market[1]

Business is set[2] to boom for the firms that help oil companies get at their prize.

When the price of oil goes up, oil firms drill[3] deeper. They also venture into harsher climes[4] and seek out unconventional sources of oil and gas that, in happier times, would be too costly to extract. National oil companies (NOCs) often lack the skills to do any of this. The world's big independent oil firms struggle[5], too. So they turn to the oil-services industry, which is set for a gusher[6] of profits. [...]

America is the centre of the boom, says James Crandell of Dahlman Rose & Co, a bank. Oil-services firms there pioneered the technique of horizontal drilling, which is used to extract shale gas from America's vast fields (conventional oil and gas are extracted using vertical wells). The same trick can be used to get at shale oil. As a result exploration and production (E&P) budgets in America are swelling.

There's more to come. Morgan Stanley, a bank, reckons[7] that shale-oil production will increase nearly fivefold[8] by 2016 to around 1.9m barrels a day. This means a huge increase in the number of rigs supplied by the oil services firms. The logistical and technological challenges of unconventional oil and deepwater drilling [...] will also boost demand. [...]

Most oil that is cheap and easy to get at has been found. Fewer and smaller discoveries mean that oil companies are forced to spend more on E&P to get at unconventional shale oil, heavy oil and tar sands as well as sinking wells[9] deep underwater. Dahlman Rose reckons that global exploration budgets will rise by some 14% in 2011, to $533 billion.

Oil-services firms have plenty of conventional work, too. Iraq is trying to boost its output. In March, Saudi Arabia, keen to maintain a buffer of spare capacity[10], said that it planned to increase its rig count by 30% by some point next year. The Saudis are not alone in their desperation to stem[11] the declining output[12] of big and ageing oil fields. This means lots more spending on technologies to arrest decline rates and on maintenance to keep older wells around the world in tip-top[13] condition. [...]

Abridged from *The Economist*
June 25, 2011.

1. Jeu de mot sur *To rig the market* (manipuler le marché) et *Oil rig* (derrick). **2.** *To be set:* être en position/bien parti. **3.** *To drill:* forer. **4.** *In harsher climes:* sous des climats plus rigoureux. **5.** *To struggle:* rencontrer des difficultés. **6.** *Gusher:* jaillissement. **7.** *To reckon:* estimer, calculer. **8.** *To increase fivefold:* quintupler. **9.** *To sink a well:* forer un puits. **10.** *Buffer of spare capacity:* réserves de production disponibles. **11.** *To stem:* endiguer. **12.** *Output:* production. **13.** *Tip-top:* au summum

4 **Complete the following expressions with words from the text, and translate them.**

a. To boost o.... . – **b.** To s... a decline. – **c.** This text is about s... o... production. – **d.** R... are necessary for deep-water d.... – **e.** Oil is sold by the b.... – **f.** The price of oil production in the US is s.... – **g.** M... work is necessary to keep rigs in good condition. – **h.** The need to invest may increase f.... .

5 **COMPRÉHENSION. Dans quelle mesure l'idée phare de Tony Hayward (document 2) s'applique-t-elle au document 3 ? (*Environ 150 mots.*)**

6 **COMPRÉHENSION. Who has published this advert, and with what objective? (Document 4 page suivante.)**

7 **COMPRÉHENSION. Vous rédigerez une note de synthèse en *250 mots environ* de ces quatre documents, montrant les causes des fluctuations, voire des crises, du secteur du pétrole, dans les pays mentionnés. Vous ferez ressortir les causes qui ont, à votre avis, les effets les plus négatifs.**

DOCUMENT 4

www.shell.com/letsgo
Détail du texte ci-contre.

How do we meet the growing energy needs of the modern world? Not just for today, but long into the future? It's a complex question to which there is no simple answer. Whatever happens collaboration is essential.

And a better mix of different, sustainable energies. At Shell we've been working with schools and universities around the world for the past 25 years on the Shell Eco-marathon – an innovative competition that challenges students to design, build and drive the most economical motorised vehicle. This year's winner achieved[2] 4,127.6km on the equivalent of one litre of fuel. It's an incredible figure. But one we hope to beat next year.

And is an example of how we're working together, to develop a mix of energies that can power and sustain all our lives long into the future. Let's broaden[3] the world's energy mix.

---

1. *To fuel:* alimenter en combustible, nourrir. 2. *To achieve:* réaliser. 3. *To broaden:* élargir.

8 **EXPRESSION. In view of these documents, of the current situation, and of any other facts you may know, are you optimistic or pessimistic about the future of oil? (*About 150 words.*)**

9 **Rédigez une lettre en anglais (*150 mots environ*) à partir des éléments suivants :** Vous êtes Mme Isabelle Fournier, directrice commerciale de la société de transports internationaux Robert Mentressangle. Vous envoyez une lettre circulaire aux services Expédition de vos clients étrangers pour leur annoncer que, à votre grand regret, votre entreprise se voit dorénavant obligée d'augmenter ses tarifs courants de 7,5 % pour les transports internationaux à partir du premier jour du mois prochain, en raison d'un accroissement de vos coûts dû à l'augmentation du prix du fuel et des frais d'entretien de vos camions. Vos autres conditions de transport restent inchangées. Vous rappelez que vos services sont particulièrement complets et performants dans toute l'Europe. Date, salutations et formules d'usage.

CHAPITRE

2

BACKGROUND

The characteristics of international trade today

Les traits contemporains des échanges internationaux

International trade is the exchange of goods, services and capital across borders. The introduction of liberal policies since World War II has boosted[1] exchanges on a global scale, all the more sharply with improvements in transport, modern production methods and NICTs (New Information and Communication Technologies) over the past decades. It is viewed as a source of economic growth as it gives firms opportunities to capture markets and expand. Countries' GDP and prosperity depend on it for a large part.

Trade regulations

Most nations had high tariffs and restrictions on international trade until the 19th century when free trade became the dominant belief among western nations.

1944: To put an end to the spiral of economic recession, protectionism and political tensions which had led up to the Second World War, the United States and Great Britain organised the Bretton Woods Conference which sought[2] to reconstruct the world monetary system through the establishment of the IMF (International Monetary Fund) and the World Bank. The monetary standard[3] for international trade became the dollar price of gold.

The WTO

In 1995, the WTO (World Trade Organisation), replacing the GATT, was set up in order to guarantee international trade agreements and the framework[4] within which these agreements were negotiated by members. It oversees[5] the rules of international trade, settles trade disputes[6] between members and organizes trade negotiations. This institution numbered 153 members in 2011. The latter meet at least every two years and have the same statutory prerogatives. Members agree to grant[7] MFN (Most Favoured Nation) status to each other in order to guarantee equal treatment in a context of competition.

The WTO is seen favourably by those who argue that it helps to raise living standards worldwide by promoting free trade and business prosperity. It is admired for its democratic functioning since all decisions are reached through negotiations and consensus.

However, it is criticized mainly because its decisions take precedence over those of local governments and benefit some countries more than others, sometimes developing countries, sometimes developed countries, depending on the arguments. It is also accused of disregarding the environment and working conditions in the poorest nations.

Free trade

Free trade is the interchange of goods and services (but not labour and capital) without the hindrance[8] of high tariffs, quotas or unilateral agreements between governments. It is based on the notion of comparative advantage, which enables businesses with the lowest costs and prices to gain a market.

The Doha rounds initiated in 2001 are trade negotiations among WTO members. They have now stalled[9] as developed and developing nations clash over the issue of lowering trade barriers and cutting subsidies, especially in agriculture.

Economically powerful nations advocate[10] free trade, which does not stop them from having recourse to selective protectionism for their strategically important industries through protective tariffs applied for example to agriculture by the United States and Europe.

Until recently, agricultural interests were in favour of free trade while manufacturing sectors supported protectionism. Now, agricultural lobbies demand special rules in the major international treaties with the result that there are more protectionist measures for agriculture than for most other goods and services.

Fair trade

Fair trade is a new concept whereby[11] trade should follow moral rules whose aim is to promote environmental sustainability[12] and fairness of trading conditions for small producers in developing countries. It is seen as an alternative to conventional international trade. It is often perceived as a political stance[13] against neo-imperialism. Various fair trade labelling organizations work together to develop this approach and organize supply chains[14] which respect their values all along the process from production to selling. Consumers in developed nations often back this approach, provided their purchasing power[15] enables them to afford fair trade products, which in most cases are tropical fruit, cocoa, tea, coffee, cotton and handicrafts[16]. However, fair trade has been accused of supporting overproduction and causing inflation in prices.

The 2008 global financial crisis

There is general agreement that the time has come to reform the financial institutions which had been set up to regulate international trade. The developing countries need improved representation when important decisions are made and there is a need for greater transparency in economic policy and in credit negotiations.

1. *To boost:* stimuler.
2. *To seek, sought:* chercher.
3. *Standard:* étalon.
4. *Framework:* cadre.
5. *To oversee:* superviser.
6. *To settle disputes:* régler des conflits.
7. *To grant:* accorder.
8. *Hindrance:* obstacle.
9. *To stall:* être au point mort.
10. *To advocate:* préconiser.
11. *Whereby:* selon lequel.
12. *Sustainability:* pérennité.
13. *Stance:* position.
14. *Supply chain:* chaîne logistique.
15. *Purchasing power:* pouvoir d'achat.
16. *Handicrafts:* produits issus de l'artisanat.

Repérer les notions essentielles

Answer the questions with the help of the text.

a. What has enabled international trade to increase enormously?

b. Why was the Bretton Woods Conference organised?

c. Why was the WTO set up?

d. What criticisms are made of the WTO and what are the arguments in favour?

e. Which countries are in favour of free trade?

f. On what issue concerning international trade is there general agreement?

Résumer le texte en français

Faites un résumé sur l'évolution des échanges internationaux à l'aide des informations ci-dessus en *150 mots environ.*

Approfondir

a. Why is it urgent to speak out for greater justice in world trade?

b. What effect has the global financial crisis of 2008 had upon international trade?

LEXICAL WORK

agreement	accord
attractive / competitive price	prix intéressant
balance of trade	balance commerciale
ban	embargo
to bargain	marchander, négocier
to barter	faire du troc
to break into a market	pénétrer un marché
breakage	casse, bris
bulk goods	marchandises en vrac
cash payment	paiement comptant
to clear goods	dédouaner des marchandises
to comply with	se conformer à, satisfaire
currency	devise
current	actuel
customs duty	droit de douane
customs procedures	formalités douanières
cutback	réduction
delay	retard
delivery time / date	délai de livraison
to dismantle	démanteler
draft	traite
to enforce	mettre en application
exchange rate	taux de change
to exceed	dépasser
export licence	licence d'exportation
export subsidies	subventions à l'exportation
to fail	échouer
fair trade	commerce équitable
forecast, prediction	prévision
foreign trade	commerce extérieur
freight rate	tarif fret
going rate	taux actuel / courant
handling	manutention
imports	importations
in time	à temps
market share	part de marché
(to) offset	compenser, compensation
on time	à la date prévue

• outsourcing	délocalisations, sous-traitance
• overseas customer	client à l'étranger
• packing, packaging	emballage
• parcel, package	colis
• (to be) profitable, to pay off	(être) rentable
• quotation	prix, devis
• to quote a price	proposer un prix
• raw material	matière première
• receipt	réception, reçu
• to run out of	manquer de, tomber à court de
• to settle	régler
• shipment	envoi
• shipping terms	conditions d'expédition
• show / fair / exhibition	salon / foire / exposition
• to smuggle	faire de la contrebande
• spoilt goods	marchandises avariées
• stake	enjeu
• to state	préciser, déclarer
• to swap	échanger
• talks	discussions, pourparlers
• target	cible, objectif
• terms	conditions
• trade barrier	barrière douanière
• trade deficit	déficit commercial
• trade surplus	excédent commercial
• unfair practice	pratique déloyale
• to work out	calculer, résoudre

USE THE LIST

1 **Complete the sentences with a word / an expression from the list, making the necessary changes, and translate the sentences.**

a. After ten hours of bargaining, they reached an … .

b. It is important that the goods ordered arrive … .

c. The factory shut down when it ran out of … .

d. We did not manage to deliver all the goods ... for the fair.

e. We were so disappointed when the talks ... .

2 **Match the following words, then use the expressions in five short sentences which you translate.**

a. to comply – **b.** value – **c.** to pay – **d.** to run – **e.** to break.

1. out of – **2.** for money – **3.** with – **4.** down – **5.** off.

GRAMMAR WORK

Le passif et « on »

Aide-mémoire grammatical, p. 252.

Analysez et traduisez les exemples suivants en employant la construction avec « on » :

1. He was given a very small office.
2. Someone left a message for you.
3. She was asked to leave.

1 **Mettez les phrases anglaises à la forme passive, ensuite traduisez-les en employant « on ».**

a. She has asked them to finish the work by tomorrow.

b. He told them that they would have to send a letter of apology.

c. Last year, they expected the increase in trade to be 5% at the most.

d. They have worked out how many cuts they would have to make.

e. We should promote international transactions on equal terms for all nations.

f. In the economically powerful nations, they advocate free trade.

g. At the next summit meeting, they will discuss fair trade.

h. Nowadays, we take the problem of trade victims very seriously.

i. We should anticipate customers' needs.

j. The advice they gave her helped her to succeed.

L'ordre des mots : la place des adverbes et expressions adverbiales et des adjectifs

▶ Aide-mémoire grammatical, p. 249.

Analysez et traduisez les exemples suivants :

1. They <u>always</u> read the financial pages in the newspaper.
2. <u>(Last week)</u>, I bought a computer <u>(last week)</u>.
3. He wants to buy <u>a big, sleek, reasonably-priced, electric</u> Japanese car.

2 Mettez les adverbes entre parenthèses au bon endroit dans la phrase.

a. He reads the financial newspaper when he arrives in the office because he has read it in the train. *(never, already)*

b. The trade agreement was adopted unanimously, to everyone's surprise. *(yesterday)*

c. Negotiations break down when everyone is expecting them to end. *(sometimes, well)*

d. The boss has organized a picnic to celebrate our good results. *(unexpectedly)*

e. He speaks two foreign languages and he will be leaving the firm to work abroad. *(very well, soon)*

3 Mettez les mots dans l'ordre correct et traduisez les phrases.

a. leather three sold I Italian beautiful expensive yesterday coats

b. week suitcase red he Chinese cheap bought plastic last a

c. shopping noisy I not in American do supermarkets overcrowded go

d. Swedish wooden a has sells large opened shop which beautiful just opened round tables.

4 Traduisez les phrases suivantes.

a. Est-ce que l'on change les devises au même taux dans les agences bancaires et dans les bureaux de change ?

b. On parle beaucoup de notre déficit en ce moment et de ce qu'on devrait faire à ce sujet.

c. Un pays comme l'Australie attire beaucoup de jeunes à la recherche d'un emploi et peut-être d'une autre façon de vivre.

d. Nous pensons exporter plus de 20 % de notre production d'ici 2016.

e. En tant que client, je m'attends à ce qu'on m'indique l'origine du produit que j'achète.

EXAM WORK

DOCUMENT 1

The greatest journey

Largely for better, sometimes for worse, our world has been defined by trade.

World trade gets a bad press: to many people globalisation seems more of a menace than an opportunity. Whether it is the threat to the environment posed by the phenomenal growth of Chinese manufacturing exports, the outsourcing of jobs by footloose[1] corporations or the re-emergence of inflation as oil heads for[2] $150 a barrel and food prices soar, trade is cast[3] as the villain[4].

By contrast, too little is heard about the positive effects of world exports that reached $14 trillion in 2006. The boost to Western living standards from all those cheap Chinese goods is taken for granted[5], while the astonishing increase in the sum of human happiness that has been wrought[6] by lifting hundreds of millions of Asians from the misery of subsistence farming into comfortable prosperity is conveniently[7] forgotten.

William Bernstein's "A Splendid Exchange" is a timely[8] and readable reminder that the desire to trade is not only one of the oldest human instincts but also the cause of many of the most important developments in our shared history. As Adam Smith observed: "The propensity[9] to truck[10], to barter[11] and exchange one thing for another is common to all men, and to be found in no other race of animals."

Mr Bernstein's purpose is to show how that trait evolved and shaped[12] the world. His story begins with Sumerian farmers who realised, some time in the third millennium BC, that the surpluses of grain generated within Mesopotamia's Fertile Crescent could be used as barter for things they did not have. Among these was copper[13] obtained from Sinai several hundred miles to the west, that could be used to make weapons[14] to repel[15] the nomadic raiders who were otherwise helping themselves to the fruits of Sumerian labour.

The author also deserves credit[16] for his willingness to take seriously the plight[17] of the victims of trade, the workers and farmers displaced by the iron rule of comparative advantage. He argues, persuasively, that it is far better to help workers affected by disruptive[18] change than it is to shield[19] industries with efficiency-destroying tariffs.

If Mr Bernstein has one overriding[20] message it is that trade "has yielded[21] not only a bounty of material good, but also of intellectual and cultural capital, an understanding of our neighbours, and a desire to sell things to others rather than to annihilate them".

Abridged from *The Economist*, July 17th, 2008.

---

1. *Footloose:* libre de toute attache. **2.** *To head for:* aller / se diriger vers. **3.** *To cast:* donner le rôle à. **4.** *Villain:* méchant, bandit. **5.** *To take for granted:* considérer tout naturel. **6.** *Wrought:* provoqué. **7.** *Conveniently:* de façon fort opportune. **8.** *Timely:* opportun. **9.** *Propensity:* tendance naturelle. **10.** *To truck:* troquer. **11.** *To barter:* échanger. **12.** *To shape:* façonner. **13.** *Copper:* cuivre. **14.** *Weapon:* arme. **15.** *To repel:* repousser. **16.** *Credit:* reconnaissance. **17.** *Plight:* situation très difficile. **18.** *Disruptive:* perturbant. **19.** *To shield:* protéger. **20.** *Overriding:* qui l'emporte sur tous les autres. **21.** *To yield:* produire, rapporter.

1 Répondez en français.

a. Que pensent beaucoup de gens du commerce international ?

b. Quels sont les effets positifs de celui-ci ?

c. Quel livre est présenté ici, et de quoi traite-t-il ?

d. Quels sont les principaux avantages et inconvénients du commerce international ?

e. Quelle solution l'auteur propose-t-il à ces problèmes ?

2 Match the following phrases and then translate the sentences.

a. As technology shrinks the globe

b. The rich countries should try to close the gap

c. Above all, the children, boys and girls alike,

d. Some people consider that it is the rich countries' duty

1. to provide food for those who are starving.

2. the need to understand other cultures becomes very important.

3. between themselves and the poor countries.

4. as well as being fed, must be educated.

3 Comment on Mr Bernstein's powerful message at the end of the text in *100 words approximately.*

DOCUMENT 2

Assessing Globalization: Benefits and Drawbacks of Trade and Integration

Globalization continues to be a divisive subject among political activists, academics[1], business leaders, and policymakers. Some look at the rapid economic and political changes taking place around the world and see injustice. Others observe these same changes and see progress.

The main economic premises[2] of globalization are generally accepted in regions throughout the world. People tend to believe their countries will benefit from trade, free enterprise, and investment by foreign companies. These views are especially common in many of the world's poorest countries, including nations in sub-Saharan Africa. However, enthusiasm for economic globalization has waned[3] considerably over the last few years in many wealthy nations, especially in Western Europe and the United States. In nations both rich and poor, however, people worry about globalization's downsides[4].

In countries throughout the world, there is broad support for key economic features of globalization. The 47-country 2007 Pew Global Attitudes survey found strong support for international trade, multinational corporations, and free

DOCUMENT 2

markets. However, the survey, conducted among representative national samples[5] in 39 countries and disproportionately urban samples in 8 countries, also found important differences across various countries and regions. Perhaps the most notable among these are the increasing signs of economic anxiety among the wealthy nations of the West.

The 2007 Pew Global poll shows that, all things considered, people consistently endorse[6] international trade. Sizeable majorities in all 47 countries said growing trade ties between countries are having a positive impact on their country. Favorable views are especially common in sub-Saharan Africa, the world's poorest region. In all 10 African countries included in the survey, over 80 percent said trade was having a positive impact.

While publics around the world generally approve of the key economic features[7] of globalization, they also have important reservations[8] about its downsides. For instance, even though they believe global trade and free markets can lead to economic growth, they realize this growth will not benefit everyone equally. As the 2007 Pew poll revealed, in many countries, there is a strong and growing concern about the gap between rich and poor.

While there are concerns that the growth associated with globalization is leaving some people behind, there are also worries about the damage growth is doing to the environment.

By Andrew Kohut, and Richard Wike, abridged from *Harvard International Review*, 2011.

---

1. *Academic:* universitaire. 2. *Premise:* hypothèse. 3. *To wane:* diminuer. 4. *Downside:* inconvénient. 5. *Sample:* échantillonnage. 6. *To endorse:* soutenir. 7. *Feature:* caractéristique. 8. *Reservation:* réserve.

4 **COMPRÉHENSION. Résumez cet article en français en *150 mots*.**

5 **Cherchez la traduction des expressions suivantes dans le texte :**

a. plus de 80 pour cent
b. dans les pays riches
c. à travers le monde
d. dans divers pays
e. parmi les militants
f. au cours des dernières années.

DOCUMENT 3

politicalcartoons.com

* *Tainted:* douteux.

6 **EXPRESSION. What opinion is expressed about fair trade in this cartoon? What motivates consumers to buy fair trade products? (*About 200 words.*)**

7 **COMPRÉHENSION. En vous appuyant sur les documents du chapitre, mettez en relief les avantages et les inconvénients de l'internationalisation des marchés. (250 *mots environ.*)**

8 **Rédigez en anglais une lettre de *150 mots environ* à partir des éléments suivants :**

Vous travaillez pour le directeur du service comptabilité d'une société française vendant des produits à une société britannique qui lui a demandé un délai de deux mois pour le paiement de la facture numéro 1727. L'entreprise britannique est cliente de votre société depuis plusieurs années mais traverse des difficultés financières en ce moment. Vous écrivez de la part du directeur qu'exceptionnellement, après étude du dossier et compte tenu de vos bonnes relations commerciales ainsi que de la régularité des paiements antérieurs, vous répondez favorablement à leur demande. Vous fixez, donc, selon leur proposition, une nouvelle échéance au 10 novembre prochain.

Date, salutations et formules d'usage.

CHAPITRE 3

The place of multinational companies

La place des firmes multinationales

BACKGROUND

Production

A multinational company (MNC) produces merchandise or provides services in more than one country. The big multinationals have budgets that exceed the GDPs (gross domestic products) of some of the countries in which they are established. They have a powerful influence in local economies and in the world economy, and they are very active in internal relations and globalisation. They now serve as the world's main conduit for the manufacturing, distribution and retailing of goods and services. The biggest multinational corporations are of American origin, but those of European origin also play a significant role in the global flow of production. A spectacular example is IKEA. The first shop which opened in Sweden in 1958 has now become a group with 316 stores in 38 countries which distributes millions of catalogues in 27 languages. Some multinational companies produce the same or similar products in the various countries in which they are located. Others provide products or services that serve as input[1] to their other establishments in other countries. Others offer diversified services.

Relations

The size of some of these multinationals means that it is not always easy for certain countries in which they are located to enforce[2] national laws. These countries, however, welcome the investment from multinational companies because it brings with it employment and training in new skills for local workers. To add to that, the technology that it brings helps improve the local infrastructure, for example the building of new roads.

Competition

In many of their dealings, the multinationals benefit from cheap labour, which reduces their costs and enables them to face the fierce competition from all around. Holding patents[3], which they have paid for, also protects them from competition, usually for up to 20 years.

Finance

Many multinationals benefit from huge financial resources with which they can fund public relations and political lobbying. Countries that are ready to welcome multinational companies compete to attract them by offering tax cuts, government help, improved infrastructures, and lax enforcement of environmental and labour requirements[4] and standards. Later, the host countries may ask for lower local prices on patented drugs or the sharing of technology knowledge.

Power

To limit the power that a multinational company may try to impose, national governments can threaten[5] to nationalise the company forcing it to sell its local assets[6] to the government or to local nationals. Local governments can make changes in local business laws and regulations which will also limit its power. The multinational company can, of course, threaten to go elsewhere, which may or may not have an effect.

Micro-multinationals

There are startups which go global very quickly. They begin by operating in different countries as small businesses, where they hire employees and market their products and services. Their growth is partly due to cheaper communications.

Business ethics

The OECD (Organization for Economic Cooperation and Development) has a list of recommendations for multinationals operating in or from countries that have adhered to the Declaration on International Investment, to remind them of the voluntary principles and standards for responsible business conduct[7]. They concern business ethics on employment, human rights, the environment, information disclosure[8], combating bribery[9], consumer interests, science and technology, competition and taxation.

There have been examples of famous brands[10] using slave labour to make products that were then sold at high prices. Fortunately, as soon as these forms of abuse were made known to the general public, the brand concerned was forced to change its policy. More and more companies are using advertising to inform the public of their ethical commitments[11] concerning human rights, climate change, various forms of pollution, etc. Besides[12] boosting the company's reputation concerning its social responsibility, it enables it to gain a foothold[13] in new markets.

1. *Input*: facteur de production.
2. *To enforce:* faire respecter.
3. *To hold a patent:* détenir un brevet.
4. *Requirement:* exigence.
5. *To threaten:* menacer.
6. *Assets:* biens, actif.
7. *Conduct:* comportement.
8. *Disclosure:* divulgation.
9. *Bribery:* corruption.
10. *Brand:* marque.
11. *Commitment:* engagement.
12. *Besides:* en plus de.
13. *To gain a foothold:* prendre pied.

Repérer les notions essentielles

Using the information above, answer the following questions.

a. What is a multinational corporation and how does it function?

b. Why do some countries welcome multinationals and how do they attract them?

c. How are the companies able to deal with worldwide competition?

d. What may the host countries have to combat sometimes and how do they set about it?

e. What recommendations has the OECD made?

f. How and why has the attitude of the MNCs to ethical issues changed?

Résumer le texte en français

Résumez ce texte en faisant ressortir les éléments qui concernent l'évolution de la place des firmes multinationales dans le monde et de leur comportement éthique (en *150 mots environ*).

Approfondir

Find two advertisements that are being used to inform the public of the ethical commitments of two multinational firms. Analyse them and say if and why they are convincing or not.

LEXICAL WORK

• to attend a meeting	assister à une réunion
• to ban	interdire
• to be in charge of	diriger, être responsable de
• border	frontière
• to break into / capture a market	pénétrer un marché
• breakdown	échec
• charity, NGO	association caritative, ONG
• to clinch a deal	conclure un marché
• code of practice	déontologie
• corporate behaviour	comportement de l'entreprise
• corporate responsibility	responsabilité d'entreprise
• counterfeiting, piracy	contrefaçon
• course of action	ligne de conduite
• to dump	vendre à perte
• employment law	droit du travail
• expertise, skill	compétence
• FDI (foreign direct investment)	IDA (investissement direct à l'étranger)
• to flood	inonder
• to flow / circulate freely	circuler librement
• to gain ground	gagner du terrain
• gimmick	astuce de vente / promotion
• to highlight	mettre en valeur
• to implement	mettre en application
• (cheap) labour	main-d'œuvre (bon marché)
• LDCs (less-developed countries)	PMA (pays les moins avancés)
• misconduct	mauvaise conduite
• outlay	investissement
• overseas / abroad	outre-mer / à l'étranger
• performance	résultats
• plant / factory	installation / usine
• political turmoil	agitation / bouleversement politique
• poverty line	seuil de pauvreté
• profitable	rentable
• prospect	perspective
• to pull out of	quitter
• rate / pace	rythme / cadence

• reliable	fiable, digne de confiance
• to rank	classer
• to recover	retrouver, récupérer
• running costs	frais de gestion
• sharply	brusquement, nettement
• slave labor	travail forcé
• to stand up for	défendre
• standard / norm	norme
• to streamline	dégraisser
• subsidiary	filiale
• success (story)	réussite
• to supply	approvisionner
• to take action	agir
• to take over	racheter (une entreprise)
• takeover bid	offre publique d'achat (OPA)
• tender	appel d'offres
• to talk about / discuss	discuter de
• to tap a new market	attaquer un nouveau marché
• to target	cibler
• to thrive / prosper	prospérer
• to wind up	liquider (une entreprise)
• to withdraw	(se) retirer

USE THE LIST

1 Which words in the list mean:

a. an amount of money invested – **b.** to go to a meeting – **c.** to aim at – **d.** to forbid?

MORE VOCABULARY

2 Match the following verbs with a particule, add a complement and translate the phrases.

a. to wind – **b.** to work – **c.** to break – **d.** to pull – **e.** to account

1. out – **2.** out of – **3.** for – **4.** into – **5.** up

α. a market – **β.** an agreement – **γ.** a solution – **δ.** a success – **ε.** a company

3 Put nouns that go with the following verbs.

Ex.: to compete: competition, competitor.

a. to produce
b. to provide
c. to improve
d. to threaten
e. to attract
f. to inform
g. to advertise
h. to exceed
i. to reduce
j. to sell
k. to cancel

GRAMMAR WORK

Les auxiliaires modaux *should / ought to, had better*

▶ Aide-mémoire grammatical, p. 231.

Analysez et traduisez les exemples suivants :

1. In my opinion, he <u>should</u> / <u>ought to</u> expand his business.
2. He <u>had better</u> invest in more machinery before it is too late.
3. They <u>should have</u> agreed to accept the project.

1 Complétez les phrases suivantes avec l'auxiliaire qui convient en effectuant les changements nécessaires, puis traduisez les phrases.

a. I think you ... (*to apply*) for that job.
b. If we do not want to lose any more business abroad, we ... (*to improve*) our international relations
c. What do you think we ... (*to do*) to encourage people to accept cultural differences?
d. They ... (*to start*) working now if they want to finish on time.
e. He ... not (*to forget*) the appointment this time. I will not give him another one!
f. Our company ... (*to think*) of advertising their green policy sooner.

L'expression du futur

Aide-mémoire grammatical, p. 242.

Analysez et traduisez les exemples suivants :

1. We are going to build a factory in Portugal.
2. It will provide 200 jobs for the local workers.
3. As agreed, we will be waiting for you at the station.
4. They are coming on Tuesday to see our new reception area.
5. They will soon have completed their project in Mexico.

2 Complétez les phrases avec un des verbes ci-dessous mis à la forme du futur appropriée, et traduisez-les.

To set up – to improve – to take off – to come – to start – to ask – to attend.

a. The CEO has announced that he ... the meeting.
b. He ... in order to discuss the new advertising project.
c. He probably ... us to work right through the weekend.
d. By the end of the year, the company's performance ..., hopefully.
e. They intend to move to Ireland next year. They ... a new firm.
f. This time next week, I ... my round-the-world trip.
g. The plane ... next Thursday at 8am.

3 Translate into English.

a. Les entreprises n'auraient pas dû emprunter autant d'argent aux banques.
b. Mon collègue, qui est un excellent gestionnaire, va partir en Australie l'année prochaine pour créer sa propre entreprise.
c. Il vaudrait mieux que vous demandiez plusieurs devis avant de prendre une décision aussi importante.
d. Les multinationales devraient participer plus activement à la campagne contre le réchauffement de la planète.
e. John aura bientôt fini de construire son entrepôt en Suède ; il en est très satisfait.
f. Nous allons commencer à vendre aux Chinois de nouveaux produits fabriqués au Pays de Galles.

EXAM WORK

DOCUMENT 1

In praise of the stateless multinational

Not without flaws[1], but infinitely preferable to the state-bound version.

If you hanker after[2] the idealistic spirit of international cooperation, talk to the boss of an emerging-market multinational. Not the boss of Gazprom, perhaps, which has behaved like an arm of the Russian State. But try Chairman Yang Yuanqing of Lenovo, who has moved his family to North Carolina to deepen his appreciation of American culture, so as to help him integrate his Chinese and American workers. Or Lakshmi Mittal, the London-based Indian boss of Arcelor Mittal, who says his multinational team of executives get on so well that he forgets there are different nationalities in the room, and who believes his firm has no nationality, instead being "truly global".

Lenovo and Arcelor Mittal are at the leading edge[3] of a new phase in the evolution of the multinational corporation. At first, companies set up overseas offices to watch over the export of goods made at home. They then built small foreign replicas of the mother ship, to cater to[4] local demand. Today the goal is to create what Sam Palmisano, the boss of IBM, calls the "globally integrated enterprise"– a single firm in which work is sourced[5] wherever it is more efficient.

For business leaders, building a firm that is seamlessly[6] integrated across time zones and cultures presents daunting[7] obstacles. Rather than huddling them together[8] in a headquarters building in Armonk or Millbank, senior managers will increasingly be spread around the world, which will require them to learn some new tricks[9].

How do you get virtual teams of workers to bond[10], for instance? The answer seems to be a lot of time spent talking – as well as the odd junket[11]. MysQL, an online database firm, holds virtual Christmas parties, at which teams around the world play games and exchange virtual gifts. And what about overcoming all those awkward[12] cultural differences?

Some people assume that stateless multinationals inevitably compete away standards[13] in a race to the bottom. It is true that multinationals tend to shop around for taxes, but in other ways they are usually sticklers[14] for good behaviour. Encouragingly, firms from emerging markets are finding that a globally integrated company needs a single culture, and that the best way to foster[15] this is to make the highest ethics anywhere in the firm the norm for everyone, wherever they are working. Anything else tends to corrode the culture.

A globally-integrated firm cannot allow corrupt practices by employees in some countries and not others, so it must outlaw them everywhere. On the other hand, it cannot enforce religious practices and holidays, or different ways of life, so it must teach tolerance.

Abridged from *The Economist*, September 20th, 2008.

---

1. *Flaw:* défaut, inconvénient. **2.** *To hanker after:* avoir envie de, rêver de. **3.** *Leading edge:* à la pointe de. **4.** *To cater to:* pourvoir à, répondre aux besoins de. **5.** *To be sourced:* être fourni. **6.** *Seamlessly:* sans faille. **7.** *Daunting:* redoutable. **8.** *To huddle together:* entasser. **9.** *Trick:* astuce, truc. **10.** *To bond:* se lier. **11.** *Odd junket:* soirée / sortie commune de temps en temps. **12.** *Awkward:* délicat, difficile. **13.** *To compete away standards:* faire disparaître les normes à force de trop de concurrence. **14.** *To be a stickler:* être pointilleux, insister sur. **15.** *To foster:* favoriser, encourager.

1 Answer the following questions:

a. Why has Yang Yuanqing moved his family to the United States?

b. How does Lakshmi Mittal describe his firm?

c. What sort of firm do multinationales want to create and what does it entail for senior managers?

d. What criticism is made of stateless multinationals and how is it answered?

e. What is the conclusion?

2 Résumez ce texte en français, en *100 mots environ.*

3 Match the following sentences and translate them.

a. Multinational trade rounds	**1.** the need to understand other cultures becomes more important.
b. As technology shrinks the world,	**2.** the difficulty of coming to an agreement.
c. Developing culture awareness is	**3.** are the foundation of the trading system.
d. Talks are still in progress because of	**4.** companies to market lower quality goods.
e. Excessive competition may encourage	**5.** an absolute necessity.

DOCUMENT 2

Why companies and campaigners[1] collaborate

Anyone who has seen television pictures of anti-globalisation riots[2] and invasions of annual general meetings would be surprised how amiable companies and campaigners can be.

Last week, on a gorgeous summer evening, as leaders of some of the world's top companies and non-governmental organisations gathered[3] on the rooftop deck[4] of London's National Theatre, it was impossible to tell them apart[5].

As their discussions proceeded, it was striking not only how well they knew each other, but also how tolerant they were of each other's foibles[6].

What brings businesses and NGOs together in the first place? Some companies meet NGOs when campaigners disrupt[7] their operations. After a period of antagonism, the companies decide it makes more sense to get to know their opponents. Other companies and NGOs begin co-operating during disasters: the Asian tsunami of 2004 and hurricane Katrina the following year were times when companies and NGOs put aside their differences to help the victims.

There are many examples of collaboration. Wal-Mart and Unilever look to the Rainforest Alliance to help them certify the coffee and tea they sell.

What is in it[8] for the companies? First, contact with NGOs provides intelligence[9]. If companies talk to campaigners, they know what the issues of the moment are. If a company waits until an NGO occupies its site and starts holding press conferences, it will struggle to catch up. If campaigners spark[10] a consumer boycott, it may never catch up. "If you ignore NGOs you end up like the fur trade, with no market at all," one company leader said.

Second, company executives have their own values; many privately agree with NGOs. More important, companies know that many of their employees sympathise with NGOs. People want to feel proud of their companies, which is hard when NGOs criticise them.

Third, companies think a relationship with an NGO gives them a seal of approval[11], which they can tell their customers and staff about.

What's in it for the NGOs? This one is simple: companies donate money. They also deliver[12]. They have staff around the world, they operate across borders and have technical expertise. The NGO representatives said their aim was to achieve results. Those they helped did not mind how. "They don't care who provides water as long as it's clean", one NGO supporter said.

Abridged from *The Financial Times*
July 8th, 2008.

---

1. *Campaigner:* militant. **2.** *Riot:* émeute. **3.** *To gather:* se rassembler. **4.** *Rooftop-deck:* terrasse (sur le toit). **5.** *To tell them apart:* les distinguer. **6.** *Foible:* petite manie. **7.** *To disrupt:* perturber. **8.** *What is in it:* Qu'est-ce qu'il y a à gagner. **9.** *Intelligence:* renseignements. **10.** *To spark:* déclencher. **11.** *Seal of approval:* approbation officielle. **12.** *To deliver:* tenir parole.

4 Answer the following questions:

a. What is so surprising about the relationship between the companies and the campaigners?

b. How can this relationship be explained?

c. What do the companies gain?

d. What do the NGOs gain?

e. What matters in the end?

DOCUMENT 3

Walmart gets first foothold in Africa

Walmart has been approved to buy South Africa's Massmart despite fierce union opposition, clearing the way for it to expand into a fourth continent.

South Africa's competition tribunal approved the multinational corporation's $2.4bn (£1.5bn) bid[1] for Massmart, which has 288 stores in South Africa and a dozen other African countries, without conditions that could have jeopardised[2] the deal. The move[3] clears the way for Walmart in a fourth continent, having already aggressively swept through America, Asia and Europe.

Supporters of the deal[4] saw it as a vote of confidence in Africa's economic growth and proof that South Africa is "open for business". But the country's powerful trade unions condemned it as likely to drive down wages and cost jobs, warning that they could respond with demonstrations, strike action and "the mother of all boycotts". The deal has been seen as a test case[5] for foreign investment in South Africa, which is home to the continent's deepest capital markets but where unions also hold huge political influence. WalMart has made inroads[6] into Brazil, China and Mexico but faced unusually strong resistance to its bid for a 51% stake in Massmart, a discount retailer that sells everything from alcohol to televisions.

The competition tribunal said that it had approved the deal, with the stipulation that Walmart must not cut jobs for two years and must work to develop local suppliers[7]. Massmart must also "give preference" to re-employing 500 workers fired last year. "The merging parties contend[8] that the merger will indeed be good for competition by bringing lower prices and additional choice to South African consumers," the tribunal said. "We accept that this is a likely[9] outcome of the merger based on Walmart's history in bringing about lower prices."

"However, the extent of this consumer benefit is by no means clear – Walmart itself has not been able to put a number to this claim[10], only that it is likely." The government and unions are concerned about Walmart's global supply network which, they argue, could lead to a flood of cheap imports, sparking[11] job losses and squeezing local suppliers.

By David Smith,
abridged from *The Guardian*,
Tuesday 31 May 2011.

1. *Bid:* offre. **2.** *To jeopardise:* mettre en péril. **3.** *Move:* décision. **4.** *Deal:* transaction. **5.** *Test case:* affaire qui fait jurisprudence. **6.** *To make inroads:* faire une percée. **7.** *Supplier:* fournisseur. **8.** *To contend:* affirmer. **9.** *Likely:* probable. **10.** *Claim:* affirmation. **11.** *To spark:* déclencher.

5 **Explain what the different points of view about Walmart expanding into South Africa are. (*About 150 words.*)**

6 **Translate the introductory sentence and the text from line 1 to line 17.**

▶ Méthodes, p. 285.

DOCUMENT 4

polyp.org.uk

7 **EXPRESSION. What are the possible interpretations of this cartoon? To what extent do you agree with the view(s) expressed in this cartoon? (*About 150 words.*)**

8 **COMPRÉHENSION. À partir des documents du chapitre, rédigez une synthèse qui expliquera de quelle nature sont les relations des multinationales avec leurs différents partenaires. (*Environ 250 mots.*)**

9 **EXPRESSION. Votre société, TipTopSport, souhaite que ses cadres supérieurs bénéficient d'une formation leur permettant d'améliorer l'efficacité de leurs projets stratégiques en Chine. Le directeur de la formation vous a demandé d'envoyer un appel d'offres à trois cabinets de conseil en management interculturel. (*150 mots environ* en anglais.)**

Vous spécifiez que les cadres concernés sont au nombre de 17 et ont quelques notions de chinois. Leurs attentes sont les suivantes : comment surmonter les malentendus et les difficultés de communication, comment adapter son management au contexte chinois et comment potentialiser les dynamiques d'équipe dans un contexte interculturel. La formation devra se dérouler à Paris en septembre prochain, puis en Chine à une date à déterminer. Vous attendez une réponse rapide ainsi qu'un devis détaillé.

Salutations d'usage.

Méthodes, p. 274.

CHAPITRE

4

The globalization of markets

La globalisation des marchés

BACKGROUND

Globalization means the internationalisation of markets all over the world due to the development of imports and exports, investment and relocation, and the setting up[1] of worldwide networks of production and information.

The globalization of the goods and services markets has opened up new and much bigger markets. Global competition has revealed new competitors (China, for example), which has disrupted[2] former strategies. The globalization of technology backed[3] by the organization of international networks has increased the speed at which innovations are spread[4]. The globalization of financial markets means that masses of capital can be transferred simultaneously.

For the rich countries, economic globalization has brought advantages for the consumer who has access to a wider range of products at lower prices. What better example than the Chinese textiles? For companies it has provided a bigger market and for shareholders a much better return[5] on their capital. The relocation abroad however by the rich countries of labour-intensive[6] industries employing mainly unskilled labour has led to job losses for thousands of workers and has also meant increased competition between the rich countries themselves.

For the emerging countries, globalization has produced rapid economic growth thanks to foreign investment, a better-paid workforce and the improvement of their scientific and technological standards and of their telecommunications.

For the poor countries, dogged[7] by famine, water shortage conflicts and disease, globalization has had little or no positive effect on their economy. The tourist industry, the world's biggest industry, provides some poor countries with income, but many of them also have to rely on international aid.

The globalization of competition today

Globalization has entered a new phase, with emerging-market companies now competing against those of the rich countries. The size of the consumer markets now opening up in emerging economies, especially in India, China, and Brazil, and their rapid growth rates will shift[8] the balance of business activity even more than the earlier rise of less populous countries such as Japan and South Korea. This dynamic new competition is changing market strategy. Emerging market firms produce goods that correspond to the new consumers' needs. The marketing of new products is organized by international managers who work with development teams in centres around the world.

The globalization of financial institutions and markets

Globalization has brought about financial fluctuations on a world scale unknown before. With no obstacle to the circulation of capital, the financing of companies and the international payments were facilitated. There are however numerous risks attached to this development. Markets have become more volatile. Systemic risks caused by big economic losses or lack of confidence are transmitted more easily to the economy as a whole, which may then precipitate financial difficulties, bankruptcies[9], the collapse[10] of the prices of certain assets, etc.

The future

The big question is how to reform the global economy to ensure better income distribution, schooling, training and healthcare[11] on a world scale. The other big question is how to re-regulate global finance in a world of self-interested sovereign states and tax havens.

1. *Setting up:* création.
2. *To disrupt:* perturber.
3. *To back:* renforcer.
4. *To spread:* répandre.
5. *Return:* rendement.
6. *Labour-intensive:* qui nécessite une main-d'œuvre importante.
7. *Dogged by:* souffrant d'un fléau endémique.
8. *To shift:* déplacer.
9. *Bankruptcy:* faillite.
10. *Collapse:* effondrement.
11. *Healthcare:* services médicaux.

Repérer les notions essentielles

Answer the following questions.

a. What does globalization represent for the rich countries? the emerging countries? the poor countries?

b. What has financial globalization created for the economy in general?

c. What needs to be changed in the future?

Résumer le texte en français

Résumez les principaux aspects de la globalisation *(150 mots environ).*

Approfondir

What are the latest issues concerning globalization today?

LEXICAL WORK

• agenda	ordre du jour / programme
• awareness	conscience, prise de conscience
• to balance	équilibrer
• to bring in / earn (money)	rapporter (de l'argent)
• capital goods	biens d'équipement
• to compete	concurrencer
• credit crunch	restrictions de crédit
• to curb / reduce	réduire / freiner
• current market price	cours du jour
• customs barrier	barrière douanière
• to cut / scrap / cancel	supprimer, annuler
• downward / upward trend	tendance à la hausse / baisse
• drop / fall	baisse / chute
• fierce competition	concurrence féroce
• floating capital	capitaux flottants / spéculatifs
• free enterprise	libre-entreprise / libéralisme
• free trade	libre-échange
• free zone	zone franche
• gap	fossé, écart
• gloomy	sombre, inquiétant
• to hinder / hamper	gêner
• to include	comprendre, inclure
• to invest	placer, investir
• investment	placement
• know-how	savoir-faire
• mainspring of the economy	moteur de l'économie
• to make a deal	conclure / faire une affaire
• to merge	fusionner
• NGO (non-governmental organization)	ONG (organisation non gouvernementale)
• output	production, rendement
• to outsource	externaliser, sous-traiter
• penalty	sanction
• price / rate	prix / cours
• prospect	perspective

• to provide for	prévoir
• to provide sb with sth	fournir qqch à qqn
• to raise funds	trouver des capitaux
• range of products	gamme / variété de produits
• regulation	règlement
• to relocate	délocaliser
• relocation	délocalisation
• to retaliate	riposter
• retaliation	riposte
• revenue, income	revenu
• to settle / sort out	régler (un problème)
• scale	échelle
• share, stock	action
• shareholder, stockholder	actionnaire
• shortage, scarcity	pénurie
• show / fair / exhibition	salon / foire / exposition
• to shrink	diminuer
• slack	(au) ralenti
• slump	forte baisse, marasme, récession
• spin-off	retombée
• Stock Exchange	Bourse
• to subsidize	subventionner
• to swamp the market	inonder le marché
• tariff	tarif (douanier)
• tax haven	paradis fiscal
• to threaten, threat	menacer, menace
• time zone	fuseau horaire
• trade talks	négociations commerciales
• trader	négociant, commerçant

USE THE LIST

1 Fill in the gaps with words from the list and translate the sentences.

a. The world is bigger now because business is carried out on a global s... .

b. T... h... offer low or zero taxes, secrecy and lax regulation.

c. The consumer can choose between a wider r... of products.

d. Unfortunately, some jobs in the rich countries are disappearing because of r... .

e. The tourist industry b... i... some r... for the poor countries.

f. Globalization can bring technical k...-h... to poor countries.

g. There is now a big g... between the rich and the poor, both within the rich countries and between the rich and poor countries.

2 **Match the following verbs with a complement and translate the expressions.**

a. to hinder – **b.** to swamp – **c.** to retaliate with – **d.** to raise.

1. the market – **2.** funds – **3.** trade talks – **4.** trade barriers.

GRAMMAR WORK

L'article défini *the* ou Ø avec les noms pluriels et les indénombrables

▶ Aide-mémoire grammatical, p. 227.

Analysez et traduisez les exemples suivants :

1. Consumers usually want lower prices.

2. The banks in this country have big problems.

3. It is urgent to help the people who are starving in their native country.

4. Poverty in a rich world must disappear.

1 **Mettez l'article défini si nécessaire dans les phrases suivantes.**

a. It is difficult to find a solution to ... widespread poverty.

b. Nowadays, ... competition is so fierce that many companies are cutting ... jobs.

c. ... global advertising means that some products are used worldwide, for example a certain drink!

d. Some people think that ... global trade is a recent phenomenon.

e. As ... technology shrinks ... world, we need to understand ... other cultures.

f. All ... trading partners usually benefit from ... trade and ... wealth it brings.

g. In some ways ... world economy was just as globalized in ... past as it is now.

h. During ... Great Depression, ... governments imposed ... trade barriers.

i. At the moment there is ... global panic as ... investors take fright at ... spreading recession.

j. Today, ... communication across ... time zones stimulates ... global trade.

k. "I'm all for ... progress, it's ... change I don't like." (Mark Twain).

Les auxiliaires modaux *may* et *can*

▶ Aide-mémoire grammatical, p. 231.

Analysez puis traduisez les exemples suivants :

1. Poverty in developing countries <u>may</u> mean that people have to emigrate.

2. Thanks to international transport, migrants <u>can</u> cross borders easily.

3. But they <u>cannot</u> always find good jobs in their host country.

2 **Ajoutez *can, cannot* ou *may* selon le cas, puis traduisez les phrases.**

a. These cheap goods from China ... swamp the market.

b. So some countries ... retaliate by raising trade barriers to protect their workers.

c. Too many people ... understand that protectionism ... threaten the consumers' standard of living.

d. Global trade ... reduce local or temporary shortages.

e. If we do not reduce our prices, we ... lose our global competitiveness.

3 **Traduisez en anglais.**

a. Il se peut que Monsieur Spruit décide de vendre son usine à cause de la concurrence de pays à bas coût de main-d'œuvre.

b. Beaucoup d'entreprises dans les pays occidentaux risquent d'être durement touchées par la concurrence mondiale.

c. L'actuel marasme économique mondial risque de durer très longtemps.

d. Les gouvernements ne peuvent pas toujours régler les problèmes économiques dus à la mondialisation.

e. L'anglais est devenu la langue utilisée mondialement pour communiquer dans presque tous les domaines.

f. Beaucoup de gens savent demander leur chemin dans une langue étrangère, mais l'accent du locuteur natif risque parfois de les empêcher de comprendre la réponse !

EXAM WORK

DOCUMENT 1

Rich nations accused of thwarting[1] new powers

Efforts by the Group of Eight [G8] to enter into a closer[2] dialogue with new economic powers such as China and India are being undermined[3] by the rich nations' unwillingness to listen fully to the emerging nations' concerns[4], according to one of their representatives.

A year ago the G8 launched what it planned as an "equal and enduring[5] partnership" with five emerging economies, but in reality – in spite of some progress – the "developed countries have basically set the agenda[6]", Lourdes Aranda, Mexico's deputy foreign minister and co-ordinator of the G8 for the five countries, believes.

She also complained in a *Financial Times* interview that the leaders of the five nations – India, China, Mexico, Brazil and South Africa – would have "not enough time" at next week's G8 summit in Japan to give their views on concerns such as spiralling food and energy prices.

Diplomats said that Japan, this year's G8 host, has been reluctant[7] to pursue the dialogue with the G5 – formalised at the Heiligendamm summit last year in Germany – for fear of acknowledging the power of China too openly. As a result, the dialogue at the July 7-9 summit has been shortened and watered down[8] by the invitation of other non-G8 countries such as Indonesia, South Korea and Australia.

She said the G5 would like to focus more on issues such as technology transfer from developed to developing countries – for instance regarding climate change – and on efforts to improve healthcare systems in poor countries.

In spite of these immediate concerns, she said the "Heiligendamm process", as the dialogue is called, has been successful as a "confidence-building measure."

Bernd Pfaffenbach, Germany's deputy economics minister and the G8's co-ordinator for the G5 dialogue, said four working groups had met several times since last year's summit. Each has a co-chair[9] from the G8 and G5. The dialogue is based on an equal footing[10].

Mr Pfaffenbach said the Heiligendamm process was a way of stressing the "common responsibility" of G8 and emerging economies for issues linked to globalisation and climate change without raising the question of expanding the G8 – an issue on which the rich nations' group was often divided.

Abridged from *The Financial Times*, July 3rd, 2008.

1. *To thwart:* contrarier, contrecarrer. **2.** *Close:* étroit, proche. **3.** *To undermine:* miner, saper. **4.** *Concern:* souci. **5.** *Enduring:* durable, qui dure. **6.** *Agenda:* programme. **7.** *To be reluctant:* hésiter, faire à contrecœur. **8.** *To water down:* affaiblir. **9.** *Co-chair:* co-présidence. **10.** *On an equal footing:* sur un pied d'égalité.

1 Répondez en français.

a. Que reproche-t-on aux pays riches ?

b. Que dénonce le vice-ministre des Affaires étrangères du Mexique ?

c. Que veut faire le G8 ?

d. Quels pays constituent le G5 et que veulent-ils ?

e. Qu'est-ce que le processus d'Heiligendamm ?
f. Dans quelle mesure a-t-il déçu au début ?
g. Dans quelle mesure peut-il réussir ?

2 **Rédigez en français un résumé de cet article en *150 mots environ.***

3 **Traduisez de "*Diplomats said...*" (l. 23) à "*... South Korea and Australia*" (l. 32).**

▶ Méthodes, p. 285.

DOCUMENT 2

Moving back to America

"WHEN clients are considering opening another manufacturing plant in China, I've started to urge[1] them to consider alternative locations[2]," says Hal Sirkin of the Boston Consulting Group. "Have they thought about Vietnam, say? Or maybe [they could] even try Made in USA?" When clients are American firms looking to build factories to serve American customers, Mr Sirkin is increasingly likely to suggest they stay at home, not for patriotic reasons but because the economics of globalisation are changing fast.

Labour arbitrage[3]–taking advantage of lower wages abroad, especially in poor countries–has never been the only force pushing multinationals to locate offshore, but it has certainly played a big part. Now, however, as emerging economies boom, wages there are rising. Pay for factory workers in China, for example, soared by 69% between 2005 and 2010. So the gains from labour arbitrage are starting to shrink[4], in some cases to the point of irrelevance, according to a new study by BCG.

"Sometime around 2015, manufacturers will be indifferent between locating in America or China for production for consumption in America," says Mr Sirkin.

BCG predicts a "manufacturing renaissance" in America. There are reasons to be sceptical. The surge of manufacturing output[5] in the past year or so has largely been about recovering ground lost during the downturn.

Even if wages in China explode, some multinationals will find it hard to bring many jobs back to America, argues Mr Pisano. In some areas, such as consumer electronics, America no longer has the necessary supplier[6] base or infrastructure. Firms did not realise when they shifted operations to low-wage countries that some moves "would be almost irreversible", says Mr Pisano.

Abridged from *The Economist*,
14 May 2011.

1. *To urge:* inciter. 2. *Location:* lieu. 3. *Labour arbitrage:* choix déterminés par les coûts salariaux. 4. *To shrink:* diminuer. 5. *Output:* production. 6. *Supplier:* fournisseur.

4 **Résumez l'article en *150 mots*, en répondant aux questions suivantes :**

a. Que préconise le cabinet de conseil BCG ? Pourquoi ?

b. À quelles difficultés les entreprises intéressées par cette évolution vont-elles faire face ?

DOCUMENT 3

The Globalization Paradox

It is dogma among economists and right-thinking members of the political and business elite that globalization is good and more of it is even better. That is why they invariably view[1] anyone who dissents from[2] this orthodoxy as either ignorant of the logic of comparative advantage or selfishly protectionist.

But what if it turns out[3] that globalization is more of a boon[4] to the members of the global elite than it is to the average Jose?

What if most of the benefits of the free flow of goods and capital across borders have already been realized, and any gains from additional globalization will be outweighed[5] by the additional costs in terms of unemployment, reduced wages, lost pensions and depopulated communities? What if global markets, to be widely beneficial, require the kind of global governance structure that does not yet exist and that most people would oppose? What if it turns out that the countries that have benefited most from free-market globalization are not those that have embraced it wholeheartedly[6], but those that have adopted parts of it selectively?

[...]

The paradox is that globalization will work for everyone only if all countries abide by[7] the same set of rules, hammered out[8] and enforced by some form of technocratic global government. The reality is, however, that most countries are unwilling[9] to give up their sovereignty, their distinctive institutions and their freedom to manage their economies in their own best interests. Not China. Not India. Not the members of the European Union, as they are now discovering. Not even the United States.

Abridged from *The Washington Post Sunday*, by Dani Roddick, March 13, 2011.

1. *To view:* considérer. **2.** *To dissent from:* être d'un avis différent de. **3.** *To turn out:* s'avérer. **4.** *Boon:* aubaine. **5.** *To outweigh:* l'emporter sur. **6.** *Wholeheartedly:* sans réserves. **7.** *To abide by:* obéir à. **8.** *To hammer out:* repéter inlassablement. **9.** *Unwilling:* peu désireux.

5 **COMPRÉHENSION. Answer in your own words: What arguments does the writer use to suggest that globalization may be criticized? Why, according to him, is there a globalization paradox? (*About 150 words.*)**

DOCUMENT 4

* *To drive nuts:* rendre fou.

6 **EXPRESSION. To what extent does the cartoon illustrate the idea that there is a "globalisation paradox"? Is it the same one as in the other documents? *(About 150 words.)***

7 **COMPRÉHENSION. Utilisez l'ensemble du corpus pour répondre à la question suivante : Quelles sont les critiques formulées à l'égard de la mondialisation ? *(Environ 250 mots.)***

8 **Rédigez un courrier en anglais *(150 mots environ)*.**

Vous êtes l'adjoint du Directeur commercial de votre société, avec qui vous devez vous rendre en Afrique du Sud, du 5 au 10 novembre, au Cap. Vous répondez à une lettre de votre agence de voyage, qui vous annonçait une augmentation de 150 euros du prix du billet d'avion et de 200 euros de l'hébergement par personne. Or, vous aviez reçu confirmation antérieure (copie jointe) de vos réservations à des prix convenus. En outre, l'annonce de cette augmentation à moins d'un mois de votre départ est contraire aux dispositions légales reprises dans les conditions générales de l'agence, lesquelles interdisent toute majoration de prix à moins de trente jours du départ. C'est pourquoi vous refusez cette augmentation.

Salutations d'usage.

▶ Méthodes, p. 274.

CHAPITRE

5

The creation of regional trading areas (European Union, NAFTA)

La constitution d'espaces économiques régionaux (Union européenne, ALENA)

BACKGROUND

The WTO and RTAs

By all accounts[1], there are 196 countries in the world today, and in 2011, 153 were member states of the World Trade Organization (WTO)[2] which encourages multilateral trading, in other words free and fair[3] trade among all its members. At the same time, Regional Trade Agreements (RTAs), which give preferential treatment to its members, have boomed in recent years. In 2011, 297 agreements were in force, and many more RTAs were scheduled[4] to be implemented[5] in the future. This means that most countries in the world belong to a regional trading area and/or have signed RTAs with several others. Free trade agreements (FTAs) and partial agreements represent 90% of these RTAs, whereas customs unions[6] (such as the EU), which have much tighter links[7], account for[8] less than 10%.

Trading blocks are usually good for consumers because they stimulate competition and investment, and help make economies of scale; they also encourage free movement of capital and labour within them.

The main regional trade or trading areas

– The European Union or EU (see below)

– The European Free Trade Association (EFTA) for non EU European countries (Switzerland, Iceland, Norway and Liechtenstein)

– The North American Free Trade Association or NAFTA[9] (see below)

– The Southern Common Market (MERCOSUR) open to Latin America members such as Brazil, Argentina, Paraguay, Uruguay, Venezuela, etc.

– The Association of South-East Asian Nations (ASEAN) includes Thailand, Indonesia, Singapore, the Philippines, Cambodia, Malaysia, Vietnam, etc.

– The Common Market of Eastern and Southern Africa (COMESA) has 20 members: Kenya, Rwanda, Congo RD, Egypt, Mauritius, Madagascar, etc.

These trade areas have widely varying business ties and aspects. Their proliferation has become a big issue, leading to a conflict between multilateralism and regionalism. However, it is difficult to stop regionalism which at least boosts free trade between its members. After all, some free trade is better than national protectionism, as the current situation of protectionist countries shows (Cuba and North Korea).

The European Union or EU

Starting with six member countries in 1958 as the **EEC (European Economic Community)**, the EU has now become one of the world's largest economic and trade blocs, and the biggest exporter of goods. It comprises[10] nearly 500 million inhabitants living in 27 countries, with three political centres (Brussels, Luxembourg and Strasbourg) and 23 official languages. It has 30% of the world's nominal GDP (Gross Domestic Product)[11], but there are big differences among the per capita[12] incomes according to the countries and the very complex taxation systems, such as VAT (Value Added Tax). It is sometimes called a fortress because it has raised many barriers against other countries' imports.

The Single Market was implemented in 1993 after the ratification of the **Maastricht Treaty**. It has created a real economic union among all member states which must be democracies adhering to free trade and free enterprise[13] and have standardized systems of laws and regulations. It guarantees free movement of people, goods, services and capital among them and enforces a common policy for trade, agriculture, fishing and regional development.

By boosting all sorts of exchanges (and not just commercial), the Single Market has improved citizens' living standards and conditions as never before in history.

The euro was the currency[14] being used by 17 countries in 2012, which were sharing the same monetary and financial policy under the authority of the European Central Bank (in Frankfurt, Germany). This rather rigid system is sometimes criticized, but it helped cushion[15] several crises, as in 2008. However it was seriously threatened by the crisis of the sovereign debt, in Portugal,

Ireland, and especially in Greece and even Spain and Italy, in 2011. This has shown the need for fiscal and budgetary harmonization in the eurozone.

The most important change in recent times is the enlargement of the EU to Eastern European countries which left the former impoverished communist bloc of the USSR, and eagerly[16] joined rich free-trading Western Europe. More European countries are applying to join, such as the Balkan states. The most controversial candidate is Turkey. And the question of a tighter political union is still unresolved, in spite of the ratification of the Lisbon Treaty in 2009.

The North American Free Trade Agreement or NAFTA

Signed between the USA, Canada and Mexico, it started operating in 1994. It has gradually eliminated most tariff barriers between them in agricultural trade (with some exceptions), and aims at increasing the flow[17] of goods in four key sectors: hogs[18], steel, consumer electronics and chemicals. It also works to increase cooperation in services, and coordination of standards, regulations and performance objectives; but its objectives are far more limited than those of the EU. It has three capitals (Mexico, Ottawa and Washington DC) and three official languages (English, French and Spanish). It is one of the world's largest trading blocs with 460 million inhabitants and the highest combined purchasing power[19] parity of its members.

It has contributed to the economic growth of its members. However, Mexican farmers have suffered because of cheap imports from the US agribusiness[20]; and American workers have lost jobs in manufacturing and assembly industries due to competition from the Mexican "maquiladoras" which are factories near the US border exploiting a cheap labour force. In addition, it has not stopped rising inequality in both Mexico and the USA.

1. *By all accounts:* d'après l'opinion générale.
2. *World Trade Organization (WTO):* Organisation mondiale du commerce (OMC).
3. *Fair:* équitable.
4. *To schedule:* programmer.
5. *To implement:* mettre en œuvre.
6. *Customs union:* union douanière.
7. *Tight link:* lien étroit.
8. *To account for:* représenter.
9. *NAFTA:* ALENA (Accord de libre-échange nord-américain).
10. *To comprise:* comprendre.
11. *GDP (Gross Domestic Product):* PIB (produit intérieur brut).
12. *Per capita:* par tête.
13. *Free enterprise:* libéralisme.
14. *Currency:* monnaie, devise.
15. *To cushion:* amortir.
16. *Eagerly:* avec empressement.
17. *Flow:* flux, circulation.
18. *Hog:* porc.
19. *Purchasing power:* pouvoir d'achat.
20. *Agribusiness:* industrie agro-alimentaire.

Repérer les notions essentielles

Répondez aux questions suivantes en français.

a. Combien de pays sont recensés aujourd'hui dans le monde, et combien sont membres de l'OMC ?

b. Quels objectifs de l'OMC sont présentés ici ?

c. Quelle est la différence entre régionalisme et multilatéralisme ?

d. Tous les pays adhèrent-ils à un espace économique régional ?

e. Les accords commerciaux régionaux sont-ils tous comparables ?

f. Nommez trois accords instituant des espaces économiques régionaux, hors Union européenne et ALENA.

g. Quelles sont les principales caractéristiques de l'Union européenne ?

h. Dégagez quelques différences structurelles importantes entre l'Union européenne et l'ALENA.

Trouvez dans le texte l'équivalent des termes suivants (attention aux articles !) :

le libre-échange – la situation actuelle – le libéralisme – appliquer une politique – s'appliquer à des pays – le niveau de vie et les conditions de vie de la population – être candidat à une adhésion – commerce équitable – la pêche – règle / règlement – usine *(2 mots)* – acier – biens de consommation électroniques.

Résumer le texte en français

Résumez ce texte en *100 mots environ*.

Approfondir

Select one of the RTAs (not the EU) mentioned in this document and carry out research about it over the Internet.

LEXICAL WORK

• antidumping suit	procès pour pratiques de dumping
• to ban (an article)	interdire (une marchandise)
• border	frontière
• border line	ligne de démarcation
• border / neighbour state	État limitrophe / voisin
• borderless	sans frontière
• boundary	limite / frontière
• to break down barriers	faire tomber des barrières
• to cancel (an agreement / a deal)	annuler (un accord)
• common goal / objective	but / objectif commun
• to comply with an obligation	respecter une obligation
• to consign / dispatch	expédier
• consignee, consigner	destinataire, expéditeur
• consignment	envoi
• customs clearance	dédouanement
• customs declaration	déclaration en douane
• customs house	poste de douane
• customs officer	douanier
• customs / export duty	droit de douane
• cutthroat / fierce competition	concurrence féroce
• debt	endettement
• (to) default	(faire) faillite, ne pas honorer (un paiement)
• to dismantle regulations	démanteler des règlements
• duty free goods	marchandises hors taxe
• to endorse an agreement	approuver un accord
• export earnings	revenus de l'exportation
• exports and imports	exportations et importations
• freight	(transport de) marchandises
• (milk) glut	excédent (laitier)
• to glut a market	saturer un marché
• to go through the customs	passer la douane
• to join a union / an organization	adhérer à une union / organisation
• loose / close tie / link	lien lâche / étroit
• offset	compensation

- to offset — compenser
- to overcome division — surmonter des divisions
- rating agency — agence de notation
- to remove borders — supprimer les frontières
- retaliatory measure — mesure de rétorsion
- to shape a new tie — former un nouveau lien
- sovereignty — souveraineté
- to strengthen border safety — renforcer la sécurité aux frontières
- to subsidize — subventionner
- subsidy — subvention
- to sue — poursuivre en justice
- timetable for unification — calendrier pour l'unification
- trade balance — balance commerciale
- trade surplus / deficit — excédent / déficit commercial
- to work out a joint constitution — élaborer une constitution commune

USE THE LIST

1 Fill in the gaps with words from the list, making the necessary changes, then translate the sentences.

a. In the EU, which is a c... union, goods can travel freely without paying c... d... .

b. In a free trade area such as NAFTA, where reciprocal preferences for goods or services are exchanged, the t... are l... since the members retain their own tariff b... on imports from other countries.

c. Thanks to NAFTA, certain goods produced entirely in one of the three member states are sold d... f... in the others.

d. Brussels now controls all s... given to a company by its national government. If a company wants to export goods, it has to c... with specific o... .

e. Most but not all FTAs are between b... s... .

f. Although China belongs to the WTO, some bad Chinese i... were recently b... .

g. In spite of NAFTA, there are still b... between its member countries.

2 Match the words below, add articles if necessary, and translate the expressions.

a. to cancel – **b.** to go through – **c.** to break down – **d.** to dismantle – **e.** customs – **f.** to join – **g.** retaliatory.

1. measure – **2.** union – **3.** barriers – **4.** officer – **5.** regulations – **6.** customs – **7.** agreement.

GRAMMAR WORK

La proposition infinitive

▶ Aide-mémoire grammatical, p. 261.

Analysez et traduisez les exemples suivants :

1. The EU wants the rest of the world to adopt its rules.
2. The paper calls on the EU to encourage other jurisdictions to follow suit.
3. The Trade Minister called for a global movement to pressure governments.
4. The customs officer asked her to complete the questionnaire.
5. The WTO urged them not to take retaliatory measures.

■ **Quels verbes ici sont suivis de la proposition infinitive ? Quels autres verbes ayant la même construction connaissez-vous ? Que remarquez-vous au sujet du pronom complément sujet du verbe infinitif, et de la place de *not* ?**

1 Reliez les deux propositions entre elles pour en faire une seule phrase que vous traduirez. Effectuez tous les changements nécessaires. Respectez les temps.

Ex.: she filled in all the forms + The customs officer asked

→ The customs officer asked her to fill in all the forms.

a. all its member countries will dismantle their protectionist regulations + The WTO expects →
b. the Interior Minister will strengthen border safety + The Prime Minister will call on →
c. they cancelled the agreement + The CEO ordered →
d. all EU countries should comply with that directive rapidly + Brussels wants →
e. governments must not subsidize ailing firms + The Commission has asked →
f. he will arrive on Monday + We expect →
g. they changed their minds + The government representative wanted →

2 Traduisez en anglais.

a. Dans le cadre de l'ALENA, le gouvernement américain veut encourager les Mexicains à acheter des produits américains.
b. Mais il ne veut pas que les Mexicains immigrent aux États-Unis.
c. On s'attend à ce que beaucoup d'immigrants retournent chez eux à cause de la crise.
d. L'OMC a réclamé que la Chine mette fin à cette féroce concurrence.
e. Le patron ne veut pas encore que nous approuvions cet accord, pourtant légal selon la législation de l'Union européenne.

f. Et il veut que nous changions le calendrier des négociations.

g. Je n'ai pas voulu qu'on poursuive la société M&N en justice : c'était inutile.

L'expression du futur après les conjonctions de temps

▶ Aide-mémoire grammatical, p. 242.

Analysez et traduisez les exemples suivants :

1. The question will become relevant when we eventually consider the prospects.
2. As soon as the Director-General comes in, people will stop talking.
3. They will listen very carefully while he is speaking.
4. Once he has finished talking, the audience will ask questions.

■ **Que remarquez-vous sur les différences de temps dans chaque exemple ?**

3 **Mettez les phrases suivantes au futur puis traduisez-les.**

Ex.: He called her back as soon as he had finished his speech.

→ *He will call her back as soon as he has finished his speech.*

= *Il la rappellera dès qu'il aura terminé son discours.*

a. The treaty was ratified when at last they agreed on its final terms. →

b. He dispatched the goods once he had filled in the clearance forms. →

c. Once the FDA (Food and Drug Administration) had decided to ban these bad products from China, it became impossible to import them to the USA. →

d. As long as those imports were cheap, consumers went on buying them. →

e. The world became a better place when they finally overcame their divisions. →

f. I sent him an email as soon as the work was completed. →

4 **Traduisez en anglais**

a. Quand j'irai aux États-Unis, j'achèterai du parfum détaxé dans les boutiques de l'aéroport.

b. Les pays de l'Union européenne ratifieront la constitution commune dès qu'ils se seront mis d'accord sur les principales conditions.

c. Tant qu'il n'y aura pas de conflit, la souveraineté de ces pays ne sera pas en danger.

d. Quand la Russie intégrera l'OMC, elle devra respecter ses obligations.

e. En particulier, lorsqu'ils auront signé les accords de propriété intellectuelle, les Russes ne pourront plus copier des œuvres originales.

f. Je passerai mes coups de fil pendant qu'il remplira les formulaires.

g. L'Asie du Sud-Est gagnera évidemment beaucoup moins de devises quand elle aura moins d'excédents commerciaux.

h. Cette décision de la Commission européenne aura force de loi quand elle aura été approuvée par le Conseil des ministres et par le Parlement.

EXAM WORK

DOCUMENT 1

Trading in the European Union

Under-floor heating system manufacturer and retailer Warmup Plc[1] is based in north-west London. The business sells its products via[2] retailers, building contractors[3] and direct to consumers, and has customers in Germany, France, the Netherlands, Cyprus, Spain, Portugal and the USA. Howard Flood, International director at the company, explains how the firm started trading in the European Union (EU).

Here's how we started building markets in the EU

Understand each market's needs

It's essential that you visit each target[4] market and walk many miles in your potential customers' shoes. You need to understand what makes them tick and what triggers[5] purchasing decisions.

While the EU is a single market, there are significant practical and cultural nuances from member state to member state. For example, in cooler climates, such as Germany and the Netherlands, most houses are carpeted, whereas in warmer countries such as Spain and Portugal, there's a greater use of floor tiling[6]. For us, that means our sales methods, features and benefits and target customers are different.

Stay close to your markets

We directly employed sales people in the local markets. They can spot[7] any issues that might arise, whether they are language related, cultural or otherwise. It's more difficult to grasp[8] these problems from the UK.

For example, in one of our markets, we were advised by our local office to make sure that we additionally shipped installation instructions in Polish - as they were seeing a rise in the number of migrant Polish workers in that area. Without that local knowledge, we would still have been providing instructions for installers in a language that wasn't native to them.

What I'd do differently

Take a closer look at country-specific regulations

We're fortunate that our product generally translates well across all EU markets as the voltages required are compatible. However, while our British Electrotechnical Approvals Board mark has been enough to meet standards in most markets, we found out that we'd need an additional local certification in France. That's slowed our progress there a little, so it would have been useful to know it was compulsory slightly[9] earlier.

Abridged from www.businesslink.gov.uk, July 5, 2011.

---

1. *Plc (Public Limited Company):* société anonyme. **2.** *Via:* par l'intermédiaire de. **3.** *Building contractor:* entrepreneur en bâtiment. **4.** *Target:* cible. **5.** *To trigger:* déclencher. **6.** *Tiling:* carrelage. **7.** *To spot:* repérer. **8.** *To grasp:* saisir, comprendre. **9.** *Slightly:* légèrement.

1 Find the equivalents in the text for:

a. to be in someone's situation – **b.** characteristic – **c.** to transport – **d.** area – **e.** advantage – **f.** necessary – **g.** to have the required features – **h.** everywhere in – **i.** obligatory – **j.** a person or business that sells goods to customers.

2 COMPREHENSION. Rédigez une note en français *(150 mots environ)* au nom de Howard Flood, le directeur des relations internationales de Warmup Plc, à l'intention d'un représentant potentiel en France, pour lui présenter sa société, en vous aidant de ce texte. Vous insisterez sur les besoins de Warmup Plc pour s'adapter au marché français en particulier.

DOCUMENT 2

Bringing NAFTA back home

At the moment it is just a thousand hectares of mud on the outskirts[1] of Monterrey, a bustling[2] industrial city in northern Mexico. Soon it should be the "Interpuerto", a customs-clearing zone to speed goods on their way to the United States via two rail lines and the motorways to which it will be connected. The aim of the $2 billion project, backed by the state government of Nuevo León and private investors, is to allow cargoes to skip[3] the long queues at customs posts on the border, 240km (150 miles to the north).

Projects like the Interpuerto matter[4] for Mexico, the economy of which depends on exporting labour-intensive[5] manufactured goods to its giant neighbour. Despite the ratifying of the North American Free-Trade Agreement (NAFTA) in 1993, within a decade Mexico's exports to the United States were overhauled[6] by those of China.

The financial crisis and recession north of the border was an even bigger blow[7]: a slump[8] in exports (down by a quarter in the first half of 2009, compared with the same period the previous year) helped to push Mexico's economy into deep recession. Recovery is now under way. But Mexicans remain gloomy about their economic prospects, according to opinion polls. And Mexican businesses worry about the world currency "war": the peso is appreciating against the dollar and, recently, against the yuan, thanks to capital inflows[9].

Yet Mexico's trade picture is brighter than it looks. Last year was less bad for Mexico than for most of the rest of the world. Although its exports shrank, they have recovered quickly. Mexico's share of the American market has grown to 12.2%—its highest level since NAFTA came into force. The rapacious expansion of China's exports has come at the expense of others, including Canada, the third NAFTA member.

This resilience[10] reflects various built-in[11] advantages. Geographical proximity has become more valuable as the price of oil (and thus transport) has risen. NAFTA exempts Mexico from the American import tariffs that clobber[12] Chinese exporters. Chinese tiles and paving stones, for instance, are cheaper than Mexican ones, averaging $5.20 per square metre against $5.29, but after paying an 8.5% tariff they end up more expensive. The same is true of cloth, glassware, chemicals and much else. The NAFTA effect is also concentrating the manufacture of smaller cars in Mexico. The country's car exports are booming as never before, up 10.5% on their level of 2008. Carmakers have announced investment of $4.4 billion over the next four years, according to the government.

China's edge[13] in labour costs is less clear-cut than it used to be. The wages of its factory workers have been rising at double-digit[14] rates in recent years. Mexican workers are highly skilled in some industries.

But the wage gap with the United States has failed to narrow as much as people hoped, complains Rogelio Ramírez de la O, a Mexican economist.

[...] More than 15 years after NAFTA, the task for Mexico is to take full advantage of the trade agreement—and to go beyond it. A sickly[15] American economy may at last provide a powerful incentive to do so. [...]

Abridged from *The Economist*, Oct 28, 2010, www.economist.com

1. *The outskirts:* la périphérie. 2. *Bustling:* très animé. 3. *To skip:* sauter, éviter. 4. *To matter:* avoir de l'importance. 5. *Labour-intensive:* à forte main-d'œuvre. 6. *To overhaul:* dépasser. 7. *Blow:* choc, coup. 8. *Slump:* forte baisse. 9. *Inflow:* afflux. 10. *Resilience:* capacité à rebondir. 11. *Built-in:* intrinsèque. 12. *To clobber:* frapper. 13. *Edge:* avantage concurrentiel. 14. *Double-digit:* à deux chiffres. 15. *Sickly:* malade.

3 Trouvez les mots ou expressions du texte signifiant :

a. faire passer rapidement
b. autoroute
c. redressement
d. être en cours
e. droit de douane
f. exportations de voitures
g. investissement
h. pessimiste
i. monnaie d'un pays
j. ne pas se produire
k. encouragement.

4 Complétez les expressions suivantes du texte, et traduisez-les.

a. to bring ...
b. to ... to do (2 possibilités)
c. an import ...
d. labour ...
e. highly ...
f. ... inflows.

5 COMPRÉHENSION. Rédigez en français une note de *150 mots environ* résumant les effets de l'ALENA sur le Mexique et les États-Unis.

6 EXPRESSION. In your opinion, and from a broader perspective, is NAFTA a good or a bad agreement for the long term economic situation of the USA and Mexico? *(About 250 words.)*

DOCUMENT 3

Evolution of Regional Trade Agreements in the world, 1948-2011

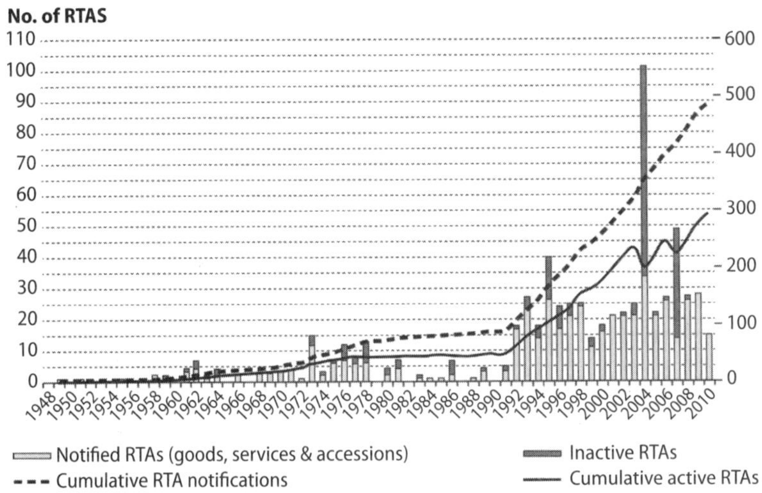

www.wto.org

7 **EXPRESSION. Write a note describing the document above. What do you notice in particular?** ***(About 100 words.)***

Méthodes, p. 271.

8 **EXPRESSION. Taking into account documents 1, 2 and 3, what can help to explain the boom in regional trade agreements in the last 20 years? Give your opinion about it.** ***(About 150 words.)***

9 **EXPRESSION. Mr O'Connor, directeur de l'hôtel *Travelinn* à Belfast, Irlande du Nord (6 Wellington Place, Belfast BT2 7GE), écrit une lettre au député européen de son secteur (Euro MP) Mr Roy Murphy, 12 Ormeau Road, Belfast, BT7 2EA.**

Mr O'Connor demande à Mr Murphy d'intervenir en faveur d'une harmonisation des taux actuellement très variables de la TVA applicable aux hôtels de l'Union européenne. Ces taux alourdissent particulièrement les prix au Royaume-Uni pour les touristes, qui préfèrent des pays moins chers comme la France (TVA de l'hôtellerie au Royaume-Uni : 17,5 %, en France : 5,5 %). Il développe des arguments en faveur de cette harmonisation fiscale dans toute l'Union européenne, en insistant également sur les avantages du tourisme pour l'emploi et la croissance économique non seulement dans l'hôtellerie et la création d'emplois, mais aussi dans les transports, etc., et même pour la notoriété de sa région. Date et salutations d'usage. *(About 150 words.)*

Méthodes, p. 274.

CHAPITRE

6

The emergence of Asian economies

La montée en puissance des pays asiatiques

BACKGROUND

Over the past few years, China and India and other Asian countries have experienced an unprecedented economic take off[1]. These Asian NICs (Newly Industrialized Countries) share common characteristics: rapid growth and industrialization, massive investments, capital formation and exports of consumer durables[2].

The Dragon: China

At the end of the 1970s, economic reforms were set up to lift the country out of poverty[3] and isolation. Over three decades, the economy of the most populous country in the world grew by 9% a year. Think about it: four fifths of the world's toys and three fifths of its clothing are made in China. It has become the second biggest economy in the world and its foreign reserves enable it to provide other economies around the world with liquidities. On the demand side, its appetite for coal, oil, iron ore[4] and steel is ravenous[5]. Since 2000, China has been responsible for 85% of the increase in world oil consumption. For all its feats[6] China's success story masks many problems such as corruption, devastating pollution and a widening[7] rural-urban gap[8].

The Elephant: India

With an 8% growth since the beginning of the 21st century, India has taken off impressively. Services (half of India's output[9]) represent a third of the labour force, and are a source of economic growth thanks to an English-speaking, low-wage graduate[10] workforce that can do the software programming and back office tasks[11] of foreign companies. Mumbai, whose port handles half of India's trade, is a dynamic economic hub[12]. With its 17 million inhabitants it will be the world's second most populated city by 2015, after Tokyo. A sense of optimism characterizes the Indians who feel that India's time has finally arrived. Dynamic companies (Mittal, Tata Group, Infosys, Wipro) are now acquiring a global competitive edge[13]. However, an infrastructure deficit renders logistics nightmarish[14]. India also suffers from rampant[15] corruption, political inertia, appalling[16] sanitation[17], power cuts, a literacy rate of 65%, child labour and strong social inequalities.

The four Tigers

Hong Kong with its natural harbour[18] is still the successful manufacturing, business and financial centre it used to be under British rule. In 1997, it was returned to Chinese rule, and it is still thriving.

South Korea's GDP growth rate is high thanks to its manufacturing strength in various sectors (automotive, steel[19], electronics, ships, robotics and petrochemicals). Its star companies, Hyundai-Kia, Samsung, Daewoo, or LG, make it one of the top ten exporters in the world. It is also a strong investor abroad, signing construction contracts in the Middle East. It has reached the ranks of Western economies and enjoys one of the highest living standards in the world, with a higher life expectancy than the Americans' and the world's highest scientific literacy rate.

Singapore boasts[20] one of the highest per capita GDPs in the world, a corruption-free administration and an efficient education system. Its exports of electronics and chemicals enable it to purchase raw materials. Its strategic seaport is one of the busiest in the world, surpassing Hong Kong and Rotterdam.

Taiwan has been industrialized since World War II thanks to Western aid; it still has a strong growth rate and its economy is based on small electronics and service companies.

The baby Tigers

Vietnam is a rising manufacturing hub that boasted a GDP growth of 7% in 2010. Its 87 million inhabitants provide a cheap labour force. However, the wealth created is not evenly[21] distributed and social unrest is brewing[22].

Thailand's economy has grown quickly over the past few years, with an average growth rate of 5.5%. It is regarded as a safe place to do business. Tourism accounts for 6% of GDP today.

Malaysia also underwent rapid development in the late 20th century and became a multi-sector economy which attracts foreign investment and exports electronics as well as crude oil[23] and gas.

Indonesia, the largest Muslim country in the world, developed rapidly in the 1990s but was most severely hit by the 1997 financial crisis. Since then it has partially recovered[24] but it suffers from political instability and inadequate infrastructure. It is the world's biggest producer of palm oil.

The Philippines is also a thriving NIC with Manila as a centre for industrial activity (food processing[25], textiles, garments[26], electronics and auto parts). Eleven million Filipino workers (who are English-speaking) emigrate all over the world to find work, and thus contribute close to 10% of GDP.

1. *Take off:* décollage.
2. *Consumer durables:* biens de consommation durables.
3. *To lift sb out of poverty:* sortir qqn de la pauvreté.
4. *Iron ore:* minerai de fer.
5. *Ravenous:* vorace.
6. *For all its feats*: malgré tous ses exploits.
7. *To widen*: agrandir, élargir.
8. *Gap:* fossé.
9. *Output:* production.
10. *Graduate:* diplômé de l'université.
11. *Task:* tâche.
12. *Hub:* centre.
13. *Competitive edge*: avantage compétitif.
14. *Nightmarish:* cauchemardesque.
15. *Rampant:* endémique.
16. *Appalling:* épouvantable.
17. *Sanitation:* hygiène.
18. *Harbour:* port.
19. *Steel:* acier.
20. *To boast:* s'enorgueillir d'avoir.
21. *Evenly:* également.
22. *To brew:* couver.
23. *Crude oil:* pétrole brut.
24. *To recover:* se remettre.
25. *Food processing:* agro-alimentaire.
26. *Garments:* habillement.

Repérer les notions essentielles

Find a word or expression which means:

a. croissance : g...
b. augmentation : i...
c. habitant (n) : i...
d. inégalité : i...
e. niveau de vie : l...
f. fournir : p...
g. santé : h...
h. acheter : p...
i. espérance de vie : l... e...

Résumer le texte en français

Faites un résumé de ce texte en *150 mots environ*.

Approfondir

Choose one Asian country and draw up a statistical fact sheet on its characteristics (capital, official language, Head of State, population numbers , birth and death rates, surface area, GDP per capita, GDP growth, inflation rate, literacy rate, etc.).

LEXICAL WORK

• apparel	habillement
• automotive parts	pièces automobiles
• boom	expansion, essor
• capital-intensive	nécessitant des investissements financiers élevés / à forte intensité capitalistique
• to catch up with	rattraper
• counterfeiting	contrefaçon
• cutting-edge	de pointe
• developing / developed	en voie de développement / développé
• double-digit	à deux chiffres
• energy-intensive	nécessitant beaucoup d'énergie / à forte intensité énergétique
• English-speaking	anglophone
• export-driven	à vocation exportatrice
• fast-growing	à croissance rapide
• garment industry	industrie de la confection
• GDP (Gross Domestic Product) growth	croissance du PIB
• ground-breaking	révolutionnaire
• growth rate	taux de croissance
• high-tech cluster	pôle de compétitivité
• illiterate	analphabète
• inequality	inégalité
• innovation-based	basé sur l'innovation
• labour-intensive	nécessitant une main-d'œuvre importante / à forte intensité de main-d'œuvre
• to lag behind	être à la traîne
• life expectancy	espérance de vie
• manufacturing-based	basé sur l'industrie
• market(-oriented) economy	économie de marché
• poverty line	seuil de pauvreté
• rampant	endémique
• standard of living	niveau de vie
• to sustain growth	maintenir la croissance
• sweatshop	atelier où la main-d'œuvre est exploitée
• to take off	décoller
• technology-intensive	à forte intensité technologique
• two-tier	à deux vitesses
• skilled / unskilled workforce	main-d'œuvre qualifiée / non qualifiée
• up-and-coming	qui monte, plein d'avenir
• warehouse	entrepôt
• well-educated	qui a fait des études

USE THE LIST

Fill in the gaps with compound adjectives taken from the list. A definition of each adjective is given to help you.

a. Taiwan has replaced its traditional ... industries such as toys and textiles by ... industries, moving them offshore to Malaysia or the Philippines. *(which requires numerous workers / which uses or produces new technologies)*

b. Taiwan benefited from the arrival of many ... Chinese who fled communism. *(who have a university diploma)*

c. South Korea has sustained a ... growth for decades. *(said of a number of at least two figures)*

d. Seoul's ... development strategy left the rural sector relatively underdeveloped despite efforts to improve rural living standards. *(which is specialised in exports)*

e. For many years, Malaysia has been one of the world's ... emerging markets. *(rising)*

f. Indian call centres rely on an ... workforce. *(who speak English)*

g. China outsources its cheap labour industrial activities to Vietnam but its ... businesses remains in China as profit margins are higher. *(using and producing a lot of capital)*

h. India is in dire need of ... reforms for entrepreneurs to overcome cumbersome bureaucratic hurdles. *(using new methods)*

GRAMMAR WORK

Les différents emplois de *as*

Aide-mémoire grammatical, p. 229.

Analysez et traduisez les exemples suivants :

1. Countries such as Malaysia and the Philippines have developed recently.
2. Many countries think of China as a source of cheap products.
3. As India lacks good roads, farmers find it difficult to sell their products.
4. As China becomes richer, so the gap between the poor and the rich is growing dramatically.

■ ***As*** **est-il préposition ou conjonction ? Quels sont ses différents sens ?**

1 Complétez les phrases suivantes avec la traduction anglaise de l'expression entre parenthèses.

a. The advent of China ... is a challenge for all countries. *(comme puissance mondiale)*

b. ... are overcrowded, roads are congested all the time. *(Étant donné que la plupart des villes)*

c. ... Singapore can accommodate up to 40 cargo tankers whereas Mumbai has something like 9 berths to accommodate them. *(Un port tel que)*

d. India's young graduates may work ... ... they speak English fluently. *(comme employés de centre d'appel / puisque)*

e. ... is developing at great speed, banks are lending more and more money to its entrepreneurs. *(Tandis que le Vietnam)*

Since, for, ago, during, while

▶ Aide-mémoire grammatical, p. 240.

Analysez les exemples suivants en observant particulièrement les temps utilisés, puis traduisez-les.

1. China has been the second most important economy in the world for a few years now.
2. Economic growth in Asia has averaged 5% since 2001.
3. A few months ago, China became the world's leading emitter of CO_2.
4. Vietnam's economy suffered during the war against the USA.
5. We visited a shipbuilding site while we were in South Korea.
6. I stayed in Malaysia for three weeks.

■ **Que remarquez-vous au sujet de la traduction de *for* ?**

2 Complétez les phrases suivantes avec la traduction en anglais des expressions entre parenthèses.

a. ..., China was one of the world's poorest countries. *(Il y a 30 ans)*

b. Korea's shipbuilding firms will enjoy a boom ... still. *(pendant de nombreuses années)*

c. ... corporate restructuring has improved the financial health of Korean companies. *(Depuis la crise de 1997)*

d. ..., the population in India will keep rising. *(Pendant les 20 prochaines années)*

e. ... the Olympic games in 2008, there was an earthquake in Sichuan, killing 90,000 people. *(Pendant que la Chine préparait)*

f. In 2008, ... toxic baby milk scandal in China, at least 300,000 infants were taken ill. *(au cours du)*

3 **Complétez les phrases suivantes en utilisant *for, since* ou *ago,* combiné avec le repère proposé entre parenthèses. Puis posez une question sur la phrase commençant par *How long* ou *How long ago,* et traduisez le tout.**

Exemples de questions : *How long has India been independent? How long ago did India become independent?*

a. China has produced inexpensive goods ... now. *(years and years)*

b. Tata Motors have been selling their Nano car ... . *(2008)*

c. China started reforming its economy more than ... . *(three decades)*

d. Taiwan's economy has been based on a strong spirit of entrepreneurship ... . *(a long time)*

e. The Philippines have lagged behind ... . *(the financial crisis)*

f. ..., all these Asian countries were colonies. *(a long time)*

g. Our Asian supplier has been making these toys ... . *(six months).*

4 **Traduisez en anglais les phrases suivantes.**

a. Leur PIB a augmenté de 6 % au cours des trois dernières décennies.

b. Depuis combien de temps Hong Kong est-il chinois ?
– Depuis plusieurs années.

c. Depuis la fin des années 1990, des pays comme le Vietnam connaissent un essor important.

d. Il n'y a pas très longtemps, comme tous ces pays étaient très pauvres, les enfants mouraient de faim.

e. Pendant dix ans, notre fournisseur nous a vendu ce riz comme étant le meilleur.

f. Cela fait combien de temps que Hong Kong est revenu à la Chine ?

EXAM WORK

DOCUMENT 1

China and India: New Innovation and Talent Forces

Most people in the U.S. and elsewhere in the West think of China and India largely as sources for inexpensive products and services. Few know that China, India, and other developing countries are taking center stage[1] in the global war for innovation and talent. Consider some important benchmarks[2]: scientists and engineers in China, India, and Russia are now producing an estimated 150,000 scientific and technical papers[3] annually, more than many Western European nations.

The rapidly developing economies also now claim[4] an estimated two-thirds of all engineers, a vital talent pool[5], while many Western countries face talent scarcities[6]. Asian scientists and students are returning home from the West in record numbers. China and India are investing heavily in research and development, with China alone spending $136 billion on R&D in 2007, second only to the U.S. and ahead of Japan.

China and India also now boast some of the world's top science and research universities. These trends have helped many Chinese and Indian companies aggregate[7] a critical mass of talent, which is having a profound impact on their ability to innovate and compete in the global economy. Tata Motors, for example, designed its new, low-priced Nano automobile almost entirely with Indian talent.

Some Western companies are keenly[8] aware of China's and India's mounting innovative capabilities and have seized upon the opportunity to capitalize on[9] the new reality. Some 70% of the employees in General Electric's Bangalore Global Research Center, for example, hold masters degrees or PhDs[10]. The 680 patents GE's Bangalore team has filed[11] since 2000 are critical to the company's global innovation efforts. Despite such votes of confidence, many multinationals still appear somewhat gun shy[12], worried about intellectual property theft, runaway[13] wage growth, and a high attrition rate[14] among engineers.

By Arindam Bhattacharya, abridged from *Business Week*, November 17th, 2008.

1. *To take centre stage:* occuper le devant de la scène. **2.** *Benchmark:* point de référence. **3.** *Paper:* article. **4.** *To claim:* déclarer. **5.** *Pool:* réservoir. **6.** *Scarcity:* pénurie. **7.** *To aggregate:* rassembler. **8.** *Keenly:* extrêmement. **9.** *To capitalize on:* exploiter. **10.** *PhD (Philosopher's Doctorate):* doctorat. **11.** *To file a patent:* déposer un brevet. **12.** *Gun shy:* qui n'assume pas ses idées. **13.** *Runaway:* galopant. **14.** *Attrition rate:* taux de départs.

1 **Sum up this article in English in *about 100 words*, justifying the title.**

2 **EXPRESSION. Rédigez en anglais le courrier suivant. *(150 mots environ.)***

Vous êtes l'adjoint(e) du directeur des relations internationales d'une société française productrice de béton, France Bétons. Celui-ci vous a demandé de rédiger un courrier pour proposer à des entreprises de fabrication de béton en Chine de créer une filiale commune afin d'exploiter le marché de la tuile en béton[1], bien plus solide que la tuile en argile[2] locale. Vous apporterez votre savoir-faire technique. Présentez brièvement votre société et joignez votre brochure technique ; proposez une rencontre : rien ne remplace le contact humain. Formules d'usage.

1. *Tuile en béton:* concrete tile. **2.** *Tuile en argile:* clay tile.

DOCUMENT 2

India starts trade talks with African countries in effort to rival China

India's prime minister and dozens of business leaders began trade talks in Ethiopia on Monday as the Asian giant strives to catch up with China in what has been dubbed[1] "the new scramble for Africa". Bilateral India-Africa trade has grown from about £620m in 2001 to £28.5bn in 2010. India's commerce and industry minister, Anand Sharma, hopes it will reach £43bn by 2012. Some 250 Indian companies have invested, mainly in telecommunications and chemical and mining companies.

But India remains about a decade behind its Asian rival. China says its two-way trade stands at £75bn, a 43.5% increase on the previous year, and up from just £620m in 1992. It has built roads, bridges, railways and power stations[2] in return for access to markets and resources. Brahma Chellaney, professor at the New Delhi-based Centre for Policy Research, told Reuters: "India is massively playing catch-up to China in Africa, and only in recent years is it trying to engage the continent in a serious way. But it is trying to build political and economic ties[3], and position itself as different to China, which has acquired the image of being a new imperial power."

The fierce competition between the pair for resources, minerals and food to fuel[4] their turbo-charged economies has been likened by commentators to the so-called scramble for Africa among European countries in the 19th century. Officials in New Delhi stress that India's links with Africa are centuries old, bolstered[5] by trade across the Indian Ocean and a million-strong Indian diaspora across Africa. But, like China before it, India has been criticised for turning a blind eye to[6] human rights abuses and corruption. Its state-owned oil company has invested in Sudanese oil, and New Delhi avoided criticising the Khartoum government at the height of the Darfur crisis.

Abridged from *The Guardian*,
by David Smith, 23 May 2011.

---

1. *To dub:* surnommer. **2.** *Power station:* centrale électrique. **3.** *Tie:* lien. **4.** *To fuel:* alimenter. **5.** *To bolster:* soutenir. **6.** *To turn a blind eye to:* fermer les yeux sur.

3 **EXPRESSION. Using document 2, write about the differences and similarities between India and China in their scramble for Africa.** ***(About 150 words.)***

4 **Translate the last paragraph into French.**

DOCUMENT 3

July 29th 2010.

The writing in Chinese means: "What do we workers want? - More money" and "When do we want it? - Now".

5 **EXPRESSION. Describe this cover from *The Economist* and explain what it implies for the world economy. *(About 200 words.)***

DOCUMENT 4

The mystery of the Chinese consumer

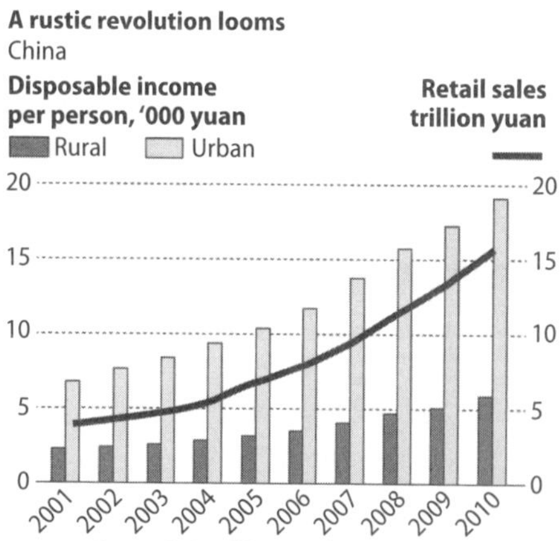

Source: National Bureau of Statistics, Lunar Capital.

From *The Economist*, July 7th 2011.

6 **EXPRESSION. Describe and analyse this bar chart. Why has it been entitled "The mystery" of the Chinese consumer? *(About 150 words.)***

Méthodes, p. 271.

DOCUMENT 5

Palm oil: the biofuel of the future driving an ecological disaster now

The numbers are damning[1]. Within 15 years 98% of the rainforests[2] of Indonesia and Malaysia will be gone. With them will disappear some of the world's most important wildlife species, victims of the rapacious destruction of their habitat in what conservationists[3] see as a lost cause. Yet this gloomy[4] script was supposed to have included a small but significant glimmer[5] of hope. Oil palm for biofuel was to have been one of the best solutions in saving the planet from greenhouse gases and global warming.

Instead the forests are being torn down in the headlong[6] rush to boost palm oil production. More startling is that conservationists believe the move to clear land for this "green fuel" is often little more than a conspiracy, providing cover to strip out[7] the last stands of timber[8] not already lost to illegal loggers[9].

Until now palm oil – of which 83% is produced in Indonesia and Malaysia – was produced for food. But the European Union's aim of cutting greenhouse gas emissions by 20% by 2020, partly by demanding that 10% of vehicles be fuelled by biofuels, will see a fresh surge[10] in palm oil demand that could doom[11] the rainforests.

Researchers from the Dutch pressure group Wetlands International found that as much as half the space created for new palm oil plantations was cleared by draining[12] and burning peat-land[13], sending huge amounts of carbon dioxide into the atmosphere.

As the risks become more obvious, there has been a growing clamour[14] for eco-labelling of "sustainable" palm oil. A "round table" of buyers, producers and environmentalists has established several key criteria that would prevent conversion of high-conservation rainforest to palm oil plantations, cut the use of fires to clear land, and mitigate[15] the conflict of plantations with wildlife and rural communities, though it has yet to be ratified. "It's vital we find financial backing for this now," said Fitrian Ardiansyah, a Worldwide Fund for Nature-Indonesia programme officer.

Jakarta is increasingly aware of the dangers. Yet as a developing country it also believes Europe must help out financially if it wants the safeguards against the downside[16] of palm oil production that will assist in cutting greenhouse gas.

Ian MacKinnon, abridged from *The Guardian*, April 4th, 2007.

---

1. *Damning:* accablant. 2. *Rainforest:* forêt équatoriale. 3. *Conservationist:* écologiste. 4. *Gloomy:* sombre, déprimant. 5. *Glimmer:* lueur. 6. *Headlong:* tête baissée. 7. *To strip out:* arracher. 8. *Stand of timber:* bosquet d'arbres. 9. *Logger:* bûcheron. 10. *Surge:* hausse. 11. *To doom:* condamner. 12. *To drain:* assécher. 13. *Peat:* tourbe. 14. *Clamour:* revendication. 15. *To mitigate:* apaiser, alléger, atténuer. 16. *Downside:* inconvénient.

7 Répondez aux questions.

a. Quel thème est abordé par le texte et quelle en est l'idée directrice ?

b. Quelles sont les conséquences de la déforestation, voire de la disparition, des forêts équatoriales ?

c. Quel espoir l'huile de palme avait-elle suscité ?

d. Quelles sont les motivations de ceux qui contribuent à la déforestation ?

e. En quoi l'Union européenne exerce-t-elle une influence sur le sort de ces forêts ?

f. Quelles mesures ont été prises et par qui pour freiner cette évolution ?

8 EXPRESSION. Comment on the dilemma illustrated here which emerging countries have to face:

Emerging countries want to develop their economies, but they have to respect the obligations of sustainable development imposed by developed countries. What can be done about it, in your opinion? *(About 200 words.)*

9 COMPRÉHENSION. Vous rédigerez une note de synthèse *(200 mots environ)* des documents 1 à 4, concernant les caractéristiques majeures des pays dont il est question ici.

10 EXPRESSION. Rédigez en anglais le courrier suivant.

Vous travaillez pour le compte d'une société malaise (Royal Asian Palm, Wisma View, 50450 Kuala Lumpur) exportatrice d'huile de palme qui est à la recherche de clients en Grande-Bretagne. Vous adressez le courrier à un importateur-revendeur qui pourra trouver des entreprises intéressées par vos produits.

Vous présentez la société et ses produits : de l'huile de palme écologique car produite selon un plan raisonné d'exploitation des sols. L'engagement de la société dans une politique de développement durable est un de ses atouts.

Vous proposez l'envoi d'échantillons afin de tester une huile plus particulièrement adaptée à la production de margarine et d'huiles de cuisson. Vous proposez des avantages commerciaux à toute entreprise prête à passer une commande importante.

Formules d'usage.

▶ Méthodes, p. 274.

CHAPITRE

7

Information and communication technologies

Les technologies de l'information et de la communication

BACKGROUND

Information and Communication Technologies or ICTs apply to any medium[1] used to record[2], broadcast[3], and manipulate information orally and/or visually: computers, hand-held computing devices, disks, CDs, DVDs, radio, cinema, television, cameras, telephones, and even paper. They include computing hardware (PCs, MP3 players, smartphones and much more), and application software, from word-processing and spreadsheets[4] to the Internet, its search engines and online services, and the World Wide Web (the consortium leading the development of technical standards and addresses for the Web). Their main characteristics today are the growing variety of services they provide and their interconnectivity. They have changed people's relationships, the economy and society.

Telecommunications

The fantastic growth in the number and sophistication of mobile or cell phones, and now smartphones, has revolutionized the world, and contributed to reducing the digital divide[5]. It has a huge impact on emerging countries in particular, by giving their inhabitants access to global information and business opportunities: many can afford[6] mobile phones, if not computers.

ICTs in emerging countries

They are playing a growing role, and especially telephones. For instance, lots of jobs have been created thanks to the call centres set up in English-speaking countries like India because of their low labour costs in order to develop telemarketing. In India too, fishermen call different ports from their boats to get the best possible prices for their fish. Millions of illiterate farmers can now do business with practically the whole country.

China has more mobile phone users now than any other country in the world. In 2008, it overtook[7] America as the country with the largest number of Internet users, one third of whom use mobile phones to go online. In 2011, it had over one billion mobile subscribers.

Mobile banking services have been introduced in various African and Asian countries. A mobile payment service introduced by Safaricom Kenya in 2007 enables subscribers to deposit and withdraw[8] money or send funds to each other by text messages[9]. Casual workers[10] and taxi drivers can be paid by phone. In Brazil, the unemployed can be notified about job opportunities by text messages. All these tools[11] and services are encapsulated[12] into one another, and become more and more sophisticated. But the problem is to make them compatible and facilitate Internet access for mobiles: this is however being made possible by smartphones and the emerging 3G and 4G (third and fourth generation) technologies. So, the potential for the mobile Internet in emerging countries in particular is enormous, as computers are much more expensive than mobile telephones.

If computers and access to the Internet are still limited there, especially in some parts of Africa, which hampers[13] business, they have been spreading fantastically in more and more countries.

Computers and the Internet

By creating e-commerce, computers and the internet have boosted and transformed the economy dramatically. They have been growing and changing too, as more and more companies today use Application Service Providers (ASPs)[14], also called Software as a Service (SaaS). This system enables clients and companies to rent, rather than buy, software used on simplified, cheaper computers. The advantage is that users no longer have to invest a lot of money in and worry about hardware, its maintenance or upgrades[15], and adapting to expensive, complex software. For example firms can perform their accounting tasks[16] through specialized services provided by Google, Yahoo, Amazon, or smaller ones like TADTechnology. The latter allow bookkeepers working individually, in large or small firms, or government organizations, to access online accounting services, applications and files[17].

Cloud computing

Some experts have called this system "cloud computing", a metaphor that refers to the Internet "clouds" depicted in computer networked diagrams, and found in outside data-centres or huge central computers. Thanks to a kind of "cloud service" for instance, your empty ink cartridge tells your mobile or laptop[18] that you need to buy a new cartridge.

Social media or networking

New Web sites like Facebook, MySpace, LinkedIn, etc, have introduced many effects, not only on society but also on business, as they can influence the decisions of consumers to buy or not, through "buzzing", blogs, "tweets", post-its, etc: a completely new trend which has sometimes become a marketing ploy. They can also boost employment and play a role in hiring people. Through them, job seekers can find jobs and companies can check on them before taking them on. Sharing music and films online can hamper these sectors by reducing their profits. But the business of online games is booming.

ICTs adapt to us, but we have to adapt to them and their ever-changing configurations. Are they our modern slaves? Or are we their slaves?

Some important reminders

When you browse[19] the Net, be cautious and critical: a lot of information may be unreliable[20], if not altogether misleading[21].

At the office especially, somebody may read your emails: never put confidential, or private, or gossipy[22] information in them. It might spread like wildfire.

1. *Medium:* support, moyen.
2. *To record:* enregistrer.
3. *To broadcast:* diffuser.
4. *Spreadsheet:* tableur.
5. *Digital divide:* fracture numérique.
6. *Can they afford it?:* peuvent-ils se le payer ?
7. *To overtake:* dépasser.
8. *To withdraw:* retirer.
9. *Text message:* SMS.
10. *Casual worker:* travailleur intérimaire / saisonnier.
11. *Tool:* outil.
12. *Encapsulated:* encapsulé.
13. *To hamper:* gêner.
14. *Service provider:* fournisseur de services.
15. *Upgrade:* nouvelle version.
16. *To perform a task:* effectuer une tâche.
17. *File:* fichier.
18. *Laptop:* ordinateur portable.
19. *To browse:* surfer sur.
20. *Unreliable:* non fiable.
21. *Altogether misleading:* totalement trompeur.
22. *Gossipy:* cancanier.

Repérer les notions essentielles

Répondez aux questions suivantes en français.

- **a.** Citez six supports de technologies de l'information et de la communication.
- **b.** Quelles sont les deux principales caractéristiques actuelles du développement des téléphones portables ?
- **c.** Quels services les téléphones portables rendent-ils dans les pays en développement ?
- **d.** Quelle évolution l'informatique connaît-elle actuellement dans les entreprises ?
- **e.** Qu'est-ce que le *cloud computing* ?
- **f.** Quels sont les deux rappels importants donnés à la fin du texte ?

Recherchez dans le texte les expressions en anglais correspondant aux expressions suivantes :

a. moteur de recherche – **b.** normes techniques – **c.** permettre l'accès à Internet – **d.** ce dernier – **e.** cartouche d'encre – **f.** se répandre comme une traînée de poudre – **g.** réseaux sociaux – **h.** le bouche à oreille.

Résumer le texte en français

Résumez ce texte en *150 mots environ*.

Approfondir

Do you have favourite Internet sites? Describe them and explain what you use them for.

LEXICAL WORK

• answering machine	répondeur-enregistreur
• attachment	pièce jointe
• B2B / business-to-business	commerce inter-entreprises
• to be cut off	être coupé
• to be on the phone	être au téléphone
• broadband	transmission à haut débit
• bug	bogue
• C2C / consumer-to-consumer	transaction(s) entre particuliers
• to call (up) / back / again	appeler / rappeler
• to crash	tomber en panne / planter
• cut and paste	copier-coller
• data (capture)	(saisie de) données
• data flow	flux de données
• device	dispositif
• to dial a number	composer un numéro
• digital divide	fracture numérique
• digital signature	signature numérique
• to download / upload	télécharger vers son ordinateur / le serveur
• e-bill / e-business	facture / commerce électronique
• to email	envoyer par mél
• to encrypt	crypter
• engaged line	ligne occupée
• ex directory (GB) / unlisted (US) number	numéro sur liste rouge
• file-sharing	partage de dossiers
• fixed (phone) line	ligne de téléphone fixe
• flat rate	forfait
• to get through to sb	obtenir la communication avec qqn
• (computer) hacker	pirate (informatique)
• to hang up	raccrocher
• to hold a conference call	tenir une téléconférence
• Internet / file server	serveur Internet / de fichiers
• junk mail	pourriel
• to key in / capture data	saisir des données
• to make / place a call	passer un coup de fil

- online-auction site — site de vente aux enchères sur Internet
- piracy, hacking — piratage
- program / software — logiciel(s)
- roaming — itinérance
- search engine — moteur de recherche
- secured transaction — transaction sécurisée
- to subscribe — s'abonner
- subscriber — abonné
- subscription — abonnement
- telephone company / operator — opérateur téléphonique
- touch screen — écran tactile
- upgrade — nouvelle version
- to upgrade — mettre à jour
- username — identifiant
- voice mail box — boîte vocale
- web grocer / retailer — épicier / détaillant en ligne
- widget — petit programme utilitaire
- wired — branché / câblé

USE THE LIST

1 Fill in the blanks with words from the list, making the necessary changes, then translate the sentences.

a. Global sales of music have dropped because of f...-s... s... which lets Internet users exchange music without paying for it.

b. For every song which is bought legally, about 20 songs are d... illegally.

c. But one Californian company compiles and sells statistics about them, because they can be useful d... .

d. More and more customers are buying their food from w... g... because they are sick of going shopping.

e. She didn't manage to g... t... to the manager directly, so she left a message on his v... m... b... .

f. We really need to u... our marketing software. Do you know a good p...?

2 Choose five words from the list which you think are important, and write sentences with them, using your dictionary or the Internet if necessary.

GRAMMAR WORK

Comparatifs de supériorité, d'infériorité, et d'égalité

Aide-mémoire grammatical, p. 236.

Analysez et traduisez les exemples suivants :

1. The date is getting <u>closer</u>.
2. There are <u>fewer</u> trees now <u>than</u> there were ten years ago.
3. They use <u>less</u> ink <u>than</u> in the past.
4. This software provides <u>more</u> services <u>than</u> that one.
5. It can be operated <u>as easily as</u> before.
6. My mobile is <u>not as</u> up-to-date <u>as</u> yours.

■ **Quels termes faut-il après un comparatif de supériorité, d'infériorité ou d'égalité ?**

■ **Quelle est la différence entre *less* et *fewer* ?**

■ **Quels sont les deux exemples de comparatif d'infériorité présentés ici ?**

1 Mettez les adjectifs suivants aux comparatifs de supériorité, d'égalité et d'infériorité en les faisant suivre de *than* ou *as* selon le cas.
Puis fabriquez trois phrases avec trois adjectifs différents mis au comparatif de supériorité, d'égalité ou d'infériorité.

Attention à la différence entre adjectifs longs et courts !

a. difficult – **b.** cheap – **c.** expensive – **d.** intelligent – **e.** slow – **f.** profitable – **g.** useful – **h.** efficient – **i.** reliable – **j.** fast – **k.** easy – **l.** convenient – **m.** high – **n.** bad.

2 Traduisez en anglais.

a. Mon service téléphonique est plus cher mais plus fiable que le vôtre.

b. Notre nouveau logiciel est plus difficile à utiliser que l'ancien, mais il est plus rapide.

c. Je ne suis pas d'accord : je l'utilise aussi facilement que l'ancien, qui était effectivement bien plus lent.

d. Les gens ont plus d'ordinateurs et de téléphones que jamais, et consomment moins de papier.

e. Les ordinateurs portables consomment moins d'énergie qu'autrefois.

f. Mon téléphone a moins de gadgets que le tien, mais le son est bien meilleur.

g. Est-ce que votre fournisseur d'accès à Internet marche aussi bien que le mien ?

Expression de la continuité : *Still, yet, no / not any longer / no more*

Aide-mémoire grammatical, p. 248.

Analysez et traduisez les exemples suivants :

1. It is no longer a joke.
2. The Internal Revenue Service still insists on that.
3. I can no longer access the Internet
4. I cannot access the Internet yet.
5. I still cannot access the Web.
6. There are no more e-mails to read.
7. He does not call us any more / longer.

3 Traduisez en anglais

a. Je n'ai plus de téléphone car il m'a été volé.
b. Vous servez-vous encore de ce logiciel pour votre informatique ?
c. Même si Bill a un téléphone mobile, il utilise encore son téléphone fixe.
d. Je n'ai toujours pas reçu votre mél : que se passe-t-il ?
e. Elle ne s'est toujours pas décidée à changer d'opérateur téléphonique.
f. Nous ne sommes pas encore abonnés à ce service.
g. Nous ne recevons plus de factures de votre service comptabilité : pour quelle raison ?
h. Le réseau informatique du bureau ne marche plus : il n'a toujours pas été réparé. Que s'est-il encore passé ?
i. Le réparateur n'est toujours pas arrivé.
j. Est-ce que vous employez encore du papier dans votre entreprise ?
k. Je n'ai toujours pas retrouvé mon mobile : où ai-je bien pu le mettre ?
l. Nous n'avons plus leur numéro de téléphone : l'avez-vous ?
m. Sheila n'utilise plus jamais cette adresse mél car cet opérateur est moins bon que le nouveau.

EXAM WORK

DOCUMENT 1

Hanging up

Reports of the death of the phone call are greatly exaggerated

While the computing cloud expands ever more, the humble phone call is in terminal decline, thanks to text messaging[1] and the mobile Internet. So, at least, say commentators in Silicon Valley. Some have already penned[2] obituaries[3]. "The phone call is dead," read a recent headline in *TechCrunch*, a blog and currently the central organ of the high-tech region. But is it really time to hang up?

There is no doubt that landline[4] calls are past their prime[5]. The time people spend talking on a fixed telephone has gone down in recent years in nearly all rich countries for which the International Telecommunication Union has data. Yet in most, this fall is more than offset[6] by the increase in mobile calls, according to a recent report by Ofcom, the British telecoms regulator (see chart).

Ofcom also found that cost, more than anything, determined how long people talk for and whether they prefer a landline or a mobile call. Should Germany's rates for wireless[7] conversation—currently twice the rate of landline calls—come down, people would certainly spend more than 112 minutes per month talking on handsets[8].

The strongest support for the notion of the disappearing phone call comes from America. Nielsen, a research firm, reports that the amount of time mobile subscribers talk has dropped to 700 minutes per month in 2010. That includes incoming calls. A survey by CTIA, a trade group, shows that the average length of a mobile call has dropped from just over three minutes to one minute and 40 seconds since mid-2007.

Less talking does not necessarily mean less phone use. According to Nielsen the number of paid texts per subscriber has grown rapidly over the same period, recently surpassing 700 per month. This is mainly thanks to the restless[9] fingers of teenagers, who are also buying more smartphones—essentially hand-held computers that let them send messages via social networks. Facebook, the world's biggest such network, recently announced that a third of its nearly 600m members access the service on their mobile phones.

Yet in Britain, where teenagers have been texting for longer, the spread of smartphones has not had the same effect, says Steve Alder, the general manager for devices at Telefonica Europe, which operates the O2 brand. British subscribers with smartphones talk 11% longer than owners of simpler handsets, Mr Alder says. The young are both more talkative and more text-hungry.

New technologies often fail to displace old ones. Research from the Kaiser Family Foundation shows that young Americans are watching more television even as they spend more time on the computer. And an old form of communication may stage a comeback in a different form. Skype, the internet phone service, is growing rapidly. In the first half of 2010 users racked up[10] 95 billion minutes in voice and video calls.

Odds are[11] that the conventional phone call will be just one of many forms of telecommunication. And for most people outside of Silicon Valley, where some entrepreneurs allegedly[12] do not even know how to use their smartphone to place a phone call, it will remain the most important one for some time to come. That should be welcomed by all those who relish[13] the gentle art of conversation—and dreaded by parents who pay the bills.

The Economist, January 1st, 2011.
www.economist.com

1. *To text a message:* envoyer un SMS. 2. *To pen:* rédiger. 3. *Obituary:* nécrologie. 4. *Landline:* ligne terrestre. 5. *To be past one's prime:* ne plus être de la première jeunesse. 6. *To offset:* compenser. 7. *Wireless:* sans fil. 8. *Handset:* récepteur. 9. *Restless:* agité. 10. *To rack up:* accumuler. 11. *Odds are:* il y a des chances. 12. *Allegedly:* paraît-il. 13. *To relish:* adorer.

1 Traduisez en anglais.

a. La plupart de ces services téléphoniques sont reliés à Internet.

b. Ce service vous permet de répondre seulement aux appels que vous voulez.

c. Ils ont choisi de drôles de noms pour séduire les jeunes.

d. Vous pouvez vous attendre à passer du temps à lire ce qui est écrit en petits caractères.

DOCUMENT 2

Still chatting away

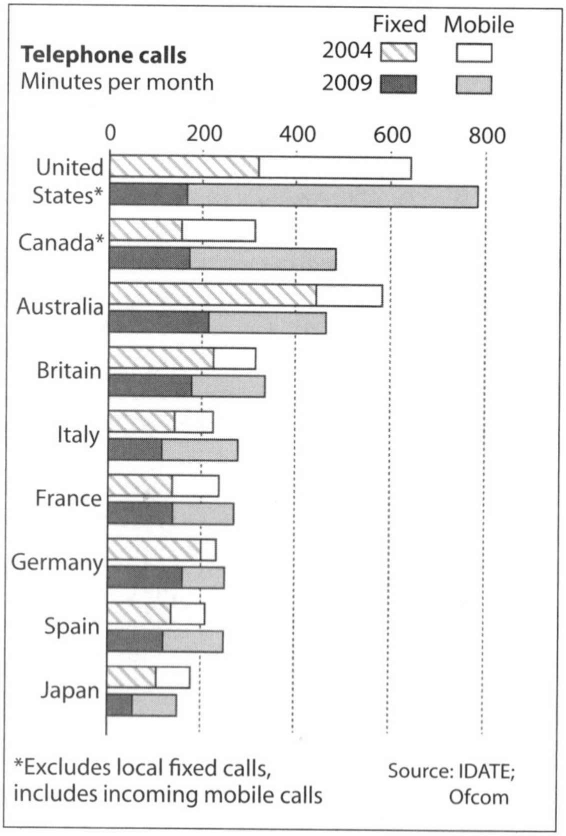

2 **Find the words or expressions in the text which could translate the following ones:**

a. Passer du temps à téléphoner.
b. Ceci comprend presque toutes les données actuelles.
c. Le téléphone n'a pas réussi à supplanter le courrier.
d. Certains smartphones permettent d'envoyer des SMS par des réseaux sociaux.
e. La plupart des gens redoutent de recevoir leur facture de téléphone.
f. Passer un appel sur son téléphone fixe.

3 **COMPRÉHENSION. Résumez ce texte et le diagramme en français (*150 mots environ*), en justifiant leurs titres.**

DOCUMENT 3

The paperless office : on its way[1], at last

No longer a joke, the "paperless" office is getting closer.

"Stephanie Breedlove and her husband founded Breedlove & Associates 16 years ago to help families who (legally) hire a nanny with the crushing burden[2] of paperwork that this entails. There are pay stubs[3] to be sent, federal and state tax returns to be filed[4], pay schedules to be updated[5] and other trails of exceedingly boring paper. Much of the firm's small office in Austin, Texas, is taken up by 100 paper-filled filing cabinets[6]. An office manager spends 25 hours a week shuffling paper[7] between desks and drawers. At peak times, says Ms[8] Breedlove, the office becomes "a sea of paper," with colour-coded stacks[9] on conference tables, floors and chairs.

With luck, this will soon be a thing of the past. Last year Breedlove decided to go paperless. It is now about halfway there, says Ms Breedlove. The constant flow of information between Breedlove and its clients now goes via e-mail, with forms attached as PDF files. The next step is to roll out[10] an online service so that clients can log on to manage their accounts. Only the Internal Revenue Service still insists on paper for some things, says Ms Breedlove, but even it claims to be going electronic soon.

Fewer trees will die and less ink will be squirted, but that is not her primary motivation, she says. It is that everyone—clients and staff—is sick[11] of paper. The clients tend to be young, middle-class families with toddlers[12]; they are good with technology and already pay bills online, use e-tickets on planes, e-file[13] their tax returns and Google recipes[14] rather than using cookbooks. And Breedlove's 16 employees are in their 20s, native to Facebook and instant-messaging and baffled[15] by the need for paper. Now everybody is happier. Next year the firm expects to be completely paperless.

[...] As new generations of office workers leave university—where their class notes and syllabuses[16] are online these days—, they take their habits with them. They like digital information because it reduces clutter[17]. It can be "tagged[18]" and thus filed into many folders[19] instead of just one physical file. It can be searched by keyword. It can be cut, pasted and remixed. It allows for easier collaboration, through features such as "track changes". It can be shared across an ocean as easily as across a desk. Increasingly, it resides in the Internet "cloud" and can be accessed from anywhere, not just in the office.

By contrast, paper tends to get torn[20], stained[21], burnt, soaked[22] and lost. [...]

The Economist, October 11th, 2008.

1. *On its way:* en route. **2.** *Crushing burden:* fardeau écrasant. **3.** *Pay stub:* fiche de salaire. **4.** *To file a tax return:* remplir une déclaration fiscale. **5.** *To update a pay schedule:* actualiser un barème de salaires. **6.** *Filing cabinet:* armoire de classement. **7.** *To shuffle paper:* remuer de la paperasse. **8.** *Ms* (*Miz* (US)): madame (mademoiselle). **9.** *Stack:* pile. **10.** *To roll out:* lancer. **11.** *To be sick of:* en avoir assez de. **12.** *Toddler:* jeune enfant. **13.** *To e-file:* envoyer un fichier par Internet. **14.** *To Google a recipe:* chercher / trouver une recette par Google. **15.** *To baffle:* déconcerter. **16.** *Syllabus:* programme d'études. **17.** *Clutter:* pagaille. **18.** *To tag (tagged):* étiqueter. **19.** *Folder:* classeur, dossier. **20.** *To tear (tore, torn):* déchirer. **21.** *To stain:* tacher. **22.** *To soak:* tremper.

4 **Write a note in English (*about 150 words*) presenting "Breedlove & Associates", stressing the fact that it is going paperless.**

What services does it provide, and what are the advantages of the paperless office?

5 **Vous allez créer un site Internet en français sur le modèle de « Breedlove & Associates ».**

Composez une courte publicité *(150 mots maximum)*, à publier sur Internet ou dans la presse, décrivant votre site et les services qu'il peut offrir, en vous inspirant du texte.

DOCUMENT 4

The virtues of life on paper in an age of technology

With more people converting to electronic calendars[1] or hovering[2] between paper and PDA[3], how we construct and coordinate our schedules is in flux[4]. And no matter how synchronized[5] our intertwined lives have become, a certain amount of calendar clashing is inevitable.

[According to] "an Exploratory Study of Personal Calendar Use," a 2008 paper from Virginia Tech[6], the march of electronic calendaring is swift and inevitable: "With the increased use of mobile devices, more and more calendaring tasks are performed off[7] the desktop computer."

Three years later, the study is already a relic, according to one of its authors, Manuel A. Perez-Quinones, an associate professor of computer science. "That was before smartphones, before Google calendar, back when you still had to plug in your PDA to sync[8]," Dr. Perez-Quinones said. "It was a whole different monster." Paper hasn't totally disappeared, he said, "but the desk and office calendar is on its way out."

This kind of prediction strikes terror in paper people. Yet there isn't necessarily a correlation between a commitment to technology and a choice of calendar. "I've got an iPad, an iPod, I'm on Twitter and Facebook and I'm talking on my BlackBerry now," said Nelson George, a cultural critic, filmmaker and producer, in a phone interview. "But that's enough. I'm an old-school paper calendar person."

Mr. George uses a datebook that fits in his back pocket. "People make comments about it," he said. "They show me their little technology. But then they sit there tapping on their device, and by the time[9] they've gone through all the log-ins and downloading, I've already flipped[10] the page."

Though it may be counterintuitive (electronic calendar keepers insist their method is more reliable than the ephemera of paper), those who use a paper calendar see it as the more durable option. Mr. George has dropped his BlackBerry in water three times—something he believes wouldn't or couldn't threaten his notebook.

Abridged from *The International Herald Tribune*, August 1st, 2011.
www.nytimes.com

---

1. *Calendar/datebook:* (ici) agenda. 2. *To hover:* voltiger. 3. *PDA:* Personal Digital Assistant (petit ordinateur de poche). 4. *In flux:* en perpétuel changement. 5. *No matter how synchronized:* aussi synchronisées que. 6. *Virginia Tech:* Virginia Polytechnic Institute and State University (in the USA). 7. *Off:* à partir de. 8. *To plug in to sync:* synchroniser en se connectant. 9. *By the time:* le temps que. 10. *To flip:* passer/tourner rapidement.

6 Complete the following sentences with words or expressions from the text and translate them:

a. My datebook is full because I have a very busy s...

b. Paper has not disappeared t... more and more people use computers.

c. I find it very difficult to g... t.... all the log-ins and downloading of my new smart-phone.

d. Young people usually have a stronger c... than older people to the new technologies.

DOCUMENT 5

People are going to be putting their information not into some device but into some service that lives in the sky.

Newsweek, November 24th, 2008.

7 **EXPRESSION. Describe and explain this picture with the help of the explanations about « cloud computing » given page 85.**

8 **EXPRESSION. Using documents 1, 2, 3 and 4, and your experience, do you think that paper will disappear altogether from offices and from our lives? *(About 250 words.)***

9 **EXPRESSION. Vous envoyez un mél (*de 150 mots maximum*) en anglais à Andrew Collins, répondant à une publicité sur son fournisseur de services BizWebCom vendus en ligne, pour demander les renseignements suivants concernant les services proposés.**

Combien de personnes au maximum peut-on joindre pour des téléconférences, partage de documents et présentations commerciales par Internet ? Quels sont les pays accessibles ? Quels sont les tarifs en euros, sachant que vous représentez une société française de 50 personnes ? Un essai est-il possible ?

Salutations d'usage dans les méls.

CHAPITRE

8

The organisation of working hours

L'aménagement du temps de travail

BACKGROUND

Historical overview

Over the 19th and 20th centuries the number of working hours gradually went down in the industrial world thanks to action from workers, trade unions[1] and collective bargaining[2]: legislation was set up to improve workers' life and situation, and give them holidays with pay. During the past few decades, most OECD countries have reduced their number of working hours also thanks to better productivity and more part-time jobs, mostly held by women. Quite a few companies have lowered both working hours and salaries in order to avoid layoffs[3] and bankruptcies following economic difficulties.

Workers' rights

In developed countries employees are now guaranteed daily breaks, weekly rests, paid (or unpaid) holidays, sabbaticals, sickness, maternity and paternity leaves, which all vary greatly from country to country. For example, British workers are entitled to[4] 28 days of paid annual leave (including or not the "bank holidays"). In the USA, there are no such things as "legal vacations" for private sector employees, but there are public holidays (such as the Fourth of July). However, American employers voluntarily grant time off[5] to employees to attract them. In all developed countries, "waiting times" (*e.g.* a fireman waiting between emergency calls) are considered as working time and paid. But there can be big differences in the legislations on paid travel, training[6], retraining, or commuting[7] times. Today, with smoking banned from the work premises[8], some companies deduct smoke breaks from their employees' paid time, which raises fierce debates.

EU countries

Member countries have set up common working time directives, but this proves complex because of the diversity of labour markets and social protection systems. Part time work has become common. Under the pressure of growing unemployment, the idea also spread that work could be shared between workers –a highly controversial issue. In France, the "Lois Aubry" became mandatory in 2000, setting a 35-hour week in all companies with more than 20 employees, in order to fight unemployment– but in the end they created relatively few jobs, and may have destroyed others.

In 2003, the European Working Time Directive (WTD) was passed to protect workers from the negative effects of long hours or disrupted[9] rest periods. A consultation in 2010 revealed that current working time rules need to be improved to facilitate local negotiations through collective bargaining.

Legislation in the United Kingdom

Adult workers cannot be forced to work more than 48 hours a week on average as long as[10] the average for 17 weeks is under 48 hours per week, according to the EU legislation. However, workers can choose to opt out of[11] the 48 hour limit but this must be voluntary and in writing. It cannot be an agreement with the whole firm's workforce.

Legislation in the USA

The Federal Labor Standards Act stipulates that employees must receive overtime pay for hours worked over 40 per workweek, but says there is no limit on the number of hours employees may work in any workweek.

The situation in Asia

Asian countries have the longest working hours in the world, legally between 44 and 48 hours a week depending on the cases. In Singapore the working week is officially capped[12] at 44 hours, but most workers do much more. In Hong Kong it is still around 50 hours on average but is gradually decreasing, though half the workers regularly work late into the evening. In China migrant workers who live in dormitories close to the factory may work up to 70 hours a week. However, this is improving.

Flexible work patterns

Workers all over the world are concerned with achieving a better work-life balance[13]. Moreover, with the "24 hour society", businesses operate[14] outside the standard hours to increase productivity and meet consumer demand. Governments in Europe implement policies which help to set up flexible working patterns, with practices such as job-sharing[15], flexi-time, teleworking and so on. However, this has a significant social and health impact, which is stronger with shift work[16] than with long hours. Part time work proves valuable for a good balance between family life and work. The prevalence of women in part time employment is due to the fact they mainly work in health, education and services where such patterns can easily be arranged. It is rare in top positions where women usually account for about 10% of managers. Involuntary part time work is slightly more common among men. The option of part-time work is more attractive for women, though "option" may be considered as ambiguous when childcare services are not available.

Stress – the new occupational disease

The Japanese, who have a long hours work culture added to company get-togethers, have invented a term which refers to death by overworking – *karoshi*. Without going to such extremes, "burn out"[17] syndromes have become an issue in many countries, and the long hours culture seems to be one ingredient but not the only one explaining why some workers end up completely exhausted, physically, nervously and emotionally.

On the other hand, many workers, especially in France, are paradoxically dissatisfied with a smaller number of working hours, as it may not mean a smaller workload[18], and might not correspond to their wishes. They can even feel more stressed than in the past.

---

1. *Trade union:* syndicat. **2.** *Bargaining:* négociations. **3.** *Layoff:* licenciement. **4.** *To be entitled to:* avoir légalement droit à. **5.** *To grant time off:* accorder des congés. **6.** *Training:* formation. **7.** *Commuting:* déplacement domicile-travail. **8.** *Work premises:* enceinte de l'entreprise. **9.** *Disrupted:* perturbé. **10.** *As long as:* du moment que. **11.** *To opt out of:* choisir de ne pas suivre. **12.** *To cap:* plafonner. **13.** *Work-life balance:* équilibre entre vie professionnelle et vie privée. **14.** *To operate:* fonctionner. **15.** *Job-sharing:* partage de poste. **16.** *Shift work:* travail posté. **17.** *Burn-out:* épuisement. **18.** *Workload:* charge de travail.

Repérer les notions essentielles

Answer the following questions.

a. What has the evolution of working hours been characterized by from the 19th century to today?

b. What aspects of work are taken into account by legislation in the 21st century?

c. What rights concerning time off are guaranteed to workers?

d. Compare the situation in the countries that are mentioned.

e. Why have new work patterns emerged?

f. What are the benefits and drawbacks of recent evolutions?

Résumer le texte en français

Résumez ce texte en *200 mots environ*.

Approfondir

What are the advantages and drawbacks of telecommuting? Give your opinion. *(About 250 words.)*

LEXICAL WORK

• absenteeism	absentéisme
• to axe jobs	supprimer des emplois
• to be out of work / unemployed	être au chômage
• bonus	prime
• to clock in / out	pointer en arrivant / partant
• coffee / tea break	pause-café / thé
• collective bargaining	négociations collectives
• to commute	aller à son travail
• to cope with	faire face à, s'en sortir
• day off	jour de congé
• downtime	temps mort
• to earn one's living	gagner sa vie
• fixed-term work contract	contrat à durée déterminée
• flexitime	horaire à la carte / variable
• freelance worker	travailleur indépendant
• full time work, timetable	travail à temps plein
• holidays with pay	congés payés
• hourly rate	taux horaire
• job losses / cuts	suppressions d'emplois
• job sharing	partage du travail
• labour laws	droit du travail
• to lay off / make redundant	licencier
• livelihood	source de revenu, gagne-pain
• maternity / paternity leave	congé maternité / paternité
• moonlighting	travail au noir
• night shift	équipe de nuit
• nine-to-five routine	horaires de bureau classiques
• overtime	heures supplémentaires
• overworked	surmené
• pay cut / rise	réduction / hausse de salaire
• to pension off	mettre à la retraite
• permanent contract	contrat à durée indéterminée
• placement / training period	stage (en entreprise)
• public / bank holiday (GB)	jour férié
• to retire	prendre sa retraite
• salary, pay	salaire

• schedule	horaire
• shiftwork	travail posté
• sick leave	congé maladie
• staggering of holidays	étalement des vacances
• study leave	congé pour formation
• teamwork	travail en équipe
• to take early retirement	partir en pré-retraite
• telecommuting / teleworking /home-working	télétravail
• teleworker	travailleur à domicile
• to temp	faire de l'intérim
• time off	des congés
• under / overstaffed	en sous- / sureffectifs
• to work long hours	faire de longues journées
• to work overtime	faire des heures supplémentaires
• to work part-time	travailler à temps partiel
• work pattern	formes de travail
• work place	lieu de travail
• workaholic	bourreau de travail
• working life	vie active
• working time regulations	réglementation du temps de travail

USE THE LIST

1 **Match the following words and add an article if necessary, then translate the phrases.** ***Ex.: to take a / the day off.***

a. to take – **b.** to work – **c.** to join – **d.** to have – **e.** to cope with

1. tea – **2.** trade – **3.** long – **4.** night – **5.** day – **6.** hours – **7.** off – **8.** shift – **9.** union – **10.** break

More vocabulary

2 **Fill in the gaps with one of the following words and translate the text :**
business – action – lessen – long – employers

A survey made in 2007 revealed that 48% of the … interviewed said stress caused by … hours and limited resources was affecting … performance, but only 5% said they were taking strong … to … this stress.

GRAMMAR WORK

Les auxiliaires modaux exprimant l'obligation et la déduction

▶ Aide-mémoire grammatical, p. 231.

Analysez et traduisez les exemples

1. I <u>must</u> get up earlier tomorrow because I've got so much to do.
2. I <u>have (got) to</u> finish this work by Tuesday because I have promised the boss.
3. My colleague has been working non-stop since last week: she <u>must</u> be exhausted! She <u>must have</u> worked 12 hours a day.
4. These two conflicting rules <u>cannot be</u> true!
5. They said they would finish the report by today; they <u>cannot</u> possibly <u>have</u> forgotten that!

1 **Complétez et traduisez les phrases avec une des formes ci-dessus.**

a. Some employees have no choice; they … work very long hours.

b. They … be extremely tired by the end of the week.

c. I would like to know more about working conditions in the 19th century so I … buy a book about the subject.

d. I suppose they … have been much harder than now, with much longer hours.

e. The company's management is going to axe jobs at the office. How awful! They … do that.

f. Bill … get up very early tomorrow morning, as he has an appointment with the Manager at 8a.m.

g. Mrs Parkin … work at the weekend again.

h. My partner has agreed to work every Sunday! She … possibly be serious!

Le *present perfect* simple et le *present perfect* progressif

Aide-mémoire grammatical, p. 256.

Analysez et traduisez les exemples suivants :

1. They <u>have</u> finally <u>completed</u> the project.
2. They <u>have been working</u> on the project all afternoon.
3. The dispute over working time <u>has just been settled</u>.
4. The boss <u>has already arrived</u> at the office.
5. He <u>has been thinking</u> of changing jobs <u>for</u> months / <u>since</u> last year.

2 Complétez les phrases suivantes avec un des verbes ci-dessous au *present perfect* simple ou progressif, et traduisez-les :
to destroy – to cut – to start – to try – to give – to suffer – to tell – to force

a. The manager ... the employees that the shop will be open seven days a week.
b. He ... to obtain permission for the past six months.
c. Many employees already ... looking for another job.
d. My colleague ... £1,000 to a charity that helps the unemployed.
e. More and more people are saying that working long hours ... their family life.
f. Unfortunately, the snow ... me to cancel my business trip.
g. They ... our working hours in the factory by a third. No holiday this year!
h. Most of the people who ... from stress say that it was due mainly to long working hours.

3 Traduisez en anglais.

a. Nous avons dû demander trois jours de congé pour aller au mariage de notre ami.
b. Il cherche un emploi depuis deux ans, et il vient enfin de trouver un travail posté de nuit.
c. Il a passé deux mois à chercher un emploi à temps partiel dans la région.
d. Je l'attends depuis deux heures. Il a dû être obligé de faire des heures supplémentaires.
e. Avez-vous fait le travail que je vous ai demandé de finir pour 5 heures ?
f. En Angleterre, les jours fériés sont depuis toujours fixés au lundi.
g. Votre femme a dû être très contente d'apprendre que vous avez eu une augmentation de salaire appréciable, sans être obligé de faire plus d'heures.

EXAM WORK

DOCUMENT 1

Work from home day: let's do it again

Working from home is a growing trend, with plans to give every employee the right to request flexible working by 2013.

Did your commute[1] seem a little quieter than normal this morning? You might have noticed a few extra seats on the train or less traffic at the usual bottleneck[2] on your drive to work. Or, perhaps you didn't bother commuting at all and took advantage of National Work From Home Day, an initiative organised by Work Wise UK.

The idea is to demonstrate that giving people the freedom to work from home from time to time can help save office costs, ease transport congestion and enable us to manage our workloads[3] more effectively.

A new analysis by the TUC[4] shows the number of homeworkers in the UK –currently around 3.7 million– fell slightly during the recession, probably because of rising unemployment levels and a general feeling of insecurity about work.

But overall, the homeworking trend is growing. Business secretary Vince Cable this week announced plans to change the law by 2013 to give every employee the right to request a flexible working pattern. It remains to be seen how many employers, particularly smaller ones, will respond to such requests, but flexible working could potentially transform the lives of many, particularly those with parental or caring[5] responsibilities.

Technology is playing a part too, with better wireless Internet connections, the emergence of smartphones and tablets as viable business tools and cheap productivity applications.

Abridged from *The Guardian*, 20 May 2011.

---

1. *Commute:* trajet domicile travail. **2.** *Bottleneck:* embouteillage. **3.** *Workload:* charge de travail. **4.** *TUC (Trades Union Congress):* Confédération des syndicats. **5.** *Caring:* soins.

1 Sum up the text answering the following questions: What is the new trend in working patterns and what makes it possible? What are its benefits? *(About 100 words.)*

DOCUMENT 2

Long hours at work may boost[1] heart-attack risk

While you may consider yourself lucky to be working long hours—or working at all—in the current economy, your diligence may be undermining[2] your health in the long run. People who work an average of 11 or more hours per day have a 67 percent higher risk of suffering a heart attack or dying from heart disease than people who work a standard seven- to eight-hour day, according to a new study in the Annals of Internal Medicine. Those who work between 10 and 11 hours per day have a 45 percent higher risk.

Routinely burning the candle at both ends may not increase heart risk by itself, but it may be an indicator of an unhealthy lifestyle in general, according to experts who weren't involved in the research. The study didn't show a cause-and-effect relationship between long hours and heart attacks, they point out, and the apparent link could be due to a number of complicated health factors, including stress, lack of exercise, and eating high-calorie takeout[3] rather than healthy home-cooked meals.

What's more, the type of work, and how much you enjoy it, may make a big difference, Kopecky says. While sitting behind a desk for 11 hours may be unhealthy, farmers are notorious[4] for working 12 or even 14 long, hard hours a day - and they tend to live longer than average, he says.

By Amanda Gardner, *Health Magazine*, healthmagazine.com, April 4, 2011.

1. *To boost:* accroître. 2. *To undermine:* amoindrir. 3. *Takeout:* plats à emporter. 4. *To be notorious for:* être connu pour.

2 To what extent are long hours related to heart attacks? *(100 words maximum.)*

DOCUMENT 3

Endless work

A study by iPass found that the majority of highly mobile workers around the world already toil[1] for more than 50 hours in an average week, with 20% working 60 hours or more. According to the latest survey, three-quarters of the 3,100 businessmen and women interviewed say they work five to 20 hours a week more than their official working hours suggest. Downtime[2] is becoming scarcer, with laptops and smartphones using ubiquitous[3] wireless broadband connections, opening up the possibility to work anywhere and at any time. Expanding airborne[4] Internet access means that workers can be tapped[5] even on traditionally tranquil flights.

Human-resource managers would understandably rejoice at what amounts to more uncompensated overtime. More surprisingly, the respondents[6] themselves seem remarkably cheery[7] about the ever longer hours. They are also unfazed[8] by the erosion of the divide between work and personal life. All but 6% believe that they are at least as productive with the flexibility to work nearly anywhere; over half say they are substantially more so. At the same time, nearly two-thirds said they found it easier to balance work and personal commitments[9], and about one in two were "marginally" or "substantially" more relaxed.

Abridged from *The Economist*, 3rd September 2011.

1. *To toil:* trimer. 2. *Downtime:* temps morts. 3. *Ubiquitous:* que l'on trouve partout. 4. *Airborne:* à bord des avions. 5. *To tap:* exploiter. 6. *Respondent:* personne interrogée. 7. *Cheery:* content, ravi. 8. *Unfazed:* pas troublé. 9. *Commitment:* engagement.

3 Résumez ce texte en français en faisant ressortir le paradoxe dont il est question *(environ 100 mots)*.

DOCUMENT 4

Do We Need Defined Hours of Work Any More?

By now, most people who work in the developed world have gotten used to the idea that the old nine-to-five routine is gradually becoming a thing of the past. Plenty of people have shifts[1] that start and end at different times, or they use job-sharing and other forms of flex-time. All of which raises a question: Are defined hours of work an anachronism that's holding us back? Or is the freedom to work whenever we want something still reserved for a select few, and/or a trap that causes us to work more rather than less?

Flexible work is something that seems increasingly popular with programmers and other online workers. Working in a startup is a much different experience [from] working in a factory. You can't throw more time[2] at a problem and expect it to get solved. That kind of approach, which management consultants like to call a "results-oriented workplace," might be fine for a creative endeavour[3] such as programming or design. But does it make any sense for other companies and industries?

Although there is plenty of research that shows both workers and companies benefit when hours are more flexible, not everyone—regardless of[4] what business they work in—is going to want to work a totally unstructured schedule. And for some people, a specific routine isn't just something that they need for external reasons: a job without defined parameters might actually increase the stress they feel and therefore make them less productive or efficient.

By Mathew Ingram, Gigaom,
September 5, 2011.

1. *Shift:* durée de travail. 2. *To throw time:* consacrer du temps. 3. *Endeavour:* entreprise/activité. 4. *Regardless of:* indépendamment de.

4 **Sum up this text, using your own words. (*About 100 words*).**

DOCUMENT 5

" Yes, we have ***flex time*** ... except when it's not convenient. "

Artist: Delgado, Roy Catalog

5 **EXPRESSION. Describe and explain the cartoon: who benefits most from flexi-time arrangements—companies or employees? *(100 words.)***

6 **En vous référant aux documents 1 à 5, expliquez quels sont les problèmes d'horaires et de temps de travail auxquels les employés doivent faire face. *(150 mots environ.)***

7 **EXPRESSION. Le directeur des Ressources humaines vous a demandé d'envoyer un questionnaire aux employés sur leur vécu et leurs désirs en matière d'horaires à la carte. *(150 mots environ, en anglais.)***

Rédigez 10 questions auxquelles les employés devront répondre pour permettre à la direction des Ressources humaines de définir de nouvelles pratiques. Commencez par une courte introduction expliquant aux employés l'objectif de ce questionnaire, et indiquez le délai de réponse maximum.

8 **Fill in the gaps with one of the following words and translate the text :** ***managers – cope – allowed – up to – cut – ensure – legislation – year – a – in hospitals – moment***

Hospitals say that ... are needed to ... compliance with European ... which says that, from August next ... , no doctors will be ... to work more than 48 hours ... week ... . At the ... , junior doctors can work ... 56 hours. Will the hospitals be able to ... when hours are ... ?

CHAPITRE

9

Changes in social protection

L'évolution de la protection sociale

BACKGROUND

Social protection covers mainly healthcare and safety, old age and retirement, unemployment and family needs. There are welfare programmes to help people cope with[2] poverty which may lead to homeless adults and children. This protection is provided by the state, by companies and/or by charities.

Health care in OECD countries

There has been a remarkable growth in international healthcare systems, public and private; a recent study showed that healthcare spending in the OECD (Organisation for Economic Co-operation and Development) had outstripped[3] GDP (gross domestic product) growth by 2 percentage points each year for the past 50 years. The costs are rising and healthcare systems everywhere are finding it difficult to meet demand. The future may see public systems paying only for core services[4] such as public health, prevention, emergency care and mental health. People will be expected to pay for expensive treatment themselves or through private health insurance.

Health care in the USA

Healthcare insurance is normally provided by private medical insurance companies or hospitals, employers or charities. In 1965 the Johnson administration created two medical insurance programs, Medicare for people over 65, and Medicaid for low-income families. As medical insurance is very expensive because of high medical costs, many people still did not have any until 2010. Then the Obama administration passed the Affordable Care Act which now makes it compulsory for all Americans to get a private, reasonably priced medical insurance, and which subsidizes low-income families to that end.

Health care in the UK

In 1948, the National Health System (NHS) was launched to provide all British citizens with free medical care, paid for by the income tax. But it gradually became both more expensive for the nation's budget and less efficient, with people's growing expectations of often costly new treatments. So in 2011 the Cameron government introduced the Welfare Reform Bill to improve the NHS.

Old age

In 2008 in Britain, the 100th anniversary of the Pensions Act[6] was celebrated, but the pensioner group is growing so fast that it is necessary to look for ways of reducing the rising cost of state pensions. There is talk of people having to work until they are 70, just as they used to. However, as people are living longer, they will still enjoy longer retirements. Unfortunately, in Britain those who have no company pension and only a state pension to live on have trouble[7] paying their bills and some of them live in such poverty that they choose between eating and heating in the winter months.

In the USA, there are many different types of pension schemes, public and private, some of which are over 100 years old. All retirees receive from a federal agency Social Security retirement benefits[8] which are based on the legally mandated contributions they made during their working careers. In addition, they may get an income from, for example, the private pension funds that they, their trade unions, and/or their employers may have contributed to. However, the value of these, sometimes very rich, pension funds fluctuates according to the way they are invested; and the growing number of senior citizens will put more and more strain on all these various systems.

Unemployment

In the United Kingdom there are Job Centres which are very helpful and guide jobseekers towards a training course, a temporary, part-time or full time job. Job seekers receive unemployment benefits which will be granted[9] according to various conditions and may be stopped in certain cases. Sometimes it is possible for the employee to relocate with some help from the firm. In the USA too unemployment compensation can be obtained, both from federal and state programs. Mobility and flexibility are now considered to be essential, but it is obviously difficult to expect these from older workers.

In many countries, there is a lack of real political will (even from trade unions) to fight unemployment among young and low-skilled people by providing effective solutions to their high rates of joblessness.

Family needs

Family allowances are granted more or less generously in many Western countries. For people managing on a low income, there are also benefits for lone parents[10], sick or disabled[11] people, those over 60, those who are caring for[12] someone who is ill or disabled, those who are registered blind, etc.

In Europe, citizens are usually taken care of by state or public organizations. In America, it is generally considered that welfare should be the responsibility of individuals themselves, or charities, or local authorities, or private institutions, but not of the federal government. Nevertheless[13], this has been changing because of the shocking growth of poverty among certain categories of people. Benefits are granted for children, low-income families or disabled people, by the federal government, by states, local authorities, etc. So there is welfare in America, but with great disparities between people and places. In the UK the Welfare Reform Bill has also changed previous welfare programmes to fight poverty and protect the most vulnerable more efficiently; its objective is to "make work pay" and encourage people to break the poverty cycle and benefit dependency. It has launched a Universal Credit System to encourage people to work longer, simplify the benefits system and make Job Centres more effective. Each country has its own benefit schemes with its own attitude towards the welfare of the population.

The Welfare State

There are structural differences between social and welfare models in Europe and the United States, but they do have something in common, which is likely to modify all the systems, namely[14] the ageing of the population, the increasing cost of welfare, and rising economic difficulties.

1. *Welfare:* avantages sociaux (*welfare state:* État-providence).
2. *To cope with:* faire face à.
3. *To outstrip:* devancer.
4. *Core service:* service de base.
5. *To turn out:* s'avérer être.
6. *Act:* loi.
7. *To have trouble:* avoir des difficultés.
8. *Retirement benefits:* allocations de départ en retraite.
9. *To grant:* accorder.
10. *Lone parents:* familles monoparentales.
11. *Disabled:* handicapé.
12. *To care for:* soigner, s'occuper de.
13. *Nevertheless*: cependant.
14. *Namely:* à savoir.

Repérer les notions essentielles

Answer the following questions.

a. Which people are concerned by social protection?

b. Why has healthcare become so costly?

c. Why is it getting difficult to provide decent retirement pensions?

d. How do unemployed people deal with their plight?

e. What aid can families get?

f. What welfare problems do our societies face nowadays?

g. Point out some differences between the European and American welfare systems.

Résumer le texte en français

Résumez ce texte en *150 mots environ*.

Approfondir

Browse the Net to find information about the welfare system of any foreign country of your choice: healthcare, unemployment, retirement schemes, and aid to families. What are its current problems and how does it deal with them?

LEXICAL WORK

• to age	vieillir
• ageism ; age discrimination	âgisme ; discrimination par l'âge
• bank (GB) / public holiday	jour férié
• to be badly off / well off	être pauvre / riche
• to be entitled to	avoir droit à
• to be in dire straits	être en grande difficulté
• to be on the dole	toucher les allocations de chômage
• to be on welfare	recevoir de l'aide sociale
• care	soin(s)
• child abuse	mauvais traitements à enfant
• company car	voiture de fonction
• compensation	indemnités
• concern	inquiétude
• to cope with	faire face à, affronter
• cost of living	coût de la vie
• day-care centre	crèche
• disablement pension	pension d'invalidité
• disease, illness	maladie
• family allowances	allocations familiales
• health and safety regulation	règle d'hygiène et de sécurité
• holidays with pay	congés payés
• income support (GB)	revenu complémentaire (pour les plus pauvres)
• income tax	impôt sur le revenu
• inland revenue	fisc
• insurance broker	courtier d'assurances
• insurance premium	prime d'assurance
• Job Centre (GB)	Pôle-emploi
• life expectancy	espérance de vie
• to live from hand to mouth	vivre au jour le jour
• life span	durée de vie
• maternity / paternity / sick leave	congé de maternité / paternité / maladie
• means-tested benefit	allocation indexée sur les revenus
• minimum wage / salary	salaire minimum
• mortgage	prêt immobilier / emprunt logement
• old age / retirement pension	pension de vieillesse / retraite
• pay-as-you-earn system	système de retenue à la source dans l'impôt sur le revenu
• to pay contributions	verser des cotisations
• pension scheme / plan	régime / système de retraite

• pensioner, retiree	retraité
• perk / fringe benefit	avantage en nature
• to pick up	se redresser
• plight	situation difficile
• poverty	pauvreté
• to protect / guarantee sb's rights	préserver / garantir les droits de qqn
• purchasing power	pouvoir d'achat
• to rescue / save / help	secourir
• senior citizen, elderly person	personne du troisième âge / âgée
• to shelter	abriter
• sickness benefit	prestation de maladie
• Social Security	système d'aide sociale (GB) / des retraites (USA)
• social worker	assistant(e) social(e)
• standard of living	niveau de vie
• tax allowance / rebate	abattement / dégrèvement fiscal
• tax form	feuille d'impôts
• the haves and the have-nots	les riches et les pauvres
• the homeless	les sans-abri / SDF (sans domicile fixe)
• the jobless / unemployed	les chômeurs
• time off / leave (of absence)	absence / congé
• trade union	syndicat
• unemployment benefit	allocation de chômage
• wealth tax	impôt sur la fortune
• welfare state	État-providence

USE THE LIST

1 **Make compound nouns by matching the following nouns and translate them.**

a. child – **b.** insurance – **c.** bank – **d.** sickness – **e.** welfare – **f.** family.

1. holiday – **2.** benefit – **3.** abuse – **4.** allowance – **5.** premium – **6.** state.

2 **Match the verbs from the first list below with the words from the second list, and translate the expressions:**

a. to be	**1.** holidays with pay
b. to cope with	**2.** on welfare
c. to be entitled to	**3.** a homeless person
d. to shelter	**4.** poverty
e. to live	**5.** from hand to mouth

3 **Fill in the gaps with words from the list and translate the text.**

Before the state pension system was created in Great Britain a hundred years ago, for many people old a... meant destitution . Nowadays, s... c... are e... to state support when they retire. Unfortunately, p... have not kept up with the c... of l..., and more and more p... are living below the poverty line. Life e... has increased, so now there is talk of raising the r... age.

GRAMMAR WORK

Les différentes constructions de *used to* : *used (not) to live, to be used to living, to get used to living*

▶ Aide-mémoire grammatical, p. 231.

Analysez et traduisez les exemples suivants :

1. People <u>used to work</u> long hours for very little pay.
2. They <u>used not to have</u> holidays with pay.
3. They <u>were used to living</u> without central heating.
4. Now they <u>have got used to living</u> in nice, warm houses.

1 **Complétez les phrases avec une des expressions ci-dessus en effectuant les changements nécessaires, puis traduisez-les.**

a. Nowadays, most people in the rich countries ... *(to be immunized / vaccinated)* against diseases which ... *(to be)* killers.

b. Mary says that for old people things ... *(to be)* worse a hundred years ago.

c. They ... not *(to have)* state pensions, so many of them ... *(to work)* until they died.

d. His grandmother did not want to live in an old people's home but she ... *(to get)* to ... *(live)* there now.

e. Old people's homes are much nicer now than they ... *(to be)*.

Les différentes constructions de *to wish*

Aide-mémoire grammatical, p. 268.

Analysez puis traduisez les exemples suivants :

1. I wish I knew more about / had known more about the various pension schemes.
2. I wish the doctor could / would give me / could have given me the new medical treatment.

2 Complétez les phrases avec une des formes ci-dessus des verbes proposés en effectuant les changements nécessaires, puis traduisez-les.

a. Mr Jones wishes he ... *(to find)* a job providing a better healthcare plan.

b. I wish I ... not *(to cancel)* my appointment at the hospital yesterday.

c. She wished she ... *(to know)* where to buy the pill advertised on TV.

d. My husband wishes the boss ... *(to give)* him longer paternity leave. Three days is too short.

e. We wish we ... *(to buy)* better health insurance, now that our daughter is seriously ill.

3 Traduisez en anglais.

a. Autrefois, en Grande-Bretagne et aux États-Unis, les médecins allaient visiter leurs malades chez eux.

b. Maintenant, comme les médecins sont moins disponibles, les malades se sont habitués à se rendre au service des urgences de l'hôpital.

c. Cette vieille dame de 90 ans est habituée à vivre seule, mais elle regrette qu'aucune assistante sociale ne vienne lui rendre visite.

d. Autrefois, les gens allaient au travail à pied ou à vélo.

e. Maintenant, beaucoup ont pris l'habitude d'aller travailler en voiture, surtout s'ils ont une voiture de fonction.

f. Ils vont devoir s'habituer maintenant à prendre les transports publics.

g. J'aimerais bien que mon employeur prenne en charge mes frais de transport.

h. Nous regrettons de ne pas avoir plus d'avantages en nature dans notre entreprise.

i. Je regrette de ne pas avoir su que l'adhésion au club de sports de la société était gratuite pour les anciens salariés partis en retraite.

EXAM WORK

DOCUMENT 1

Carry on camping

French workers' perks[1] are under scrutiny

IN MOST of Europe, works councils[2] deal with such dull matters as working hours and safety. In France they are ministries of fun. Comités d'entreprise together spend €11 billion ($15.5 billion) a year on treats[3] for workers such as half-price beach and ski trips, camping holidays for families and Christmas hampers[4].

At Électricité de France (EDF), a big utility[5], the comité d'entreprise is so big and rich, with thousands of employees, that it has its own comité d'entreprise. It is believed to have more press officers[6] than EDF itself. Each year it has about €500m to spend. Even that is not enough; in 2009-10 union officials went over their budget, leaving a cash deficit of €130m. The comités d'entreprise of Air France, France Télécom and Euro Disney have also overspent wildly[7] in recent years, triggering investigations.

"When you have all that money, it can go to your head," confides the head of one council. And if the company makes up[8] the deficit, as many do, what incentive is there to scrimp[9], he asks? Luxurious facilities are a particular weakness. Air France's comité d'entreprise, which found itself in financial difficulties last year, is now under pressure to sell Domaine de Lassy, a leisure centre outside Paris which was formerly a stud[10] farm owned by the Aga Khan.

Even by French standards, EDF's comité d'entreprise is exceptional. In 2009 it became the first works council to buy a listed company, André Trigano, a lossmaking camping firm. The cash it spent—around €60m—would have covered much of its recent loss.

Scandals at some of the biggest comités d'entreprise have given all a bad name. The former head of Air France's works council has even called for reform. But employees need not fear. In a country where workers routinely take bosses hostage[11], no one wants to meddle with[12] their right to go camping.

The Economist, May 28th, 2011.

---

1. *Perk:* avantage en nature. **2.** *Works council:* comité d'entreprise. **3.** *Treat:* gâterie. **4.** *Hamper:* bourriche, panier garni. **5.** *Utility:* entreprise de service public. **6.** *Officer:* responsable. **7.** *Wildly:* de façon extravagante. **8.** *To make up:* compenser. **9.** *To scrimp:* se serrer la ceinture. **10.** *Stud:* étalon. **11.** *To take sb hostage:* prendre qqn en otage. **12.** *To meddle with:* se mêler de.

1 **Find the words or expressions in the text that mean:**

a. réclamer – **b.** l'ancien patron – **c.** installations luxueuses – **d.** une base de loisirs – **e.** déclencher – **f.** subir des pressions – **g.** une société cotée en bourse – **h.** autrefois – **i.** un voyage à moitié prix.

2 **Résumez ce texte en *100 mots environ.***

DOCUMENT 2

Intern[1] Nation: How to Earn Nothing and Learn Little in the Brave New Economy[2] (from a book by Ross Perlin)

The most widespread trend in the world of working for nothing is the explosion of white-collar and no-collar[3] interning. Not only is interning the fastest-growing job category, it is also fashionable [...]. In Intern Nation, Ross Perlin, a survivor of serial internships on three continents, describes the lengths to which graduates[4] must go to secure[5] an unpaid intern position (often the first of many) that might help them build a CV or get a foot in the door. An auction[6] market has even sprung up to sell these positions to the highest bidder[7]. A Versace internship fetched[8] $5,000 at auction, temporary blogging rights at the Huffington Post[9] went for $13,000, and someone paid $42,500 for a one-week stint[10] at Vogue. At one Californian outfit[11], Dream Careers, 2,000 internships all over the world are sold annually. You can buy an eight-week summer position for $8,000 (a placement in London will set you back[12] $9,500).

[...] The educational value of these gigs[13], whether organised by an operation like Dream Careers or a university careers centre, is notoriously slight[14]. The work is usually menial[15]; it's rare for interns to receive any structured training. The biggest beneficiary is, of course, the employer. On Perlin's estimate, corporate America enjoys a $2 billion annual subsidy from unpaid internships. He also confirms that a large number of full-time jobs have been converted into internships, while formerly paid internships have morphed[16] into unpaid ones. An estimated 37 per cent of internships in this country are now unpaid or below the minimum wage; the figure is 50 per cent in the US.

Andrew Ross, abridged from *The London Review of Books*, May 19th 2011.

---

1. *Intern:* stagiaire. **2.** *Brave new economy:* after the famous ironic phrase from *The Tempest* by Shakespeare: "Oh brave new world" (which was not brave at all). **3.** *White-collar and no-collar:* normally the expression is white-collar and blue-collar (office and factory workers); here it is ironic, again. **4.** *Graduate:* étudiant de 3e cycle. **5.** *To secure:* obtenir. **6.** *Auction:* vente aux enchères. **7.** *Bidder:* enchérisseur. **8.** *To fetch:* aller chercher. **9.** *Huffington Post:* journal d'informations américain publié uniquement sur le Net. **10.** *Stint:* période de travail spécifique. **11.** *Outfit:* boîte (entreprise). **12.** *To set back:* revenir à/coûter. **13.** *Gig:* boulot temporaire. **14.** *Slight:* léger. **15.** *Menial:* subalterne. **16.** *To morph:* se transformer.

3 **Complete the sentences below with the following words and expressions from the text, making the necessary changes:**

widespread – trend – placement – to spring up – training – formerly – subsidy

a. This utility has called for state ... to improve its employees' welfare.
b. It is difficult to find a good, well paid job if you have no ... .
c. The British word for internship is ... .
d. Unemployment is now ... in many developed countries.
e. The job market was not so bad, ...
f. There is now a rising ... towards part-time employment.
g. New jobs are most encouragingly ... in this promising sector.

4 **Résumez ce texte en *100 mots environ.***

5 **EXPRESSION. If you have already worked as an intern in an organization, write a report about it, describing your experience. How did you find your internship/placement? What did you do? Did you earn anything, and did you get any fringe benefits? *(About 250 words.)***

DOCUMENT 3

www.guardian.co.uk

TUC : Trades Union Congress (confédération des syndicats britanniques)

6 **COMPRÉHENSION. Rédigez une note de synthèse faisant ressortir dans quelle mesure le document 3 illustre le document 2. *(100 mots environ.)***

DOCUMENT 4

Default[1] retirement age of 65 to end in Britain, ministers confirm.

"I would scrap[2] the concept of retirement altogether[3]. Only people who are not physically or mentally capable of working should be paid by the state - this would ease the burden on taxpayers and employers, improve quality of life of older people and curtail[4] the private pensions industry which is little more than smoke and mirrors." Alan Findley, Consett

"I am 61 this month and I work in administration and welcome the scrapping of DRA, because I am more than capable of working after 65 and want to do so. I don't think because you reach 65 that you are incapable of carrying out your work –I do think this is age discrimination. I know that in manual jobs this would be difficult but in an office environment it would pose no problem and we would also be paying NI[5] and tax and not putting a burden on the government." Val Redden, Swansea

"I am a small to medium size business owner. We need clear guidelines –not everyone aged over 65 is fit[6] enough to keep working after 65. I suspect no win no fee lawyers[7] will be rubbing their hands[8] with this ambiguous legislation. It is hard enough for young people to obtain employment: this has got to have an impact on that sector as well." Trevor Brooks, Woking

"I for one[9] totally disagree with the retirement age of 65. I personally think that it should be a choice whether somebody wants to keep working past the retirement age;

"I for one[9] totally disagree with the retirement age of 65. I personally think that it should be a choice whether somebody wants to keep working past the retirement age; and those that wish to retire at an early age should be allowed to do so. I would like the government to show the public a statistic showing those in favour of the retirement age being raised to support their evidence[10]. In my opinion it's a way for the government to pay less out, as ... people are living longer." Leslie Mahon, Leeds

"I am 65 in December this year and this is a real help –I work for a local authority, I am a father of 11 and 13-year-olds, and retaining my job is important if possible. I work as a social worker and social work manager and it is absolutely discriminatory if I were to be put out to grass[11] on the basis of age. If I can do the job competently, then it is my human right not to be dismissed on the grounds of age, and I absolutely agree that when I am no longer competent to do so I hope I recognise this early enough... " Tom Coy, UK

www.bbc.co.uk

---

1. *Default:* normal, par défaut. 2. *To scrap:* supprimer. 3. *Altogether:* complètement. 4. *To curtail:* réduire. 5. *NI:* National Insurance (contribution sociale payée par tous les travailleurs britanniques). 6. *To be fit:* être en forme. 7. *No win no fee lawyer:* avocat qui ne touche d'honoraires que s'il gagne le procès (illégal en France). 8. *To rub one's hands:* se frotter les mains. 9. *I for one :* moi, personnellement. 10. *To support their evidence:* pour renforcer leur témoignage. 11. *To put out to grass:* mettre sur la touche.

7 COMPRÉHENSION. Rédigez une note de synthèse (en français) de ces blogs réagissant à la décision du gouvernement britannique de mettre fin au concept d'âge normal (par défaut) de départ à la retraite. *(150 mots environ.)*

8 EXPRESSION. Vous rédigez un blog personnel au sujet de l'âge de départ à la retraite, en comparant la situation dans divers pays que vous connaissez. *(Environ 100 mots.)*

9 EXPRESSION. Comment on documents 1, 2, 3 and 4: to what extent can social protection be fair or unfair? What factors may account for all these differences, in your opinion? *(About 250 words.)*

10 EXPRESSION. Rédigez la lettre suivante adressée à Mr Trevor Dixon, CEO of Applied Web Systems, 772 Colusa Avenue, El Cerrito, CA 94530-2392, USA, dans le cadre de négociations d'embauche dans sa société.

Vous le remerciez de l'offre de salaire intéressante qu'il vous a faite pour un emploi qui vous tente a priori. Toutefois, avant d'accepter définitivement, vous voulez connaitre les avantages sociaux auxquels vous aurez droit : assurance maladie, accident du travail et décès, plan de retraite complémentaire à capitalisation ou revenus garantis (de quelle caisse s'agit-il, et comment est-elle gérée), conditions de travail (congés rémunérés, éventuellement crèche d'entreprise et services proposés sur le lieu de travail, etc.), aide au logement, voiture de fonction, stock-options, etc. Salutations et formules d'usage. *(150 mots environ.)*

CHAPITRE

10 Competition and the law

La concurrence et le droit

BACKGROUND

The market economy and competition

Market economies are based on free trade, free enterprise, and above all on fair competition, which is seen as the best way to guarantee lower prices with better goods for consumers. Fair competition, however, is not natural and has to be guaranteed by strict laws. Any business (whatever[1] its legal status, size and sector) must therefore respect these laws, so that it can meet its obligations, assert[2] its rights and protect its own position against unfair competition.

Competition law in the European Union

EU competition or antitrust laws (Articles 81 and 82 of the EC Treaty) prohibit two main types of anti-competitive activity:
– **anti-competitive agreements:** they are agreements which prevent, restrict or distort[3] competition (or are meant to), and might affect trade in the EU. These agreements, usually secret, are between major competitors who directly or indirectly fix purchase or selling prices, or any other trading conditions (for example discounts or rebates[4]) ; or who limit or control production, markets, technical development or investment (for example, setting production quotas); or who share markets or sources of supply; or apply dissimilar conditions to similar transactions.
– **abuse of dominant position:** if a business has a large (40 or 50%) market share, it can be in a dominant position. What is illegal is abuse of this dominance by imposing unfair trading prices, exclusivity, excessive pricing, refusal to supply or provide access to essential facilities[5], tying sales[6], etc.

All EU member states have their own anti-trust laws. In the UK, they are chapters 1 & 2 of the Competition Act[7] of 1998, and the Enterprise Act of 2002.

Antitrust authorities in the EU

For the EU, anti-trust laws are enforced[8] by the Commission in Brussels, through a specialized Commissioner. Each country has its own body; in the UK, it is the Office of Fair Trading (OFT).

Suppressed April 2014. now The Competition and Market authorities (CMA).

Antitrust laws in the United States

Contrary to what many people think, the US market economy is very strictly controlled and regulated. In addition[9] to state[10] anti-trust laws, there are three major federal ones:

– **the Sherman Antitrust Act** (dating back to 1890), guarantees a free market economy, and outlaws[11] trusts, cartels, monopolies and other combinations and conspiracies that unreasonably restrain interstate trade. This includes agreements among competitors to fix prices, rig[12] bids[13] and allocate[14] consumers;

– **the Clayton Act** is a civil statute[15] passed in 1914 and amended in 1950. It prohibits mergers or acquisitions that are likely[16] to lessen[17] competition;

– **the Federal Trade Commission Act** (1914) which prohibits unfair methods of competition, created the powerful Federal Trade Commission (FTC), an independent antitrust agency.

Antitrust authorities in the US (or "trustbusters")

The FTC lawyers protect consumers from violations of antitrust acts and unfair business practices.

The Federal Department of Justice (DOJ) and its Antitrust Division investigate possible antitrust activities, prosecute[18] and punish their authors severely. These authorities can interact: for example, the DOJ's sanctions can be appealed[19] before the FTC.

Contravention of these laws

Whether[20] in the EU or in the USA, firms which breach[21] these laws can face hefty fines[22] from the authorities, or expensive actions for damages[23] from customers and competitors who can show that they have been harmed by anti-competitive behaviour. In some cases, companies accused of being monopolies have had to split[24]. This was the case for example of American Telephone and

Telegraph (AT&T) in 1984. Microsoft had to pay a huge fine[25] to the EU Commission in 2008. Some individuals may even receive criminal sanctions.

Some forms of behaviour are considered anti-competitive in one country but not in another: for example comparative advertising is unlawful in some EU countries (France, in particular), but authorized in others such as the USA.

1. *Whatever:* quel que soit.
2. *To assert:* affirmer.
3. *To distort:* dénaturer, fausser.
4. *Discount / rebate:* remise / rabais.
5. *Facilities:* équipements, installations.
6. *To tie sales:* imposer des ventes liées.
7. *Act (of Parliament or Congress):* loi.
8. *To enforce:* mettre en application.
9. *In addition:* en plus.
10. *State:* État (l'État fédéral est divisé en 50 États).
11. *To outlaw:* déclarer illégal.
12. *To rig:* truquer.
13. *Bid:* enchère, réponse à un appel d'offres.
14. *To allocate:* (se) répartir / partager.
15. *Statute:* loi.
16. *Likely:* susceptible.
17. *To lessen:* diminuer.
18. *To prosecute:* poursuivre en justice.
19. *To appeal:* faire appel de.
20. *Whether:* que ce soit.
21. *To breach:* enfreindre.
22. *Hefty fine:* lourde amende.
23. *Damages:* dommages et intérêts.
24. *To split:* éclater.
25. *Huge fine:* lourde amende.

Repérer les notions essentielles

Answer the following questions.

a. What is this text about?
b. Why is competition guaranteed by strict laws, and in which countries?
c. What must firms do regarding competition?
d. What is competition protected by in the EU, the UK and the USA?
e. What is prohibited, in particular?
f. Point out some similarities and differences between competition law in the UK, the EU, and the USA.

Résumer le texte en français

Résumez ce texte en français (*100 mots environ*), à l'aide de vos réponses aux questions.

Approfondir

Browse the Net to find more information about antitrust law in the EU, the UK, the US or another country.

Do you know of another company which has recently been penalized for breaking competition law in one of these countries?

LEXICAL WORK

• agreement / cartel	entente / cartel
• to be guilty of	être coupable de
• to be liable (in / under law) (for)	être civilement responsable (de)
• to be responsible for	être responsable de
• to bring / file a lawsuit against sb	poursuivre qqn en justice
• case law	jurisprudence
• to charge (with)	accuser (de)
• to claim (for) damages	réclamer des dommages et intérêts
• to claim one's innocence	clamer son innocence
• class-action suit (US)	recours collectif en justice
• to compensate (sb for sth)	indemniser (qqn pour qqch)
• compensation	dédommagement, indemnisation
• to complain (to a court of justice)	se plaindre, déposer une plainte, saisir la justice
• corporate lawyer	juriste / avocat d'entreprise
• counterfeit	(un) faux
• to counterfeit	contrefaire
• counterfeiting	contrefaçon
• criterion (criteria)	critère(s)
• defendant	défendeur
• to defraud sb of sth	escroquer qqch à qqn
• to file a complaint	déposer une plainte
• to impinge on sb's rights	porter atteinte aux droits de qqn
• to infringe a regulation / sb's rights	enfreindre un règlement / les droits de qqn
• infringement, impingement	violation, infraction, transgression
• to investigate	enquêter
• legal department	service du contentieux
• to levy a fine on sb	infliger une amende à qqn
• litigation	procès, litige, contentieux
• loss of earnings	manque à gagner
• to make charges against sb	porter des accusations à l'encontre de qqn
• to make up for (a loss)	compenser (une perte)
• patent	brevet
• to patent	breveter
• penal / civil law	code pénal / civil
• penalty	peine, pénalité, amende
• plaintiff	plaignant
• prohibition	interdiction
• registered trademark	marque déposée
• to report a crime	signaler un délit / une infraction
• sentence, conviction	condamnation
• to set a precedent	faire jurisprudence

- to settle a legal dispute — régler un contentieux
- sharp / stiff / tough competition — concurrence vive / dure / rude
- to sue sb (for damages) — poursuivre qqn (en dommages-intérêts)
- suit, lawsuit, litigation — procès, action en justice
- to take over a company — racheter une société
- to testify — témoigner

USE THE LIST

1 Fill in the gaps with words from the list above, making the necessary changes, then translate the sentences.

a. Amazingly, selling c... luxury articles in some EU countries openly is tolerated, which creates unfair competition.

b. And yet, c... is considered a c... o... by EU law.

c. The sellers of c... are l... to be c... with a crime.

d. Our company has been harmed by unfair competition and will have to c... to a c... of J... .

e. We will have to ask our l... to f... a c... .

f. Hopefully, we will be able to c... for d... because of a serious loss of earnings.

g. But it will be difficult to assess the c... for this loss.

h. By t... o... their only serious competitor, this multinational risks being c... with trying to monopolize the market.

i. He was disqualified from being a company director following his c... for breach of Chapter I of competition law.

j. In the USA, many people s... businesses for sometimes huge d... .

k. The d... tried to settle the case out of court by paying c... money.

2 Fill in the gaps using a dictionary if necessary.

Noun	Verb	Noun	Verb
a. ...	to prohibit	**g.** ...	to restrain
b. agreement	...	**h.** bid	...
c. competition	...	**i.** ...	to prosecute
d. breach	...	**j.** ...	to sue
e. monopoly	...	**k.** patent	...
f. ...	to investigate	**l.** ...	to defend

3 Choose five words from these lists which you think are important, and write sentences with them.

GRAMMAR WORK

Les subordonnées de but

Aide-mémoire grammatical, p. 265.

Observez et traduisez les exemples suivants :

1. This law was voted to protect competition.
2. In order to safeguard our interests, we will have to investigate the case.
3. He pleaded guilty so as / in order not to have to undergo a long trial.
4. A company must know the law so that all its employees can respect it.

■ **Quelles différences remarquez-vous ?**

■ **Attention au modal obligatoire après *so that* !**

1 **Reliez les deux propositions des phrases ci-dessous en y introduisant les constructions ci-dessus pour exprimer le but (attention aux temps !). Puis traduisez les phrases.**

Ex.: *Bestdrugs took over its main competitor because it wanted to make economies of scale.*

→ *Bestdrugs took over its main competitor to make economies of scale.*

Bestdrugs a racheté son principal concurrent pour faire des économies d'échelle.

a. The consumers sued the company because they wanted to get better value for money.

b. Because it wanted to know if there was collusion between the competing firms, the government launched an investigation.

c. You must fill in a form if you want to claim damages.

d. If you wish to get a refund, you will have to apply for it.

e. The FTC has set an example since it does not want this to happen again.

f. We must stop trading with them if we do not want to lose any more money.

g. Because they want significant compensation, these consumers are going to file a class action suit.

h. They will do it as they want companies not to repeat those mistakes.

i. Brussels took action because it thought counterfeiters should stop selling counterfeits in certain EU countries.

Expression de la quantité

▶ Aide-mémoire grammatical, p. 263.

Observez et traduisez les exemples suivants :

1. They spent millions / thousands / hundreds of dollars.
2. The operation cost them €3bn = three billion euros.
3. This will require a lot of capital / efforts.
4. How much (money) will they need?
5. How many patent medicines do they produce?
6. One never has too much money / too many guarantees.

■ **Quelles différences remarquez-vous ?**

2 **Complétez les phrases suivantes avec une expression de quantité, en effectuant les changements nécessaires (ajout de *-s*, *of*, ou article).**

million – much – many – lot – hundred – thousand.

a. How ... jobs have been eliminated because of this take-over? – Unfortunately, three ... at least.

b. How ... work went into preparing this report? – ..., I am sure.

c. Too ... people came to attend the trial, so they could not all get in.

d. The drugmaker spent over four ... dollars to develop this new drug.

e. This online bookshop has already sold two ... copies of that novel.

f. Unfortunately he did not get ... royalties out of his book.

g. Too ... trustbusting may drive ... companies out of business, and therefore destroy ... jobs.

h. This company will need ... of ... dollars to take over its main competitor. – I would say as much as eight ... ... dollars.

3 **Traduisez en anglais.**

a. Pour gagner beaucoup d'argent, il faut beaucoup travailler.

b. Il y a des centaines de millions de citoyens dans l'Union européenne, savez-vous combien ? – 500 millions

c. La Commission de Bruxelles fait beaucoup pour protéger les intérêts des 500 millions de consommateurs européens.

d. Il a gagné dix-huit millions d'euros en revendant sa société à un concurrent. Cela fait vraiment beaucoup d'argent pour un seul homme.

e. Le P-DG a tout de suite annoncé la nouvelle afin que les autorités anti-trust ne poursuivent pas la société en justice.

f. Beaucoup d'entreprises se plaignent qu'il y a trop de concurrence dans le monde entier, et font du lobbying pour qu'il y en ait moins.

EXAM WORK

DOCUMENT 1

EU threatens drugmakers with antitrust action

• *Investigation exposes widespread competitive failure*
• *Commission will not hesitate to take action, Kroes says*

Neelie Kroes, Europe's most senior competition official, has attacked drug firms for using the courts to delay[1] or block the development of cheaper generic versions of their medicines, pushing up bills for taxpayers.

The competition commissioner said the preliminary results of a year-long investigation into the industry exposed widespread[2] competitive failures. "We find that competition in this industry does not work as well as it should," Kroes said.

In a 400 page report published today she pointed to the practice of multiple patent[3] applications for the same drug and protracted[4] litigation[5] and settlement[6] deals with generic producers that delayed cheap products reaching patients and health services across Europe.

She estimated such tactics by drug firms cost EU healthcare[7] providers in 17 member states about € 3bn[8] (£2.5 bn) between 2000 and 2007. "It is still early days, but the commission will not hesitate to open antitrust cases against companies where there are indications that the antitrust rules may have been breached," Kroes said.

Responding to Kroes on behalf of[9] the industry, the European Federation of Pharmaceutical Industries and Associations (EFPIA) said: "The report does not adequately recognise the complex and highly regulated nature of the pharmaceutical market in Europe and misses[10] the opportunity to address the real issues impeding[11] innovation. The report also overstates[12] the level as well as the reasons for delays in generic market access." EFPIA said it was frustrated that Kroes "mischaracterized[13] the industry as anticompetitive" despite providing no evidence[14] of competition infringements.

Furthermore, owners of original drugs often intervened in national procedures for the approval of generic medicines, resulting in typical[15] delays of around four months.

Generic drug companies have long complained that they have trouble getting their products to market in Europe. Generics account for just over 40% of the market by volume in Europe, against more than 60% in the United States. One drug industry insider said: "The patent system is the lifeblood[16] of innovation."

Simon Bowers, www.guardian.co.uk:business, November 28th, 2008 (abridged).

---

1. *To delay:* retarder. **2.** *Widespread:* très répandu. **3.** *Patent:* brevet. **4.** *Protracted:* qui n'en finit pas. **5.** *Litigation:* procès. **6.** *Settlement:* règlement. **7.** *Healthcare:* service de santé. **8.** *Bn (billion):* milliard. **9.** *On behalf of:* au nom de. **10.** *To miss:* rater. **11.** *To impede:* empêcher. **12.** *To overstate:* exagérer. **13.** *To mischaracterize:* accuser à tort. **14.** *Evidence:* preuves. **15.** *Typical:* habituel. **16.** *Lifeblood:* élément vital.

1 **Rédigez un résumé de cet article en français *(100 mots environ).***

2 **Comment on this document. Which side do you agree with: the EU or drugmakers? Why? Do you think that pharmaceutical companies should be exempt from competition law? Why or why not? *(About 200 words.)***

DOCUMENT 2

Seven High Tech Companies Face Antitrust Wage-Fixing Class Action

San Francisco, CA: Siddharth Hariharan, a former software engineer at Lucasfilm and founder and CEO of InEarth, has filed a class action lawsuit charging that several of the nation's leading high-tech companies violated antitrust laws by conspiring to fix the pay of their employees and entering into "No Solicitation"[1] agreements with each other. The complaint seeks restitution for lost compensation and treble[2] damages for the anti-competitive employment practices of Adobe Systems Inc., Apple Inc., Google Inc., Intel Corporation, Intuit Inc., Lucasfilm Ltd., and Pixar.

"My colleagues at Lucasfilm and I applied our skills, knowledge, and creativity to make the company an industry leader," stated Mr Hariharan. "It's disappointing that, while we were working hard to make terrific[3] products that resulted in enormous profits for Lucasfilm, senior executives of the company cut deals[4] with other premiere[5] high tech companies to eliminate competition and cap[6] pay for skilled employees."

The complaint alleges the conspiracy among defendants[7] consisted of 1) agreements not to actively recruit each other's employees; 2) agreements to provide notification when making an offer to another's employee (without the knowledge or consent of that employee); and 3) agreements to cap pay packages[8] offered to prospective[9] employees at the initial offer.

Starting in 2005 with Lucasfilm and Pixar, and continuing until at least 2009 with all defendants, the companies entered into "No Solicitation" agreements with knowledge of the overall conspiracy and with the intent to reduce employee compensation. As additional companies joined the conspiracy, competition among participating companies for skilled labor decreased. Compensation of defendants' employees was less than what would have prevailed[10] in a properly functioning labor market where employers compete for workers.

The complaint for damages follows an investigation last year by the United States Department of Justice into similar misconduct by defendants. After that investigation was made public, defendants agreed to end the anticompetitive agreements. However, no compensation was provided to employees of defendants. This class action was filed to seek lost pay for the employees who were targeted by defendants' conspiracy.

The lawsuit was filed in California Superior Court in Alameda County. Mr Hariharan seeks to represent a nationwide class of all employees who were harmed by defendants' unlawful agreements.

www.lawyersandsettlements.com

---

1. *No solicitation:* non sollicitation (engagement à ne pas embaucher un employé d'un concurrent). **2.** *To treble:* tripler. **3.** *Terrific:* fantastique. **4.** *To cut a deal:* passer un marché. **5.** *Premiere:* de premier plan. **6.** *To cap:* plafonner. **7.** *Defendant:* prévenu. **8.** *Pay package:* salaire total. **9.** *Prospective:* futur/potentiel. **10.** *To prevail:* l'emporter.

3 **Rédigez une note résumant ce texte en *150 mots environ* en faisant ressortir les griefs et les demandes des plaignants. N'oubliez pas les faits de base : lieu et identités des protagonistes.**

DOCUMENT 3

www.rudebarbs.com

1. *Grim:* sombre. 2. *To bust up:* démanteler. 3. *Ma & Pa business:* petite entreprise familiale. 4. *Textbook example:* exemple classique.

4 **Décrivez cette caricature. Qui est caricaturé, et pourquoi ?**

5 **COMPRÉHENSION. Après avoir pris connaissance des trois documents, rédigez une note de synthèse sur les avantages et inconvénients du droit de la concurrence qui y sont présentés ; concluez en donnant votre opinion *(250 mots environ).***

6 **EXPRESSION. Rédaction d'une lettre d'accompagnement *(covering letter) (150 mots environ).***

Vous êtes Mme Clémentine Lafarge et travaillez pour la Papeterie d'Eymoutiers (route de Nedde, 87120 Eymoutiers) qui fabrique du carton ondulé et exporte beaucoup vers le Royaume-Uni, où elle détient 10 % du marché. Votre entreprise projette d'y racheter une usine de carton ondulé, la société UDM, 40 Framewood Road, Slough, SL36PJ, UK. Vous êtes chargée de rédiger la lettre d'accompagnement du dossier contenant tous les documents et précisions nécessaires qui va être envoyé à l'Office of Fair Trading (Fleetbank House, 2-6 Salisbury Square, London EC 4Y8JK). Vous demandez confirmation que ce rachat est bien compatible avec la loi britannique sur la concurrence, car après l'opération, votre part du marché au Royaume-Uni représentera 13 % au maximum : vous ne serez donc en principe pas en contravention avec les règles de la concurrence applicables. Vous espérez une réponse rapide de confirmation. Date et salutations.

CHAPITRE

11 Legal business structures in France

Les formes juridiques de l'entreprise (française)

BACKGROUND

There are two main kinds of businesses in France:

– **unincorporated ones**, which have no legal personality but have a legal status and carry out commercial or economic activities. They are the *Entreprise individuelle (EI)*, and the recently created, simpler and cheaper system called *Auto-Entreprise*, the equivalent of the sole trader in the UK, possible if the turnover is less than €35,000 a year;

– **incorporated**[1] **ones**, which have a legal personality, and have to complete[2] more extended registration formalities. The capital of incorporated companies belongs to the shareholders[3] who can control the business (to a certain extent[4]) through their voting rights at the annual general meeting, and have a right to the payment of dividends. They elect (or dismiss[5]) the management of the company and approve (or not) the accounts presented by the chairman/woman. They appoint a statutory auditor[6] to control the accounts and publish the financial reports.

There are seven main types of incorporated companies.

The *Société anonyme* (SA)

The *SA* must have at least seven shareholders (no maximum number). The shareholders' liability[7] is limited to their capital contributions.

*SA*s have two possible management and control structures:

– **either a Board of 3 to 18 Directors**[8], elected by the shareholders, which determines and oversees the company's activities. It elects the Chairperson[9] and appoints the CEO (Chief Executive

Officer[10]), who may often be the same person. The Board can also dismiss them;

– **or a Supervisory Board**[11] elected by the shareholders, in charge of controlling the management. It appoints the Management Board which collectively manages the company, with a President representing the company.

If the **shares** of the *SA* **are quoted/listed** on the Stock Exchange[12], the minimum capital is €225,000. *SAs* are usually the largest non state-owned companies in France, and may be compared to the British PLCs (Public Limited Companies).

If the **shares are not listed**, the minimum capital is **€37,000**.

The *Société par actions simplifiées* (*SAS*)

This business structure is increasingly used especially by small and medium-sized companies or by foreign corporations setting up subsidiaries[13] in France, because it provides more freedom in the internal organization of power. The minimum capital is €37,000, held by at least 2 shareholders whose liability is limited to the amount of their contribution. It cannot be quoted on the Stock Exchange. It is headed by a President appointed by the shareholders, who may be a salaried employee. The shareholders are given considerable freedom in decision-making, according to the articles of incorporation, and more or less similar rights as within the *SA*. The ***SASU*** (*Société par actions simplifiée unipersonnelle*) is like a *SAS* but with a single shareholder, often a corporation.

The *Société à responsabilité limitée* (*SARL*)

It is the most widespread[14] type of company in France, because it offers many advantages to small businesses, such as a small capital requirement (€1 minimum), and a limited number of shareholders (from 2 to 100). It cannot be listed on the stock exchange. It is run by one or several *gérants*. The shareholders' rights are not very different from those of the *SA*, and their liability is also limited.

The *Entreprise unipersonnelle à responsabilité limitée* (EURL)

This is like a *SARL* but with one shareholder only, who may be the manager or who may appoint a manager.

The *Société en nom collectif* (SNC)

It is the oldest type of company in France, and may be compared to the American or British General Partnership. It is particularly adapted to businesses with a very small number of members, and is often preferred to the *SARL* because of its more flexible management structure. There must be at least 2 shareholders, who are liable for all debts and obligations, and may thus lose their personal assets[15]. The capital (no required minimum) is divided into shares. The shareholders are often the managers. The *SNC* is not listed on the Stock Exchange.

The *Société en commandite simple* (SCS) and the *Société en commandite par actions* (SCA)

They are not very common, especially the *SCS*. They resemble Limited Partnerships. The *SCA* must have a minimum capital of € 37 000, but the *SCS* has no minimum capital, and they are not listed on the Stock Exchange. They must have at least 2 shareholders (no maximum), and have general partners with no limited liability but more rights to the management of the company; they also have limited partners whose liability is limited. They are often owned by families who want to keep control of the business.

1. *To incorporate:* constituer une société sur le plan légal.
2. *To complete:* remplir complètement.
3. *Shareholder:* actionnaire.
4. *To a certain extent:* dans une certaine mesure.
5. *To dismiss:* révoquer.
6. *Statutory auditor:* commissaire aux comptes.
7. *Liability:* responsabilité légale ou financière.
8. *Board of directors:* conseil d'administration.
9. *Chairperson:* président.
10. *Chief executive officer:* directeur général.
11. *Supervisory board:* conseil de surveillance.
12. *To quote/list on the stock exchange:* coter en Bourse.
13. *Subsidiary:* filiale.
14. *Widespread:* répandu, courant.
15. *Personal assets:* bien meubles, patrimoine.

Repérer les notions essentielles

a. What are the two main legal forms of businesses in France?
b. Which is the smallest and easiest to set up?
c. To whom do incorporated companies belong?
d. How do they control its management?
e. How is the company's capital controlled in a *Société anonyme*?
f. Why is the *SAS* legal form used more and more often?
g. Which is the most common type of company?

Résumer le texte en français

Résumez ce texte en *150 mots environ.*

Approfondir

Find a French company which has a Web site (in English if possible), and study its structure, capital amount, name of Chairperson and CEO, and as many legal aspects about it as possible.

LEXICAL WORK

• active partner	associé gérant / commandité
• to allot, allotment	répartir, répartition
• articles of association	statuts de la société
• board minutes	procès-verbal des délibérations
• to break up a company	démanteler une entreprise
• business concern	fonds de commerce
• to disclose	révéler
• economies of scale	économies d'échelle
• equity capital	fonds propres
• fixed / locked up capital	capital fixe / immobilisé
• to form a quorum	constituer un quorum
• general partner	commandité / associé gérant
• to go public	entrer en Bourse
• to hold a meeting	tenir une réunion / assemblée
• IPO (Initial Public Offering)	introduction en Bourse
• law firm	cabinet d'avocats
• limited partner	commanditaire
• loophole in the law	faille juridique
• majority owner	actionnaire majoritaire
• memorandum of association	acte constitutif de la société
• to merge	fusionner
• merger	fusion
• nominal / registered capital	capital social
• parent company	société mère
• proceedings of a meeting	délibérations d'une assemblée
• provisions	prescriptions statutaires
• public utility (company)	société de service public
• to put on the agenda	mettre à l'ordre du jour
• registered office	siège social
• rules and regulations	réglementation
• sleeping partner	commanditaire, bailleur de fonds
• small or medium-sized firm	PME (petite ou moyenne entreprise)
• society / (non-profit) organisation	association (à but non lucratif)
• state-owned firm	entreprise nationalisée / publique
• subscribed capital	capital souscrit
• subscriber	souscripteur
• take-over	acquisition
• to take over	acquérir
• to vote by proxy	voter par procuration
• voting right	droit de vote

USE THE LIST

1 Fill in the gaps with words from the list above, then translate the sentences.

a. The advantage of merging for companies is that they can then make e... .

b. To set up a company, people need to prepare a m... and a... of association.

c. Companies go p... by selling shares on the Stock Exchange: they then become PLCs.

d. First they have to make an IPO = ...

e. Today, it is the s... and m... ... companies that create the most jobs.

f. A g... p... takes part in the management of the partnership.

g. A l... p... cannot lose more than the amount of his investment.

h. When a shareholder cannot come to the Annual General Meeting, he can vote by p... .

i. We now have a q... , so we can lawfully start the meeting.

j. They took advantage of a l... in the law to pay less tax.

2 Match the following words to make expressions, then translate them.

a. sleeping	**1.** right
b. take-over	**2.** the agenda
c. to put on	**3.** utility
d. majority	**4.** expert
e. business	**5.** concern
f. public	**6.** partner
g. voting	**7.** owner

3 Choose five words in the list which you think are important and write sentences with them.

GRAMMAR WORK

Les discours direct et indirect

▶ Aide-mémoire grammatical, p. 238.

Observez et traduisez les exemple suivants :

1. "What we did first," Judy explained, "was to incorporate the business".
2. "The advantage of a partnership is that it is easy to establish," she said.
3. Steve told her that what they had done had been an excellent idea.
4. She said that a partnership is / was easy to set up / their partnership had been easy to set up.
5. He suggested that they might find it easier to do that.

■ Remarques

– Il vaut mieux employer *She told me* au discours indirect, et *She said / explained* au discours direct.

– Attention aux changements de temps, ponctuation, pronoms et déterminants, marqueurs de temps et de lieu, etc., lorsque l'on passe du discours direct au discours indirect et vice-versa.

1 Indiquez si les phrases ci-dessous sont au discours direct ou indirect, puis faites-les passer d'un discours à l'autre, en effectuant les changements nécessaires.

Ex.: Steve told Judy that it was important to define their legal structure.

→ *He said: "It is important to define our legal structure."*

a. He explained that he wanted to set up a company with her.

b. He added that he had a new idea to develop and that he needed her help.

c. He told his colleague that they might make a lot of money out of it.

d. Judy answered: "Yes, but it will be extremely hard to work together."

e. She added: "We must talk to a lawyer first of all."

f. She asked him what would happen if they did not agree on something.

g. The lawyer said that it was essential to define their relations from the start.

h. He asked them what form of partnership they wanted to set up.

i. He then asked: "Where do you want to have your registered office?"

j. They answered that it would be easier to have it in one of their homes.

Place des adverbes négatifs

▶ Aide-mémoire grammatical, p. 249.

Observez et traduisez les exemples suivants :

1. Not everybody is against that law.
2. Small companies have never experienced such difficulties in the past – Neither have big ones.
3. Not only is this law inconvenient for small companies, but it is costly too.

■ Remarque

La place de l'adverbe négatif varie selon l'intention du locuteur, et détermine celle du verbe ou de l'auxiliaire verbal si l'adverbe est mis au début de la proposition.

2 Mettez les mots ci-dessous dans le bon ordre, et traduisez les phrases.

a. shareholders / to / meeting / came / all / Not / the / annual

b. only / investment / Not / lucrative / will / this / be, but / tax / it / will / deductible / be.

c. France / merger / had / to / in / We / seen / big / such / a / never – had / Neither / they / Europe / in

d. too / it / but / disclosed / he / find / loophole / law / only / find / a / in / Not / he / did

e. all / bills / laws / voted / into / Not / are

3 Traduisez en anglais.

a. Mon avocat m'a déclaré qu'il pensait que cette loi ne serait jamais votée.

b. Tous nos investisseurs n'ont pas accepté de mettre de l'argent dans notre nouvelle société.

c. Le Directeur général m'a dit qu'il avait besoin d'un avocat pour changer les statuts de son entreprise.

d. Il m'a demandé si j'en connaissais un bon.

e. M. Martin n'aurait jamais dû se lancer dans une entreprise pareille, me dit-il, et son associée non plus.

f. Non seulement cet actionnaire n'est pas venu à l'assemblée générale annuelle, mais il n'a même pas voté par procuration.

EXAM WORK

DOCUMENT 1

How French business structures determine the management style

French companies tend towards rigid hierarchy and functionality within which system the PDG (CEO) holds great sway[1]. The PDG determines in a singular[2] way the future direction of the company. This vision is then disseminated down the line for implementation[3] by more junior management. Senior management, therefore, tends towards the directive, rather than the collaborative, as might be found in such countries as the Netherlands or Sweden.

The power often vested[4] in the hands of the PDG obviously adds impetus[5] to a centralist approach, which is already discernible in many other aspects of French life. Below the PDG will be found a strict hierarchy of managers, organised along rigidly functional lines of responsibility.

To those from a less hierarchical background, this approach often seems to be eminently well suited for operations which are performing well and producing results. The weaknesses of the system may only become apparent when problems arise and quick responses are called for[6]. With little buy-in[7] having been sought lower down the line, a sense of personal responsibility could be found lacking[8].

www.WorldBusinessCulture.com

1. *To hold sway:* avoir de l'emprise. 2. *Singular:* individuel. 3. *Implementation:* mise en œuvre. 4. *To vest power:* assigner du pouvoir. 5. *To add impetus:* renforcer. 6. *To call for:* rendre nécessaire. 7. *Buy-in:* investissement. 8. *Lacking:* qui manque.

1 Answer the following questions.

a. What are the main characteristics of French business structures?

b. What impact does this have on the French management style?

c. What are the good and bad aspects of this system?

2 Résumez ce texte en français en *100 mots environ.*

DOCUMENT 2

Setting up a business[1] in France

Every year thousands of foreigners are tempted to set up a business in France, often thinking that they can prolong their holidays here. Unfortunately, what were dreams often turn into nightmares and the number of foreigners who have succeeded in business is remarkably low.

Even for the French, setting up a business is renowned to be incredibly tough[2]. Compared to the U.K. and the U.S. there is an enormous amount of complicated paperwork[3], not just to set up the company, but also to run it afterwards. The only solution is to "waste" money on lawyers and accountants in the hope that they do a good job, or do the best you can yourself. Be warned, the French authorities have no sympathy for people starting out in business and if you do things wrong, you can get into serious trouble. The notion of making mistakes, but doing so in "good faith" isn't recognized here: if you do something incorrectly, however innocently, you won't be let off the hook[4].

If your company eventually fails, you may well end up being responsible for the liabilities, even though the structure of the company appeared to offer "limited liability."

www.parisfranceguide.com
Publisher: Fiona Lazareff
(Business/Talking shop-setting up a business in France)

---

1. *To set up a business:* créer une affaire. **2.** *Tough:* dur. **3.** *Paperwork:* paperasse. **4.** *To let off the hook:* lâcher, laisser partir.

3 **Que pense l'auteur de ce texte concernant la création d'une société en France ? Pour quelles raisons ?**

DOCUMENT 3

San Francisco Book Company

Phil Wood, co-owner and manager of the San Francisco Book Company, came to Paris three years ago. His belongings[1] consisted, among other things, of two thousand books he wanted to sell. A year and a half later, the San Francisco Book Company first opened its doors to the public.

"Basically there are always going to be problems. My first problem was that I couldn't be a *gérant* (director) of a French company, because I am not a citizen of an EU member-country. To be a *gérant* I had to either find someone who was a EU citizen to be my *représentant légal* or get a *carte de commerçant étranger* which would automatically entitle me to[2] a *carte de séjour*. I was in a Catch 22 situation[3]; to be a legal resident, I had to have a *carte de commerce*, which in turn required that I be the *gérant* of a company that existed. In order to register a company, it must have a *gérant*! It was crazy. On the whole, people kept telling me it was impossible to do what I wanted to do. In the States when you start up a business, people congratulate you. But as an American friend of mine who lives here is fond of saying: 'In France *No* is not the end of the conversation, it's the beginning'."

"In terms of running a business here in France, I'm not at all bitter. Quite the contrary. It is all about understanding the system, trying to cooperate with the authorities and filling out the forms[4] correctly. In France paperwork is much more important than in the U.S., and that's something we Americans have a hard time[5] understanding. We just want to get the thing done, whatever it is[6]. However, I've come to accept that ultimately[7] there's something to be said for[8] the French way of doing things."

Abbey Books

On July 1st 1989, Brian Spence opened Paris' first English/French-Canadian combined bookstore, the Abbey Bookshop.

"The biggest differences between the French and the Canadian systems are that business life is much more controlled and regulated here. Here you absolutely have to have an accountant, whereas in Canada

I only used an accountant once a year. On the other hand the administration nowadays are taking a more cooperative attitude as opposed to the confrontational one it had ten years ago. Things are changing."

www.Parisfranceguide.com
Publisher: Fiona Lazareff
(Business/Talking shop-setting up a business in France)

1. *Belongings:* ce que l'on possède. **2.** *To entitle to:* donner droit à. **3.** *Catch 22 situation:* situation inextricable. **4.** *To fill out a form:* remplir un formulaire. **5.** *To have a hard time doing:* avoir du mal à faire. **6.** *Whatever it is:* quoi que ce soit. **7.** *Ultimately:* pour finir. **8.** *There is something to be said for:* cela a du bon.

4 **Traduisez le texte intitulé Abbey Books (2e partie du document 3).**

Méthodes, p. 285.

5 **Résumez les deux parties de ce document *(150 mots environ).***

DOCUMENT 4

"BEHIND EVERY GREAT BUSINESS DEAL IS A COMPANY LAWYER ADVISING AGAINST IT."

6 **Answer the following questions.**

a. What and whom does this cartoon satirize?

b. Why would a company lawyer advise against a business deal, and against what sort of deal?

7 **COMPRÉHENSION. Rédigez une note de synthèse de tous ces documents, en faisant ressortir les avantages et inconvénients du système juridique français des entreprises pour un étranger voulant créer sa société en France *(250 mots environ)*.**

8 **EXPRESSION. Vous rédigez un courrier en anglais destiné à un avocat américain.**

Vous envisagez d'introduire votre société (qui se développe très vite) sur un marché boursier américain pour y lever des capitaux. Vous demandez à l'avocat quelles sont les conditions requises pour effectuer cette introduction, comment changer vos statuts, quel est le capital minimum et quel impact cela aura sur la vie sociale de votre entreprise : rapports investisseurs-dirigeants, assemblées générales, constitution du conseil d'administration, etc. *(200 mots environ.)*

▶ Méthodes, p. 274.

CHAPITRE

12

Company organization

L'organisation de l'entreprise

BACKGROUND

The great secret of success

In an increasingly complex and volatile world, the key to a company's success is its high-performance organization which brings it an enormous competitive advantage.

What makes for a high-performance organization?

A company must have a clear, well adapted organization or flow chart[1] showing who does what and who reports to whom. Organization charts show graphically the firm's formal structure concerning authority, functions and relations. There are several types: the most common are hierarchical, but there are also matrix and linear structures (see below), etc. They define staff members' positions, tasks and duties, so as to avoid overlapping[2].

The best organization will be efficient only if it has the right person in the right place. Above all, the quality of the workforce is essential: in addition to[3] being motivated, competent and hard-working at all levels of the hierarchy, they must also be talented and have a dynamic personality. Diplomas and skills are not enough.

Coordination and integration

The real power of any organization arises from its capacity to coordinate and integrate people, activities and systems. The various departments should communicate and work closely[4] with one another: for example Sales with Accountancy, Manufacturing with Information Technology, Marketing with R&D (Research and Development). The organization should also help to encourage and integrate innovations which are essential to growth, and combine them with a global approach in the case of multinationals. The hierarchy must therefore be flexible and open to new, creative and even revolutionary ideas.

Management's role

Managers should encourage coordination and integration. They must develop a strategy, encourage feedback, and conduct an analysis of the major activities (selling, marketing and advertising, order[5] taking, invoicing[6], product development and manufacturing, project management, purchasing[7], maintenance, customer service, shipping[8]) in order to identify ways to make them more efficient, cheaper and faster. They also have to define functions and responsibilities, supervise recruitment, decide on lay-offs[9] when necessary (even if they often do so reluctantly[10]), improve the company's social policy to motivate the staff, and control quality to keep customers happy. Above all they must be charismatic leaders. Some top managers have shaped not only their companies but also the economy: Henry Ford who invented Fordism, Lee Iacocca, who rescued Chrysler Corporation, and Jack Welch who turned GE (General Electric) into an impressive multinational.

Making decisions

Leadership consists in making decisions, which is a difficult art: designing the organization and the strategy, assigning the right tasks[11] to the right people clearly, making them accountable[12], as well as checking and tracking[13] the impact of the decisions made. Research shows that only 15% of companies have an organization good enough to help them outperform[14] others. That is why many firms seek help from business organization consultants, such as the well-known American (and international) ones McKinsey or Arthur D. Little.

Various types of organization charts

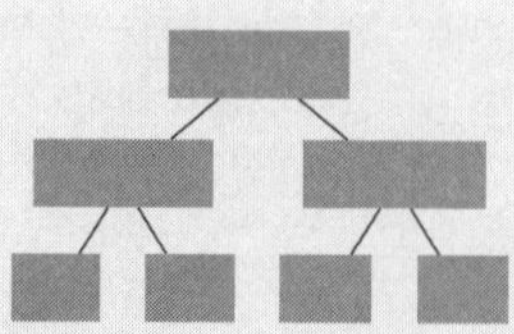

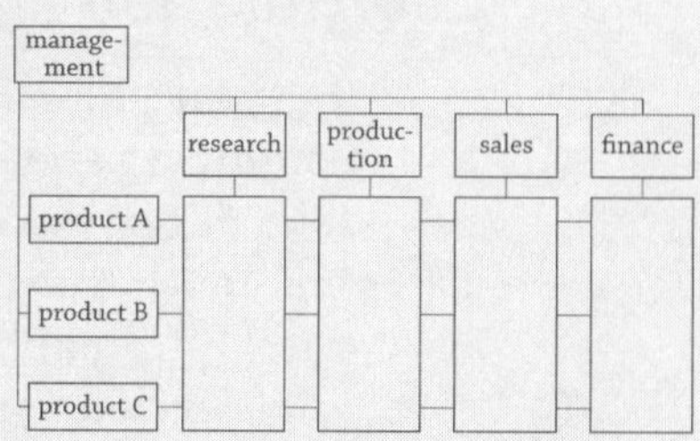

– **The hierarchical chart** (left) is the most classical one.

– **The matrix pattern**[15] (right) combines functional and product areas within the organization to obtain the advantages of each.

Teams of functional personnel (e.g.[16] research, finance, technology, sales and marketing) report to a manager with project responsibility. Functional personnel also report to their functional bosses, who are responsible for maintaining the quality of functional performance. Within[17] the matrix, functional personnel report to two bosses, which requires on their part a lot of understanding and cooperation.

– **Linear or flat organization** has few or no middle managers between employees and top management, because well-trained workers are supposed to be more productive when they are involved in the decision-making process, rather than supervised by several layers[18] of management. This is possible essentially in small firms or in units within big ones. Feedback is often quicker than in other organizations.

1. *Organisation / flow chart:* organigramme.
2. *Overlapping:* chevauchement.
3. *In addition to:* en plus de.
4. *Closely:* étroitement.
5. *Order:* commande.
6. *Invoicing:* facturation.
7. *To purchase:* acheter.
8. *Shipping:* transport de fret.
9. *Lay-off:* licenciement.
10. *Reluctantly:* avec réticence.
11. *To assign a task:* assigner une tâche.
12. *Accountable:* responsable (de ses actes).
13. *To check and track:* vérifier et suivre à la trace.
14. *To outperform:* faire mieux que.
15. *Matrix pattern:* modèle matriciel.
16. *e.g.:* par exemple.
17. *Within:* à l'intérieur de.
18. *Layer:* couche.

Repérer les notions essentielles

Answer the following questions.

a. Name and describe six different company departments mentioned above.

b. What is an organization or flow chart and what are the three main types?

c. How can companies be well organized?

Match the words in the lists below to form compounds then translate them.

a. one – **b.** middle – **c.** competitive – **d.** product – **e.** decision-making.

1. development – **2.** manager – **3.** another – **4.** advantage – **5.** process.

Résumer le texte en français

Rédigez un résumé *(150 mots environ)* de ce texte.

Approfondir

Using the Internet, find information about the organization of a successful company.

LEXICAL WORK

• accountancy	comptabilité, expertise comptable
• accounting control	contrôle de la comptabilité
• accounts department	service comptabilité
• to acquire / buy out	acheter, acquérir
• to appoint to a position	nommer à un poste
• appointment	nomination, rendez-vous
• to be on the payroll / staff	faire partie du personnel salarié
• board of Directors	conseil d'administration
• brainstorming session	réunion de réflexion informelle
• buy-out / acquisition	rachat d'entreprise
• to chair a committee / meeting	présider un comité / une réunion
• Chicago-based corporation	société sise à Chicago
• deputy / assistant-manager	directeur adjoint
• divestment	scission
• downsizing	réduction d'effectifs
• effective / successful / efficient	performant
• efficiency / competitiveness	efficacité ; compétitivité
• facilities	équipements
• to headquarter a company	établir le siège social d'une société
• human resources (HR) department	direction des ressources humaines (DRH)
• lean structure	structure dégraissée
• management accountant	contrôleur de gestion
• management audit	contrôle de gestion
• management operating system	système intégré de gestion
• to manufacture / produce	fabriquer ; produire
• marketing (department) manager	chef du service Marketing
• to merge, merger	fusionner, fusion
• middle manager	cadre moyen
• non-executive director	directeur administratif
• PR (Public Relations) department	service de la communication
• premises	locaux (de la société)
• to promote	promouvoir
• purchasing manager	directeur du service Achats
• rank and file	personnel de base
• to resign, resignation	démissionner, démission
• restructuring	restructuration
• rules and regulations	règles
• to sell out	revendre
• senior / executive manager	cadre supérieur
• senior staff	ensemble des cadres supérieurs
• subordinate	subordonné
• subsidiary	filiale

• team leader / spirit	chef / esprit d'équipe
• to temp	travailler en intérim
• temporary worker	travailleur intérimaire
• top management / manager	cadre(s) dirigeant(s)
• trainee	stagiaire
• turnover of capital / staff	rotation des capitaux / du personnel
• to upgrade	revaloriser
• vice-president (US)	chef / directeur d'un service
• warehouse	entrepôt
• workshop	atelier
• to write off an operation	passer une opération par profits et pertes

USE THE LIST

1 Complete the lists below with the corresponding verb or noun from the word list.

Verb	Noun
a. to acquire	…
b. to …	appointment
c. to resign	…
d. to …	temporary worker
e. to train	…
f. to merge	…

2 Complete the sentences below, making the necessary changes, then translate them.

a. Companies can grow externally thanks to M&As (… and …).

b. Mrs Watson has just been a… to the p… of H… R… manager.

c. Finn and Co Ltd has just opened a s… in Singapore.

d. Bill Graves, one of the v…-p…, has just r… because he disagrees completely with the manager's strategy.

e. Our f… really need to be modernized.

f. Jane, our t…, is so efficient that we should offer her a permanent p… .

g. T… w… do not always want permanent jobs because they wish to remain free.

h. How can we have a more s… organization?

i. In 2005, the company moved to new p… in Swindon, Wiltshire.

j. They w… o… the $50 000 as a dead loss.

GRAMMAR WORK

Les articles indefinis *a* / *an*, *some* / Ø

Aide-mémoire grammatical, p. 227.

Analysez, puis traduisez les exemples suivants en mettant (ou pas) l'article qui convient en français :

1. She works as a manager at MTV Networks, a division of Viacom, an American media group.
2. She must find Ø new ways of doing things.
3. This chain of shops sells some expensive clothes, and Ø others that are quite cheap.
4. That company knows how to save Ø time and money.
5. A firm cannot operate without an accountant.
6. Can I ask you some questions?

1 **Ajoutez *a, an, some* ou Ø selon le cas, puis traduisez. Vous avez parfois le choix, mais la traduction sera différente.**

a. B&A, ... well-known company, is ... tough competitor for us.

b. It sells ... top quality material.

c. They have ... excellent strategy and even ... bilingual managers.

d. ... people do all their shopping there.

e. Our firm flies ... goods to America, and ships ... others by boat.

f. As ... accountant he is very efficient, but as ... colleague he is ... very unpleasant man.

g. You cannot enter the USA without ... passport and ... visa.

h. This shop sells ... new designs twice ... month.

i. We made ... big profit last year.

j. Have you got ... change, please?

2 **Traduisez les phrases suivantes en anglais.**

a. Nous avons des clients très fidèles.

b. Et nous avons aussi quelques clients très riches.

c. Mais certains clients ne sont jamais contents.

d. On ne peut pas gérer une entreprise sans stratégie.

e. Il y a des gens qui n'ont jamais de monnaie, ni même d'argent sur eux.

f. Cette entreprise a des salariés très efficaces, mais certains veulent partir.

g. Une cliente est venue sans carte de crédit et sans argent, et n'a évidemment pas pu acheter les articles qu'elle avait repérés.

La forme en *-ing* après toutes les prépositions et certaines expressions

Aide-mémoire grammatical, p. 244.

Analysez et traduisez les exemples suivants :

1. This company makes a lot of profit while keeping prices low.
2. It thrives by breaking all the rules.
3. We look forward to meeting the new manager.
4. The Chairman was exhausted after chairing the committee for four hours.
5. The CEO may have a lot of difficulty (in) restructuring the firm.
6. It is not worth restructuring it in fact.
7. In addition to being competent, the staff must be motivated.

■ Remarque

To have a lot of difficulty (in) doing peut être remplacé par *to find it difficult to do*, ou *to struggle to do*, moins lourds, et suivis de l'infinitif.

3 Complétez les phrases ci-dessous avec les verbes mis à la forme voulue :

resign – work – understand – start – take – make – spend – be – listen – renovate.

a. We will outperform our competitors by ... better organized than them.
b. The employee put an end to his troubles by ... .
c. They find it difficult ... the whole issue.
d. How can they work while ... to music?
e. Is it worth ... a lot of money on ... our premises?
f. I look forward to ... work soon with that company.
g. One can rarely earn a lot of money without ... risks.
h. He often has difficulty ... decisions, which is bad for leadership.

4 Traduisez les phrases suivantes en anglais.

a. Cela vaut la peine de restructurer notre service en plus de rénover les bureaux.
b. Il faut prendre un rendez-vous avant de venir voir le directeur du marketing.
c. Vous ne pouvez pas rentrer dans nos locaux sans badge.
d. Dans les entreprises, les salariés ont bien du mal à être performants sans esprit d'équipe.

EXAM WORK

DOCUMENT 1

Zara Thrives[1] by Breaking All the Rules

How the Spanish apparel[2] chain gets new designs into stores in two weeks while keeping costs low.

ARTEIXO, SPAIN. Many U.S. apparel retailers are choking[3] on slow-moving inventories as consumers hold back[4] on spending. But Spain's Inditex, whose Zara chain pioneered cheap chic, is zipping ahead[5]. The $13.8 billion company, which is closing in on[6] Gap for the title of world's biggest clothing retailer, has nearly quadrupled sales, profits, and locations[7] since 2000. This year, Inditex plans to expand by up to 640 stores. [...]

Inditex's secret? Besides selling relatively cheap clothes, which fit the times, the company maintains an iron grip[8] on every link in its supply chain. That enables it to move designs from sketch pad[9] to store rack[10] in as little as two weeks. This "fast fashion" way of doing things has become a model for other apparel chains, such as Los Angeles-based Forever 21, Spain's Mango, and Britain's Topshop, which is set to open in New York next year.

Inditex has spent more than three decades perfecting its strategy. Along the way it has broken almost every rule in retailing[11]. At most clothing companies, the supply chain starts with designers, who plan collections as much as a year in advance. At Inditex, Zara store managers monitor what's selling daily – and with up to 70% of their salaries coming from commission, there's a lot of incentive to get it right. They track everything from current sales trends to merchandise customers want but can't find in stores, then shoot[12] orders to Inditex's 300 designers, who fashion what's needed instantly.

Higher pay at the plant

Typically[13], apparel chains outsource the bulk[14] of production to low-cost countries in Asia. Inditex produces half of its merchandise in factories in Spain, Portugal and Morocco, keeping the manufacturing of the most fashionable items in-house while buying basics such as T-shirts from shops in Eastern Europe, Africa and Asia. Wages are higher at Inditex – its factory workers in Spain make an average of $1,650 a month, vs. $206 in China's Guandong province. But the company saves time and money on shipping. Also, Inditex's plants use just-in-time systems developed in cooperation with logistics experts from Toyota Motor, which gives the company a level of control that would be impossible if it were entirely dependent on outsiders.

In addition, Inditex supplies every market from warehouses in Spain. Even so, it manages to get new merchandise to European stores within 24 hours, and, by flying goods via commercial airliners, to stores in the Americas and Asia in 48 hours or less. [...]

For rivals hoping to mimic[15] Inditex's results, analyst Luca Solca of Sanford C. Bernstein has a bit of advice: Don't follow the Zara pattern halfheartedly[16]. "The Inditex way is an all-or-nothing proposition that has to be fully embraced to yield results."

By Kerry Capell, abridged from *Business Week*, October 20th, 2008.

---

1. *To thrive:* prospérer. **2.** *Apparel:* habillement. **3.** *To choke:* s'étouffer. **4.** *To hold back:* se retenir. **5.** *To zip ahead:* aller de l'avant. **6.** *To close in on:* rattraper. **7.** *Location:* emplacement. **8.** *Iron grip:* main de fer. **9.** *Sketch pad:* cahier d'esquisses. **10.** *Store rack:* présentoir de vêtements en boutique. **11.** *Retailing:* vente au détail. **12.** *To shoot:* envoyer une rafale. **13.** *Typically:* généralement. **14.** *The bulk:* la plus grosse partie. **15.** *To mimic:* imiter. **16.** *Halfheartedly:* à moitié, à contrecœur.

1 **Rédigez une note en français *(150 mots environ)* décrivant l'organisation de la société Inditex. Quels sont les secrets de son succès ?**

DOCUMENT 2

Lost Battles in Company Organization

ABB, the Swedish-Swiss engineering conglomerate, was lauded[1] in the 1990s by business-school professors, consulting gurus and business journalists: ABB, the first truly transnational corporation, had invented a new organisational form that represented the 'prototypical post-industrial organisation'. ABB was repeatedly voted Europe's most respected industrial company. Admiration for its chief executive, Percy Barnevik, ran ahead even of the ratings[2] of the company.

In 2002 ABB's revenues and profits collapsed, and the company struggled to[3] survive under a mountain of debt. The decentralised management structure Mr Barnevik created for the company's far-flung[4] units ended up causing conflicts and communication problems between departments. The qualities of charisma, boldness and vision that had once won plaudits[5] for Barnevik were now portrayed as arrogance, aggression, resistance to criticism. Of course, neither ABB's organisation nor Barnevik's personality had changed: what had changed was the company's results, and hence the lens[6] through which the organisation and the personality were viewed.

Similarly Enron was perceived as a model of a new style of corporate organisation when its stock[7] price was rising and a hotbed[8] of corporate corruption when it went bust[9]. The financial innovation that until 2007 was a sophisticated mechanism for spreading and minimising risk was in 2008 perceived as an unmanageable source of instability in the world financial system.

The mistake is to make inferences about the relationships between outcomes[10] and processes when we cannot observe and do not understand the processes themselves. [...] The organisation that was Enron spread its activities widely, and no chief executive could have controlled its operations, or did.

Obliquity by John Kay (published in 2011), www.johnKay.com

1. *To laud:* porter aux nues. 2. *Rating:* estimation. 3. *To struggle to:* avoir du mal à. 4. *Far-flung:* éloigné. 5. *Plaudits:* applaudissements. 6. *Lens:* prisme. 7. *Stock:* action. 8. *Hotbed:* foyer. 9. *To go bust:* faire faillite. 10. *Outcome:* résultat.

2 **Résumez ce texte en dégageant les traits principaux de l'échec des deux organisations décrites ici. *(100 mots environ.)***

DOCUMENT 3

**Bottleneck* : goulot d'étranglement.

Scott Adams, *The Dilbert Principle*,
© United Feature Syndicate Inc, 1996, p. 56.

3 COMPRÉHENSION. Rédaction de note de synthèse (*150 mots environ*, en anglais).

Vous montrerez pourquoi, d'après les documents 1, 2 et 3, il n'y a pas de modèle d'organisation universel. Quel est finalement le meilleur système ?

4 EXPRESSION. Rédaction de courrier (*150 mots environ*).

Vous êtes Peter Taylor, directeur commercial d'une chaîne de magasins de vêtements pour hommes à Londres. Vous écrivez à l'un de vos fournisseurs chinois pour vous plaindre de retards de livraison. En effet, cela fait quatre fois de suite en deux mois que vous recevez vos commandes de vêtements avec plus de quinze jours de retard. Vous lui demandez de remédier à ce problème en réorganisant soit son service Expéditions, soit son service Production. En tout état de cause, vous n'accepterez plus de tels retards à l'avenir. Vous attendez ses explications.

Date et salutations d'usage.

▶ Voir Méthodes, p. 274.

DOCUMENT 4

A business case for[1] women

Women in developed economies have made substantial gains in the workplace during recent decades. Nevertheless[2], it's still true that the higher up in a company you look, the lower the percentage of women.

But some companies have moved successfully to increase the hiring, retention and promotion of female executives. Their initiatives have included efforts to ensure that HR policies aren't inadvertently biased[3] against women or part-time workers, to encourage mentoring and networking, to establish (and consistently monitor at a senior level) targets for diversity, and to find ways of creating a better work-life balance[4]. Changes like these have a price, but there are business advantages to making them – above and beyond[5] the branding benefit[6] that might accrue[7] to companies viewed as socially progressive.

Research in Europe and the United States suggests, for example, that companies with several senior-level women tend to perform better financially. Hiring and retaining women at all levels also enlarges a company's pool[8] of talent at a time when shortages[9] are appearing throughout[10] industries.

In recent years, McKinsey has done extensive work on the relationship between organizational and financial performance and on the number of women who are managers at the companies we've studied. Our research has shown, first, that the companies around the world with the highest scores on nine important dimensions of organization – from leadership and direction to accountability[11] and motivation – are likely to have higher operating margins[12] than their lower-ranked counterparts do. Second, among the companies for which information on the gender of senior managers was available, those with three or more women on their senior-management teams scored[13] higher than did companies with no senior-level women.

Abridged from *The McKinsey Quarterly*, www.mckinsey quarterly.com, September 2008.

1. *Business case:* méthode de gestion de projet ; *case for:* arguments en faveur de. 2. *Nevertheless:* néanmoins. 3. *Biased:* qui a des préjugés. 4. *Balance:* équilibre. 5. *Above and beyond:* par-dessus et par-delà. 6. *Branding benefit:* avantage d'une bonne image de marque. 7. *To accrue:* profiter. 8. *Pool:* réservoir. 9. *Shortage:* pénurie. 10. *Throughout:* dans l'ensemble de. 11. *Accountability:* responsabilité financière. 12. *Operating margins:* marges d'exploitation. 13. *To score:* marquer des points.

5 **Traduisez le titre et du début jusqu'à « ... *better work-life balance* » (l. 16).**

6 **Répondez en français aux questions suivantes portant sur les documents 4 (ci-dessus) et 5 (page suivante).**

a. Que montrent ces documents en ce qui concerne la place des femmes dans l'entreprise en Europe et aux États-Unis ?

b. Quels sont les arguments en faveur d'un accroissement du rôle des femmes ?

c. Que recouvre le terme *diversity,* à votre avis ?

d. Quels sont les neuf critères montrant une organisation efficace ? Dans quelle mesure sont-ils influencés par la présence de femmes ?

DOCUMENT 5

More effective

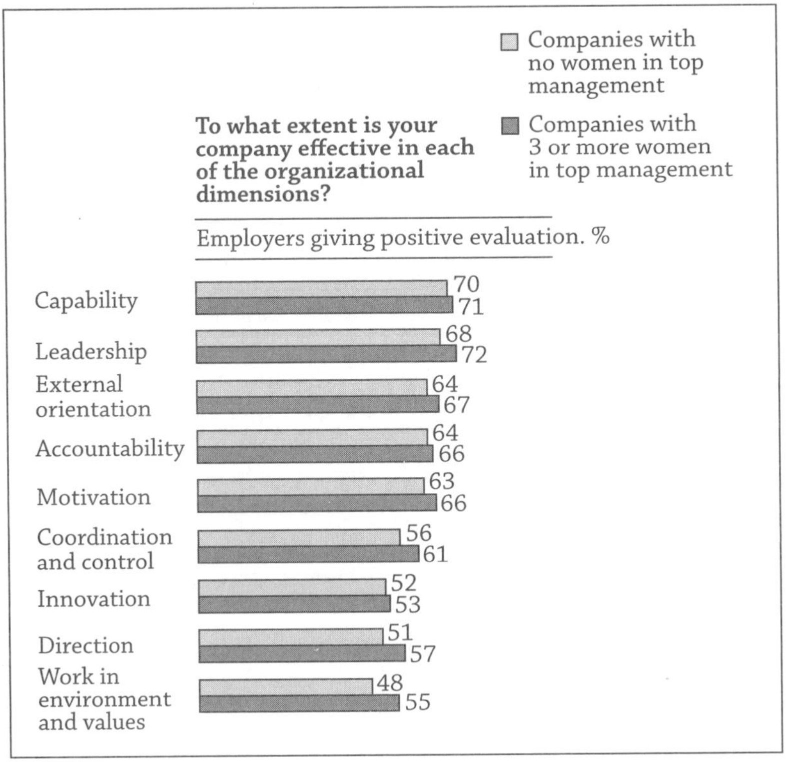

www.mckinseyquarterly.com/Organization/Strategic_Organization, December 12th, 2008.

7 EXPRESSION. The manager of the Human Resources Department in your company has asked you to write a report making suggestions for creating "a better work-life balance" in your department, especially for women.

What changes could be made in the organization?
What "price" could these changes have, and what could make up for it?
(About 250 words.)

CHAPITRE

13

The main functions of companies

Les grandes fonctions de l'entreprise

BACKGROUND

The six main functions of a company are: production, research and development, marketing and sales, administrative operations, human resources and strategic planning. Other approaches include financial management, information technology, or controlling whether progress complies with[1] plans. All operations are carried out by various departments which work together. In small companies, functions may be performed by one or two people. It is also possible to make a distinction between internal functions such as production, logistics or computing and external functions such as advertising, market research or hiring chartered accountants[2]. However some functions can be both internal and external, like public relations.

Producing implies developing products and managing the production process. Marketing consists in doing market research, pricing, packaging, advertising, selling and distributing. Administrative functions are carried out by management and financial departments. The hiring process is central to HR departments, but so are a host of other crucial ones, like training or industrial relations. Strategic planning is carried out by the Board of Directors, but staff may have their say.

All companies play a key role in the economy of a country. Their main role is to produce goods or services. However, they are far more involved in society as a whole because they pay salaries and taxes and participate in social protection, to various degrees according to the countries where they operate.

Corporate culture

The corporate culture of a company will determine the way it works within each department and between departments themselves. The way employees work, think and act has direct repercussions on the company's success. Visible issues such as dress codes, schedules or job titles shape this culture, but also less visible issues like promotion, innovation and values.

Dynamism and wealth creation

By producing goods and services, companies create wealth. Places where setting up a company is easy are usually dynamic and offer more job opportunities to workers. The wealth created is not technically speaking the product or service themselves or even the profit but the whole transformation process. This is called added value and its impact is not solely[3] dependent on the size of the company. Companies are required to place financial interests above competing[4] interests, sometimes even the public good, if they do not want to go bankrupt. In such a perspective, the only way to make an ever larger profit is by reducing cost, discouraging competition and downsizing[5] or outsourcing[6] production, even. That is why some consider multinational corporations as the villains of the global economy. However, in spite of such criticism, they promote prosperity as a whole. Governments usually impose economic regulations to control prices or to protect smaller companies from unfair competition.

CSR : corporate social responsibility[7]

All companies are connected with their environment and are accountable to[8] their stakeholders, or more simply have to respect social regulations. First, their employees not only need to be paid decent wages but also expect recognition, rewarding[9] jobs, training opportunities and career plans. Also, by law, companies have to respect a certain number of rules, such as offering safe working conditions or not discriminating against employees on criteria of gender[10] or race. Secondly, many ethically-minded companies today play a role in the fight against unemployment or the protection of the environment. Their various stakeholders (customers, suppliers[11], local communities) expect them to participate in social progress. Governments may offer tax breaks[12] to motivate greener[13] behaviour, like reducing CO_2 emissions.

Innovation

Creativity and innovation are the cornerstones[14] of competitiveness in a globalised economy. Larger companies usually allocate far more resources to R&D (Research and Development) than small ones, in spite of a few now famous firms that started in garages and grew into multi-million businesses. However, money is not the only mainspring[15] of innovation – it requires management methods that facilitate risk and creativity, efficient team work, and a good sense of customers' needs. A combination of luck and flair are part of the recipe[16] too. There should not be too many regulations which might hinder[17] creativity.

Mindsets

The world we live in is shaped, for better or for worse, by companies and brands. Many young people dream of working for huge firms whose brand image radiates[18] all over the world whereas others would like to find professional opportunities in smaller structures.

1. *To comply with:* être en conformité avec.
2. *Chartered accountant:* expert-comptable.
3. *Solely:* uniquement.
4. *Competing:* contradictoire.
5. *To downsize:* réduire les effectifs.
6. *To outsource:* délocaliser.
7. *CSR:* RSE, responsabilité sociale de l'entreprise.
8. *Accountable to:* responsable devant.
9. *Rewarding:* gratifiant.
10. *Gender:* sexe (masc. ou fém.).
11. *Supplier:* fournisseur.
12. *Tax break:* réduction d'impôts.
13. *Greener:* plus écologique.
14. *Cornerstone:* pierre angulaire.
15. *Mainspring:* moteur.
16. *Recipe:* recette.
17. *To hinder:* freiner.
18. *To radiate:* rayonner.

Repérer les notions essentielles

Answer the following questions.

a. How many functions do companies have?
b. Why is corporate culture such an important element?
c. List the different roles played by companies.
d. What is an ethically-minded company?
e. Do governments play a role in the decisions of private companies?
f. What are the best conditions for innovation to be fruitful?

Résumer le texte en français

Résumez ce texte en *150 mots environ*.

Approfondir

Would you prefer to work for a large company or a small one? Justify your choice by showing the relative advantages and / or disadvantages of each.

Choose one of the six functions mentioned at the beginning of the background and say what it consists in. *(About 150 words.)*

LEXICAL WORK

• (de)regulation	(dé)réglementation
• to amortize equipment	amortir des équipements
• at the cutting edge	à la pointe du progrès
• to be export-oriented	être orienté vers l'exportation
• to be hard-hit	être durement frappé
• to be in operation	fonctionner
• blue- / white-collar worker	col bleu / blanc
• booming	prospère
• to boost	stimuler
• branch / subsidiary	succursale
• brand image	image de marque
• business ethics	éthique des affaires
• business	les affaires
• businessman / woman	homme / femme d'affaires
• to buy out / to take over	racheter / acquérir une entreprise
• to cancel / call off a project	annuler un projet
• commitment	engagement
• company, firm, business	entreprise, société
• competitiveness	compétitivité
• corporate	relatif à l'entreprise
• employee	employé, salarié
• to enjoy a leading position	avoir une position de premier plan
• ethical investment	investissement éthique
• to go global	se mondialiser
• growth	croissance
• head office	siège social
• investment	investissement
• labour force	main-d'œuvre
• to launch a product	lancer un produit
• to lay off / make redundant	licencier
• mainspring of the economy	moteur de l'économie
• to make a profit	faire des bénéfices
• to manufacture	fabriquer
• market share	part de marché
• to merge	fusionner
• a merger	une fusion
• to operate efficiently	fonctionner efficacement
• to outsource	délocaliser, externaliser
• plant, works, factory	usine
• to produce	produire
• productivity gain	gain de productivité

• profit-making, lucrative	rentable
• to relocate	(se) délocaliser, déménager
• shortage	pénurie
• slowdown	ralentissement économique
• slump	marasme économique, récession
• to stay competitive	rester concurrentiel
• to subcontract	sous-traiter
• team	équipe
• technological breakthrough	percée technologique
• the service sector	secteur des services
• the steel / chemical industry	secteur de l'acier / chimique
• to turn a company around	remettre une entreprise sur pied
• wealth	richesse
• to yield	produire, rapporter

USE THE LIST

1 Utilisez les mots suivants, dérivés de *compete*, pour compléter les énoncés. Certains pourront être utilisés plusieurs fois.
compete – competitive – competitively – competitiveness – competitors – competition – competing – competed.

a. Hypermarkets ... with each other in order to gain market shares.

b. The music industry has had to face stiff ... from the Internet.

c. When goods are at a ... price, consumers tend to go for them.

d. The company proved the ... and quality of its services.

e. If our cars are ... priced, we will be able to sell more.

f. By reducing costs, the company kept its ... edge over its ... .

g. ... in business is supposed to benefit the consumer, provided there is no illegal collusion of interests.

h. ... for a market can be an exciting challenge

2 Utilisez les mots suivants, dérivés de *produce*, pour compléter les énoncés. Certains pourront être utilisés plusieurs fois.
products – produce – production – produced – producing.

a. Our factory has been ... smart cards for ten years.

b. This toy factory has not ... enough dolls to satisfy demand.

c. China exports more and more consumer ... like toys or electronic goods.

d. Our Polish ... sites ... at a higher rate thanks to new German robots.

e. Finished ... come off the assembly line.

f. The latest model will go into ... by the end of next year.

GRAMMAR WORK

Les pronoms relatifs : *who / whom / which / ∅*

▶ Aide-mémoire grammatical, p. 258.

Observez les exemples suivants et traduisez-les :

1. A manager is a person <u>who</u> runs a company.
2. They want to invest in markets <u>which</u> will be profitable.
3. The sales manager ∅ / <u>whom</u> I work with is called Mr Jones.
4. This is a problem ∅ / <u>which</u> we must solve everyday.

■ **Qu'est-ce qui détermine le choix entre *who*, *whom* et *which* ?**

■ **Dans quel cas peut-on omettre le pronom relatif (∅) ?**

1 Complétez avec *which* ou *who(m)*. Indiquez dans quelles phrases il est possible d'omettre le pronom relatif.

a. Businesses ... lose money may go bankrupt.

b. The new employees ... the recruiting manager hired will have to be trained.

c. Our production site was visited by investors ... would like to buy company shares.

d. The new premises ... were inaugurated last week are quite pleasant to work in.

e. The financial statement ... the young trainee mislaid has finally been found.

f. The report shows that workers ... commute for more than two hours a day are highly stressed.

Comment traduire le pronom relatif français « dont »

▶ Aide-mémoire grammatical, p. 258.

Observez les exemples suivants et leur traduction en français.

1. Bookkeepers <u>whose work</u> has to be accurate should be well-paid.

→ Les comptables <u>dont le travail</u> doit être exact devraient être bien payés.

2. This factory produces 1,000 cars a day, <u>half of which</u> are exported to Belgium.
→ Cette usine produit 1 000 voitures par jour, <u>dont la moitié</u> est exportée vers la Belgique.
3. Where are the office supplies <u>(which) I need</u> for my report?
→ Où sont les fournitures de bureau <u>dont j'ai besoin</u> pour mon rapport ?

■ **Dans quel exemple le pronom relatif français « dont » permet-il :**
– de préciser une sous-partie d'un ensemble ?
– d'exprimer la possession ?
– de reprendre la préposition française « de » ?

■ **Observez les trois équivalents anglais de « dont » dans chacun de ces cas.**

2 **Complétez les phrases suivantes par la traduction de l'élément entre parenthèses.**

a. Here are the files … yesterday. *(dont je t'ai parlé)*
b. A company … is positive is attractive for investors. *(dont la croissance)*
c. They have defined many objectives, … will have to be reached before the end of the year. *(dont beaucoup)*
d. Workers … are not clearly defined become less efficient. *(dont les missions)*
e. Unemployment, … , has been increasing since last year. *(dont les gens ont peur)*
f. Managers … are purely operational cannot foster innovation. *(dont les stratégies)*

3 **Traduisez en anglais.**

a. Les investissements que nous avons faits en Écosse ont rapporté 6 %.
b. Les employés qui travaillent dans le secteur des services sont les plus nombreux.
c. La fusion dont nous avons parlé n'aura pas lieu avant l'année prochaine.
d. Les salariés dont les emplois sont menacés veulent faire grève.
e. Nos succursales, dont la plupart sont situées en Asie, sont prospères.

EXAM WORK

DOCUMENT 1

On your bike

Obesity and high oil prices are good news for the world's biggest bikemaker.

Two wheels good

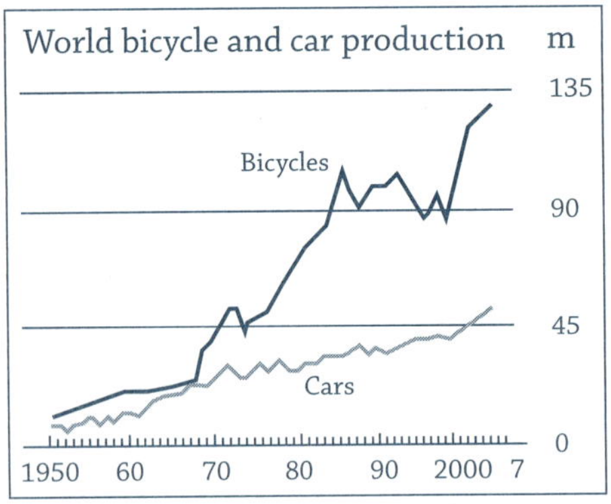

m = million

Source : Earth Policy Institute

These are tough[1] times for carmakers, many of which are labouring[2] under high oil prices, slowing demand and financial weakness. For makers of human-powered, two-wheeled vehicles, by contrast, business is booming. Giant Manufacturing, the world's largest bicycle-maker, sold a record 460,000 units last month and is heading for[3] its best year ever. Such is the demand for bikes that shortages were reported in New York earlier this year. In Taiwan, Giant's home market, supply[4] is tighter still: for many models, buyers put down deposits months before their bikes come off the assembly line.

After a slow 2006, sales took off[5] last year in Europe and America as fuel prices shot up[5]. Suddenly a bicycle seems like the remedy for many modern ills[6], from petrol prices to pollution and obesity. Each market has its own idiosyncrasies[7]. Europeans mainly use bikes for commuting[8], but have the odd habit of ignoring models made explicitly for that purpose in favour of sleeker[9], faster models which are then expensively modified. Americans prefer off-road[10] BMX trail bikes. Taiwanese demand is led by racing-style bikes used for exercise.

Giant, as the largest producer, makes everything for every market. Its share price has held up fairly well despite stockmarket turmoil[11] and dramatically higher costs for raw materials[12], notably aluminium. Strong demand and a desire for better bikes have allowed bikemakers to pass higher material costs on to buyers. Since 2004 wholesale prices[13] of bikes have gone up by 23% in Europe, 45% in America and almost 50% in Asia, even as thousands of low-cost factories in China, including some run by Giant, churn out[14] boatloads[15] of cheap bikes.

Abridged from *The Economist*, September 20th, 2008.

1. *Tough:* rude. **2.** *To labour:* peiner. **3.** *To head for:* se diriger vers. **4.** *Supply:* offre. **5.** *To take off / to shoot up:* décoller. **6.** *Ills:* maux. **7.** *Idiosyncrasy:* particularité. **8.** *To commute:* faire la navette (*commuting:* migrations pendulaires). **9.** *Sleek:* élégant. **10.** *Off road:* tout terrain. **11.** *Turmoil:* soubresaut. **12.** *Raw material:* matière première. **13.** *Wholesale price:* prix de gros. **14.** *To churn out:* produire en série. **15.** *Boatload:* cargaison.

1 Answer the following questions.

a. Using the graph and the text, compare the situation of carmakers and bikemakers.

b. What does the article reveal about Giant, the Taiwanese bikemaker?

c. How does Giant adapt to the market and to the economic situation?

2 EXPRESSION. Passez une commande aux conditions habituelles à la société South Lake Bicycles, un distributeur du fabricant de vélos Giant.

South Lake Bicycles est situé aux États-Unis (121 W. Washington Street, Mineola, FL 34755).

Vous souhaitez lui acheter pour votre centre de vacances (The Old Bicycle Inn, Lake County, 315 West Main Street, Tavares, FL) :

– 15 vélos pour femme, modèle Aerynn Advanced, en bleu ;

– 20 vélos pour homme, modèle Trinity Alliance, en gris ;

– 30 vélos pour enfant, modèle XTC Junior Light, en rouge.

Date et salutations d'usage.

DOCUMENT 2

The challenges of innovation

Indifference, hostility, and isolation are among the major obstacles to a healthy innovation environment.

Indifference. In most companies, just about all the cards are stacked against[1] the nurturing[2] of innovation, especially the kinds of new ideas that generally lead to major changes in the marketplace. While just about every CEO and senior executive of a company pays lip service[3] to innovation, many do not really mean it. The majority of executives make it to top positions by being very good operational managers. But as executives rise up in the organization, other skills become increasingly important. They need to transition from being a manager to being a leader. Management is about business results and processes. Leadership is about people. The key quality you need in good leadership is passion – the urgency to attack and solve the complex problems that all organizations face. To do so, you need to be surrounded by highly talented people, and you need to find a way to transmit your passion to them, so they will buy into[4] your vision of the future, and come up with innovative solutions to the challenges of achieving[5] the vision.

Hostility. But some managers go beyond[6] indifference. Their initial reaction to any new idea is negative, if not[7] downright[8] hostile. This is particularly true if the idea comes from someone outside their own organization. Such hostile behavior is hugely detrimental to a healthy innovation environment.

Isolation. But perhaps even more important, a collaborative approach[9] to innovation helps provide the energy and emotional support that new ideas need in their very early stages. New ideas are almost always rough[10] and ill-formed[11] at first. In my experience, nothing works better than bouncing ideas off other, supportive people[12]. This back-and-forth dialog[13] is crucial in helping to shape the idea into something more concrete, understandable, and actionable[14].

A spirit of innovation and collaboration does not come naturally to an organization. For such a spirit to take hold[15], it must become an integral part of the company's culture. None of this is easy, but it is what a company must do if it truly wants to create a healthy environment in which innovation can flourish[16].

By Irving Wladawsky-Berger, abridged from *Business week*, August 22nd, 2008.

---

1. *To stack all the cards against:* tout jouer contre. **2.** *To nurture:* cultiver. **3.** *To pay* *lip service:* manifester un intérêt de pure forme. **4.** *To buy into:* adhérer à. **5.** *To achieve:* concrétiser. **6.** *Beyond:* au-delà de. **7.** *If not:* voire. **8.** *Downright:* franchement. **9.** *Approach:* démarche. **10.** *Rough:* brouillon. **11.** *Ill-formed:* mal formé. **12.** *To bounce ideas off sb:* soumettre ses idées à qqn. **13.** *Back-and-forth dialog:* échange nourri. **14.** *Actionable:* réalisable. **15.** *To take hold:* prendre racine. **16.** *To flourish:* s'épanouir.

3 **Answer the following questions.**

a. What is the general attitude of CEOs towards innovation?

b. What is the difference between a manager and a leader?

c. Why is passion necessary to achieve innovation?

d. How do CEOs who are hostile to innovation react?

e. Why is team work a key factor in healthy innovation?

DOCUMENT 3

The path to successful new products

Businesses with the best product-development track records[1] stand apart from their less-successful peers in three crucial ways.

Is your company finding it hard to develop new products? If so, you might try learning from the masters.

We found—after surveying more than 300 employees at 28 companies across North America and Europe—that the businesses with the best product-development track records do three things better than their less-successful peers[2]: They create a clear sense of project goals early on, they nurture[3] a strong project culture in their workplace, and they maintain close contact with customers throughout a project's duration.

The teams in our study that embraced these tactics were 17 times as likely as the laggards[4] to have projects come in on time, five times as likely to be on budget, and twice as likely to meet their company's return-on-investment targets.

While we focused on companies in the automotive, high-tech, and medical-device industries, we believe that product makers of all stripes could benefit from our work.

Here is a closer look at what we found:

Keep it focused

Whenever project requirements were clearly defined and communicated to teams before kickoff[5], the project had a greater chance of success.

In our survey, 70 percent of the people working on high-performing projects—those that ranked[6] in the top quarter of a performance index linking best practices to outcomes[7]—said they had a clear view of the project's scope from the beginning, compared with just one-third of poor performers. We found that not thinking through a project's scope early on—say an appliance maker asks developers to design a new cooking range[8] in the four-burner category but then later expands the project to include ranges with six burners—can create delays.

The teams with a clear understanding of project requirements appeared better able to make trade-offs[9] between product performance and things like cost, time to market, and project risk. Only 19 percent of poor performers said they had the necessary information to make those decisions.

Top performers also focused more intensely than low performers on staffing[10] projects with the right people: 47 percent of the former researched employees' skill sets before the project kicked off to ensure the project team was well rounded[11]. None of the low performers did.

Nurture a project culture

The top-performing companies in our survey also nurtured a strong project culture by making product development a priority. They made more of an effort than the laggards—39 percent versus 12 percent—to minimize staffing disruptions[12] due to external demands and to staff projects adequately. When people with critical skills become overburdened[13], they often decide on their own which of their many projects is the most important, a decision best made at the management level.

Two-thirds of top performers compared with 39 percent of poor performers said team members focused more on the success of the project than on satisfying the needs of their job function when those interests competed. They also were more likely than the laggards—44 percent versus 17 percent—to give team leaders responsibility for reviewing team members' job performances.

Three years ago, a North American medical-device maker in our study began an effort to stem[14] market-share losses. Recognizing that one of the company's underlying problems was that project culture was weak, the device maker gave senior team leaders ownership of projects from beginning to end, as well as authority over staffing, personnel reviews and, in some cases, profit-and-loss responsibility. The new structure encouraged leaders to make better decisions, resolve conflicts quickly and reduce delays.

Talk to the customer

The successful innovators in our study kept in close contact with customers throughout the development process. More than 80 percent of the top performers said they periodically tested and validated customer preferences during the development process, compared with just 43 percent of bottom performers. They were also twice as likely as the laggards to research what, exactly, customers wanted. That made them better able to identify and fix design concerns[15] early on, minimizing project delays.

The medical-device maker we mentioned created a matrix to identify and weigh the importance of various product features[16] to different customer segments. It then tested trade-offs between product performance and things like price by bringing in surgeons and other medical specialists to use the product in simulated clinical settings. That allowed the team to fine-tune[17] the product well before launch[18].

The result? Three years after starting its effort to shore up[19] market share, employee satisfaction with product development increased, time to market improved for all projects—up to 40 percent in some cases— and overall gross margin rose six percentage points.

Mike Gordon, Chris Musso, Eric Rebentisch, and Nisheeth Gupta, *McKinseyQuarterly*, January 2010.

---

1. *Track record:* résultat. **2.** *Peer:* pair. **3.** *Nurture:* cultiver. **4.** *Laggard:* traînard. **5.** *Kickoff:* démarrage. **6.** *To rank:* se classer. **7.** *Outcome:* résultat. **8.** *Cooking range:* cuisinière. **9.** *Trade-off:* compromis. **10.** *Staffing:* le personnel. **11.** *Well rounded:* harmonieux. **12.** *Disruption:* perturbations. **13.** *Overburdened:* surchargé. **14.** *To stem:* endiguer. **15.** *Design concerns:* des problèmes de conception. **16.** *Feature:* caractéristique. **17.** *To fine tune:* régler avec précision. **18.** *Launch:* lancement. **19.** *To shore up:* consolider.

4 **Quels sont les secrets des entreprises qui réussissent, selon ce texte ? Pourquoi ? *(Environ 200 mots.)***

5 **Complétez les phrases avec les verbes ci-dessous mis à la bonne forme (Ving / to V / V) : make - keep - succeed - ask - innovate**

a. Companies that adopt clear guidelines are more likely ... successfully.

b. Corporations without a strong project culture find it hard ... .

c. If your customer's needs are undefined, try ... them questions.

d. Project managers need accurate information ... the right decisions.

e. Successful teams elaborate new ideas by ... close contact with customers.

DOCUMENT 4

Small business faces a gauntlet of obstacles

a)

© John Pritchett.

b)

© andertooons.com

6 **EXPRESSION. Both cartoons show that running a business is no easy job. Using them and drawing from your knowledge of the corporate world, write about the various difficulties that companies run into. *(About 200 words.)***

7 **COMPRÉHENSION. Après avoir pris connaissance de tous les documents du chapitre, rédigez en français une note de synthèse *(250 mots environ)* sur les stratégies des entreprises pour innover et assurer leurs fonctions.**

CHAPITRE

14

Companies and their stakeholders

Les partenaires de l'entreprise

BACKGROUND

A company has internal stakeholders[1] (management, shareholders, employees) and external stakeholders (customers, suppliers, bankers, the various local and national bodies[2], society as a whole and even the media). This means that companies evolve in and depend on a complex environment where exchanges take place all the time.

Customer satisfaction

Customers have to be taken very seriously as their loyalty is fundamental for a company's success. In order to scrutinize customer behaviour and track purchasing patterns[3], data-tracking loyalty schemes[4] are set up by big retailers, and cookies are put on computers by commercial web sites. Special offers, coupons, reductions and so on are also used to build customer loyalty[5].

Reliable[6] suppliers

Suppliers of raw materials or goods, hauliers[7] or shipping[8] agents, security and maintenance companies, experts, telecommunication firms, advertising agencies... There is no end to the list of suppliers that companies work with. If one of them fails for any reason, the company will be in trouble[9]. Transport strikes[10] or the bankruptcy of a vital supplier may affect business badly. Just-in-time[11] strategies help to reduce inventory or warehousing costs, or to adapt to fluctuating customer demand by manufacturing built-to-order[12] products.

Bankers

Banks may be considered as suppliers as they provide capital, in the form of loans, without which no company could meet its financial obligations. Companies have to be able to pay wages or bills even before they make any profit, so that is why their working capital[13] or cash flow[14] depend on bank loans. Bankers need to check whether the companies they lend money to will be profitable but they also take a risk when granting loans[15].

The workforce

With the decline of the manufacturing sector in many Western countries, the number of jobs held by blue collar workers has dropped. The vast majority of companies in Great Britain today are in the service sector and usually need greater numbers of employees. Another strong evolution has been the increasing presence of women in the labour market, which has led companies to reconsider work patterns and introduce flexibility, as women now want to achieve a satisfactory balance between work and family life.

Trade unions

Their role is to defend the interests of employees (wages, working hours and conditions) through bargaining[16], or by resorting to industrial action or strikes when there is a dispute[17]. Unions have now lost some of their clout[18] in various countries like Great Britain or France. In 1979, when Margaret Thatcher was elected, union participation in the UK was around 80%. This number has fallen to 30% in public services and 12% in the private sector today.

Communication strategies

In an increasingly complex environment, it is vital for modern companies to define various communication strategies adapted to each category of their stakeholders. By creating a distinctive brand image[19], companies gain a good reputation and improve the perception of their products by consumers, employees, and shareholders. Consultancies[20] now provide assistance in marketing, public relations, advertising, the preparation of media interviews or crisis communication. That is what happens when a company is faced with problems such as product recalls[21] or hostile takeover bids[22]. Communication is not just a one-way process, so companies need to analyse the feedback[23] from stakeholders as well.

1. *Stakeholder:* partenaire, partie prenante (terme vulgarisé par J.K. Galbraith dans *The New Industrial State*, 1967).
2. *Body:* organisme.
3. *Purchasing pattern:* habitude d'achat.
4. *Data-tracking loyalty scheme:* récolte de données *via* un système de carte de fidélité.
5. *To build up customer loyalty:* fidéliser la clientèle.
6. *Reliable:* fiable.
7. *Haulier:* transporteur routier.
8. *Shipping:* transport (maritime ou autre).
9. *To be in trouble:* avoir des ennuis.
10. *Strike:* grève.
11. *Just-in-time:* flux tendu.
12. *Built-to-order:* fabriqué sur commande.
13. *Working capital:* fonds de roulement.
14. *Cash flow:* marge d'autofinancement.
15. *To grant a loan:* accorder un prêt.
16. *Bargaining:* négociations (collectives).
17. *Dispute:* conflit.
18. *Clout:* influence.
19. *Brand image:* image de marque.
20. *Consultancy:* cabinet-conseil.
21. *Product recall:* rappel de produit.
22. *Takeover bid:* offre de rachat.
23. *Feedback:* retour de l'information.

Repérer les notions essentielles

Answer the following questions.

a. Why do companies have so many stakeholders?
b. Why and how should companies pay attention to customers?
c. What is expected from suppliers and why?
d. What is the role of banks in the corporate world?
e. What characterizes today's workforce?
f. What is the role of a trade union?
g. Why do companies rely on modern communication strategies?

Résumer le texte en français

Résumez ce texte en français, en *150 mots environ.*

Approfondir

Do some research on the topic by answering the following questions.

a. What various strategies do advertisers use to appeal to consumers?
b. What is your opinion about the increasing number of loyalty cards that are issued by retailers and services today?
c. What is implied by the term "brand image"? Why is this image so important? Give examples of company brand images.

LEXICAL WORK

• to advertise	faire la publicité de
• advertisement, commercial	publicité
• advertiser	publicitaire
• advertising	publicité (secteur)
• after-sales service	service après-vente
• agency / branch	succursale
• bank manager	directeur de banque
• bargain	bonne affaire
• brand image	image de marque
• to build up customer loyalty	fidéliser la clientèle
• to buy in bulk	acheter en gros
• consumer	consommateur
• corporate culture	culture d'entreprise
• CSR	RSE (Responsabilité Sociale des Entreprises)
• customer / client	client
• dealer	concessionaire, revendeur
• to deliver	livrer
• delivery	livraison
• delivery delay	retard de livraison
• delivery terms	conditions de livraison
• delivery time	délai de livraison
• to dispatch	expédier
• employee	employé / salarié
• goods	marchandises
• to grant a loan	accorder un prêt
• grassroots / rank and file	base
• haulage company	transporteur routier
• industrial dispute	conflit social
• industrial tribunal	conseil des prud'hommes
• labour market	marché du travail
• to launch a campaign	lancer une campagne
• to make a complaint	faire une réclamation
• to make a loan	faire un prêt
• to meet expectations	satisfaire des attentes
• merchant / investment bank	banque d'affaires
• middleman	intermédiaire
• partner	associé
• prospective customer	client potentiel
• quality standard	norme de qualité
• reliable	fiable

• representative	représentant
• responsibility	responsabilité
• retailer	détaillant
• sales	soldes
• shareholder	actionnaire
• to ship	transporter des marchandises
• skilled worker	ouvrier qualifié
• to sponsor	parrainer
• sponsorship	mécénat, parrainage
• stakeholder	partie prenante, partenaire
• strike	grève
• supplier	fournisseur
• supply chain	chaîne logistique
• take out a loan	faire un emprunt
• to target consumers	cibler les consommateurs
• trade union	syndicat
• to trust	faire confiance à
• union member	syndiqué
• unionist	syndicaliste
• venture capital	capital risque
• workforce	main-d'œuvre
• working population	population active
• works council	comité d'entreprise

USE THE LIST

Use words from the list to fill in the gaps, then translate the sentences.

a. To create customer l..., companies acknowledge r... for mistakes. This is why efficient a... s... services are popular among c... . They t... companies that not only provide r... services but also find solutions when problems occur.

b. A... are people who promote new products by placing an a... which may be seen on television. A... is an interesting activity because you have to find good ideas in order to a... such or such a product and to t... different categories of consumers.

GRAMMAR WORK

Les noms dénombrables et indénombrables

Aide-mémoire grammatical, p. 247.

Analysez et traduisez les exemples suivants :

1. Companies do business with dozens of stakeholders.
2. In all countries, small businesses are more numerous than multinationals.
3. Our main supplier is a small catering business.
4. If you lose your job, you will be out of work.

- **Les noms soulignés sont-ils dénombrables ou indénombrables ?**
- **En traduisant, remarquez les différents sens de certains noms selon leur catégorie.**

1 **Dites si les mots suivants sont indénombrables, dénombrables, ou les deux.**

loan – trust – commitment – advice – information – progress – time – growth – job – work.

2 **Utilisez les mots de l'exercice précédent pour compléter les phrases en effectuant les changements nécessaires. Ensuite traduisez les phrases.**

a. The company's relations have to be based on ..., but within reason.

b. It takes ... to build a positive brand image.

c. Banks grant ... to companies which want to invest in development.

d. We sent our customer the invoice three ... but he didn't pay us.

e. Some retailers try to collect as much ... about their customers as they can.

f. A lot of ... has been achieved targeting customers according to their needs.

g. The shareholders expect rapid ... of the company's turnover.

h. For people out of ..., it is difficult to accept that they have lost their ... .

i. Economic ... is due to many factors such as demography and monetary policies.

j. Companies now publish their ... to respecting Human Rights.

k. Good bankers provide reliable ... for their customers to make the right choice.

L'expression de la quantité

Aide-mémoire grammatical, p. 262.

Analysez et traduisez les exemples suivants :

1. As they had a little money, they were able to buy presents for the whole family.
2. When consumers have little money, they cannot afford to buy luxury products.
3. Banks tend to lend less money these days.
4. A few days ago, they launched their marketing campaign.
5. A shop that has too few customers cannot make enough profit.
6. They have fewer customers than before because of the crisis.

3 Complétez les phrases suivantes avec *less* ou *fewer*.

a. There were ... customers than usual.
b. There should be ... advertising on TV.
c. Ten years ago, there were ... advertisements at the cinema.
d. They have been exporting ... wool from Australia.
e. I was given ... advice than I expected.

4 Traduisez les phrases suivantes.

a. Il y a aujourd'hui moins d'entreprises dans les petites villes anglaises.
b. Ils auront peu de temps pour améliorer leur image de marque.
c. Le magasin m'a accordé quelques réductions sur mes achats de Noël, avant les soldes.
d. L'entreprise a fait moins de bénéfices l'année dernière.
e. La publicité a probablement moins d'influence sur les consommateurs que l'on ne croit.
f. Un peu de confiance est nécessaire dans les relations avec les fournisseurs.
g. Peu de clients ont fait confiance à cette société de vente par correspondance.
h. Cette banque accorde trop peu de prêts à ses clients.
i. Il y a quelques années, peu de gens faisaient leurs achats par Internet.

EXAM WORK

DOCUMENT 1

The College Credit Card Trap

Credit card companies are aggressively targeting college students, many of whom are naive about money matters and vulnerable to predatory offers that can get them permanently mired in debt[1].

According to an eye-opening[2] survey by the United States Public Interest Research Group, some students reported receiving hundreds of credit card offers in a year. The report also described how companies lure[3] cash-starved[4] students with gifts of clothing and free food. In one flagrant case in Ohio, students who showed up[5] for the food were required to fill out credit card applications before they could eat.

A half-dozen states have placed restrictions on how credit cards can be marketed at public colleges. Congress is considering sensible bills[6] that would restrict the amount of credit and the number of cards that students could be offered. Lawmakers should also focus on the lucrative and often secret deals that universities and their alumni[7] associations regularly cut[8] with credit card companies.

Those deals often grant companies the exclusive right to market to a college's students. In some cases, the colleges get a cut[9] of what the students spend, which makes the school a partner in the plundering[10] of young peoples' meager assets.

Abridged from *The New York Times*, October 17th, 2008.

---

1. *Mired in debt:* endettés jusqu'au cou. **2.** *Eye-opening:* révélateur. **3.** *To lure:* attirer par la ruse. **4.** *Cash-starved:* désargentés. **5.** *To show up:* arriver. **6.** *Bill:* projet de loi. **7.** *Alumnus (pl.: alumni):* ancien étudiant. **8.** *To cut a deal:* signer un contrat. **9.** *Cut:* part. **10.** *To plunder:* piller.

1 **Résumez le texte en anglais en *100 mots environ.***

2 **Traduisez le titre et de *"Credit card companies..."* (l. 1) à *"... before they could eat."* (l. 15).**

Méthodes, p. 285.

DOCUMENT 2

Three Steps to Calming Angry Customers

Niceness is now arriving at major airports. At John F. Kennedy International Airport in New York, 500 employees are being taught to be, well, pleasant. It's easier said than done when faced with frustrated passengers hurling abuse[1] two inches from your face.

How do you calm down an angry customer while building the customer's loyalty to the airline? Tom Murphy, director of the Human Resiliency Institute at Fordham University, has created a three-step process with this challenge in mind. Here are Murphy's three steps:

1. **Turn down the volume.** When a customer's voice rises, Murphy recommends you lower[2] yours. He explains this sends a signal to the brain that helps reduce anxi-

ety for both your customer and you. Make eye contact to engage[3] your customer. Demonstrate that you are actively listening by nodding your head[4] and not interrupting. This demonstrates a commitment[5] to resolving the problem.

2. **Offer information.** According to Murphy, people under stress hate to be left in the dark[6]. They want to feel as if you are focused on their problem, not on something else. You must give them the facts and be specific.

3. **Brainstorm options.** In step three, an airport employee is told to brainstorm[7] alternatives with the passenger to meet his needs. Think about it. A passenger isn't upset because the plane is delayed; he is upset because he might miss a crucial meeting and lose an account[8].

Murphy believes that airport workers – from parking attendants[9] to ticket-counter employees – can use his method to take the edge off[10] frustrated travelers, and in doing so, help the airline and airport gain a competitive advantage.

Abridged from *Business Week*, by Carmine Gallo, June 13th, 2008.

---

1. *To hurl abuse:* lancer des injures. 2. *To lower:* baisser. 3. *To engage sb:* établir un contact avec qqn. 4. *To nod one's head:* hocher la tête. 5. *Commitment:* engagement. 6. *To leave sb in the dark:* laisser qqn dans l'ignorance. 7. *To brainstorm:* passer en revue. 8. *Account:* client. 9. *Attendant:* gardien. 10. *To take the edge off:* calmer.

3 Cherchez dans le texte des traductions pour ces mots :

a. en colère
b. passager
c. fidélité
d. processus
e. défi
f. s'élever / monter
g. cerveau
h. stressé
i. concentré
j. précis
k. d'autres choix possibles
l. satisfaire un besoin
m. retardé
n. manquer / rater
o. voyageur

4 Faites un résumé du texte en français en *120 mots environ*.

5 EXPRESSION. Rédigez le courrier de réclamation suivant, destiné au service clientèle d'une compagnie de transports aériens.

Vous aviez un billet d'avion pour un voyage d'affaires de Paris-Charles de Gaulle à Stockholm le 25 juin dernier, et, bien qu'étant à l'heure, vous n'avez pu monter dans le vol prévu pour des raisons de surréservation. De plus, l'employé à l'accueil ne vous a pas traité(e) avec beaucoup d'égards. Cet incident vous a fait manquer un rendez-vous avec un client. Vous exigez des explications et l'indemnisation à laquelle la réglementation européenne sur les droits des passagers aériens vous donne droit. Formules d'usage.

DOCUMENT 3

Just good business

Illustration by Ian Whadcock.

Whether[1] through electronic screens, posters or glossy[2] reports, big companies want to tell the world about their good citizenship[3]. They are pushing out the message on their websites and in advertising campaigns. Their chief executives[4] queue up to speak at conferences to explain their passion for the community or their new-found commitment[5] to making their company carbon-neutral[6].

Since there is so much CSR (Corporate Social Responsibility) about, you might think big companies would by now be getting rather good at it. A few are, but most are struggling[7].

CSR is now made up of three broad layers[8], one on top of the other. The most basic is traditional corporate philanthropy. Companies typically allocate about 1% of pre-tax profits to worthy[9] causes because giving something back to the community seems "the right thing to do". But many companies now feel that arm's-length[10] philanthropy – simply writing cheques to charities – is no longer enough. Shareholders want to know that their money is being put to good use, and employees want to be actively involved in good works.

Money alone is not the answer when companies come under attack for their behaviour[11]. Hence the second layer of CSR, which is a branch of risk management. Starting in the 1980s, with environmental disasters such as the explosion at the Bhopal[12] pesticide factory [in 1984] and the *Exxon Valdez*[13] oil spill[14], industry after industry has suffered blows[15] to its reputation. [...] So, often belatedly[16], companies respond by trying to manage the risks. [...]

The emphasis[17] on opportunity is the third and trendiest layer of CSR: the idea that it can help to create value. "Doing well by doing good" has become a fashionable mantra[18]. Businesses have eagerly adopted the jargon of "embedding[19]" CSR in the core[20] of their operations, making it "part of the corporate DNA[21]" so that it influences decisions across[22] the company.

Abridged from *The Economist*, January 17th, 2008.

---

1. *Whether:* que ce soit. **2.** *Glossy:* sur papier brillant. **3.** *Citizenship:* citoyenneté. **4.** *Chief executive:* Directeur général. **5.** *Commitment:* engagement. **6.** *Carbon-neutral:* non producteur de CO_2. **7.** *To struggle:* avoir du mal. **8.** *Layer:* niveau. **9.** *Worthy:* méritant. **10.** *Arm's-length:* distant. **11.** *Behaviour:* comportement. **12.** *Bhopal:* an Indian town. **13.** *Exxon Valdez:* name of the oil tanker that struck a reef in Alaska in 1989. **14.** *Oil spill:* marée noire. **15.** *To suffer blows:* prendre des coups. **16.** *Belatedly:* tardivement. **17.** *Emphasis:* insistance. **18.** *Mantra:* devise. **19.** *To embed:* insérer. **20.** *Core:* cœur. **21.** *DNA:* ADN. **22.** *Across:* dans toute.

6 **Answer the following questions.**

a. How does the picture illustrate the text? (Useful vocabulary: to fly a kite: *faire voler un cerf-volant;* organic: *bio;* coat hanger: *cintre.*)
b. How do companies generally communicate on their ethical commitments?
c. Is it easy for companies to adopt CSR (Corporate Social Responsibility)?
d. What are the three ways of behaving ethically for a company?
e. Why are shareholders dissatisfied with conventional philanthropy?
f. What is the impact of environmental catastrophes on companies?
g. What impression does the last paragraph convey about CSR in companies today?

DOCUMENT 4

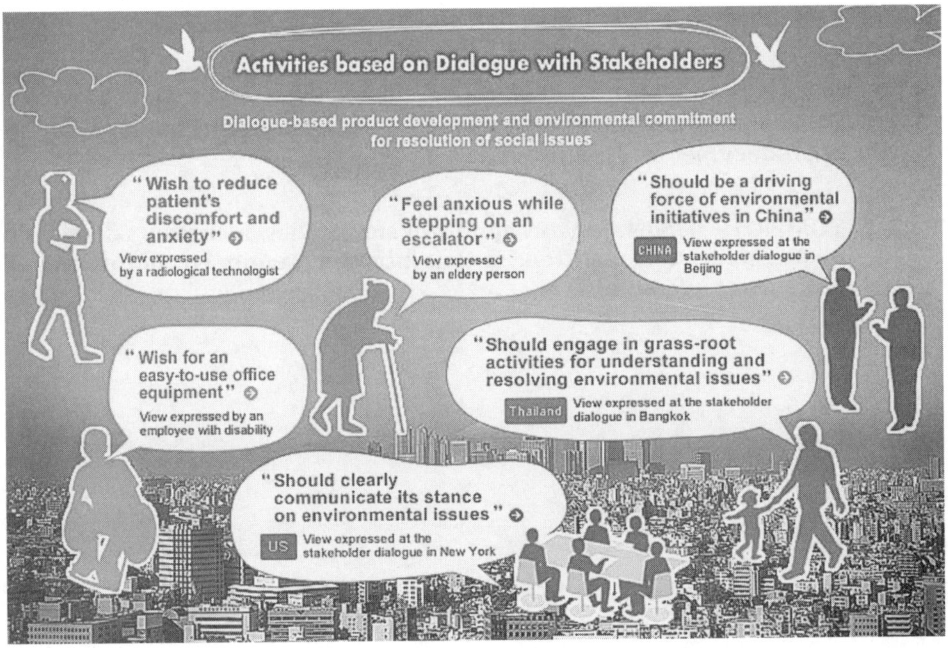

www.toshiba.com

7 **Describe this poster published by Toshiba. What did Toshiba want to convey when it published this document? *(About 200 words.)***

DOCUMENT 5

"Make sure everything is done ethically. Within reason, of course."

© Andrew Toos / www.CartoonStock.com

* *Within reason:* dans les limites de ce qui est raisonnable.

8 **EXPRESSION. Comment on the cartoon. To what extent does it apply to the other documents? *(150 words.)***

9 **COMPRÉHENSION. En vous appuyant sur tous les documents du chapitre, expliquez pourquoi les entreprises ont intérêt à prendre en compte leurs divers partenaires. *(250 mots.)***

CHAPITRE

15 Setting up a company

La création d'entreprise

BACKGROUND

Why set up[1] a company?

There are several reasons for becoming an entrepreneur. Some people reject the hierarchy and want to be their own boss; others want to create their own job; others have an idea for making a better or an innovative product, filling a market niche, offering a more competitive service, or launching a new activity; and finally others want to earn a lot of money (which does sometimes happen).

Indeed you can make a fortune legally by founding a company and eventually selling it to another one, or taking it public, that is to say selling its shares or stocks[2] on the Stock Exchange[3]. This was the case of Bill Gates who set up Microsoft Corporation in 1975, Steve Jobs who founded Apple Inc. (= Incorporated) in 1976, or Richard Branson with Virgin Group Ltd (= Limited) that started as Virgin Records in 1970, and many more. The well-known system of stock-options helps founders and employees to become shareholders/ stockholders of the company: if the latter[4] is successful, they will become rich after taking big risks.

The necessary conditions

First, the key to success in starting a business is differentiation which gives the entrepreneur a competitive advantage. A lot of hard work, courage, optimism, and resilience[5], in short an entrepreneurial spirit are also necessary. This is found unevenly[6] in countries and depends on their entrepreneurial culture, which is particularly developed in the USA. Entrepreneurs are modern heroes: they are the driving force[7] behind economic growth, and the start-ups that they launch are now a bigger source of job creation than large firms. In modern western[8] countries that have understood the value of this activity, it can be quick, cheap and relatively simple! Would-be[9] entrepreneurs also need sound management skills[10], must prepare their project carefully and employ specialists in accounting, marketing, R&D, production, etc. The "one-man/woman show" may lead to failure[11].

Entrepreneurs create needs, business people just satisfy them.

How to set up a company?

1) **Work out[12] a business plan** containing the following elements which are summed up in the Executive summary at the beginning.

– Business description: describe the mission, objectives, value proposition, business model and key assets[13] such as patents, intellectual property, or licences.

– Market analysis: give details about the potential market (with market surveys) and the competition.

– Marketing and sales: define the market segmentation and sales organization.

– Personnel: describe the management team and staff organization.

– Financials: forecast[14] the financial needs and expected profit, with an income statement, a balance sheet, and a statement of cash flow.

2) **Carry out the business registration formalities**.

In the UK, you can do this online in just three hours by logging on[15] to the official site www.companieshouse.gov.uk. You can then order or download the statutory forms[16], fill them up and return them, indicating your company's name, specifying your sector of activity and registered office[17], and what type of company you want to set up or legal status you have chosen. Your company will then be registered and you will get a Certificate of incorporation, and the Memorandum and Articles of association[18]. You will also need to open a bank account, get a phone number and an e-mail address, take out insurance, etc.

3) **On the financial level**, there is no need to be rich to set up a company! It is better at first to use your personal savings[19], however small[20], than to get a bank loan; then family and friends can invest in your business. Subsidies[21] may be obtained. If a lot of capital is needed, for instance in high-tech or biotech, a business angel[22] or venture-capitalist may fund[23] the project. But the capital and profits will have to be shared with the co-investors.

1. *To set up:* créer.
2. *Share, stock:* action.
3. *Stock Exchange:* Bourse.
4. *The latter:* cette dernière.
5. *Resilience:* capacité à rebondir.
6. *Unevenly:* inégalement.
7. *Driving force:* moteur.
8. *Western:* occidental.
9. *Would-be:* potentiel.
10. *Sound management skills:* solides compétences en gestion.
11. *Failure:* échec.
12. *To work out:* élaborer.
13. *Key asset:* atout clé.
14. *Forecast:* prévision ; *to forecast:* prévoir.
15. *To log on:* se connecter.
16. *Statutory form:* formulaire légal.
17. *Registered office:* siège social
18. *Memorandum and Articles of association:* statuts de la société.
19. *Savings:* économies.
20. *However small:* si petites soient-elles.
21. *Subsidy:* subvention.
22. *Business angel:* investisseur providentiel.
23. *To fund:* financer.

Repérer les notions essentielles

Répondez en français.

a. Quelles sont les raisons de créer une entreprise ?

b. Quelles sont les conditions nécessaires pour réussir ?

c. Comment peut-on créer sa société d'une façon générale ?

d. Que faut-il faire au Royaume-Uni ?

e. Quels sont les aspects financiers de la création d'entreprise ?

Résumer le texte en français

Résumez ce texte en français *(150 mots environ)* en vous aidant de vos réponses aux questions précédentes.

Approfondir

Do you know an entrepreneur or a start-up? Write a report about him/it.

Try to find out how to set up a corporation in the USA, or a company in France or in another country of your choice, with the help of the Internet. Present it as clearly and methodically as possible.

Find information (for instance on the Internet) about a small company which you have heard of, and write a report or presentation about it.

LEXICAL WORK

• assets and liabilities	actif et passif
• balance sheet	bilan
• bankruptcy / failure / default	faillite / cessation de paiement
• to be self-employed	être à son compte / indépendant
• capital intensive	à forte intensité capitalistique
• cash deficit	déficit de trésorerie
• cash expenses	sorties de fond
• cash flow	capacité d'autofinancement
• to close / wind down	fermer ses portes
• competitive advantage / edge	avantage compétitif / concurrentiel
• to disclose	révéler, divulguer
• early stage investor	investisseur de début
• equity capital	fonds propres
• equity financing	financement par augmentation de capital
• to fail	échouer
• financial forecast	budget prévisionnel
• franchisee	franchisé
• franchiser	franchiseur
• freelancer	travailleur indépendant
• to go bankrupt / bust	faire faillite
• to go public	entrer en Bourse
• to grow / develop	croître, se développer
• growth market	marché porteur
• to have a stake in	avoir des intérêts / de l'argent investi dans
• to hold shares	détenir des actions
• income statement	compte de résultats
• to incorporate	constituer (une société)
• IPO, Initial Public Offering	introduction en Bourse
• joint venture	co-entreprise
• LBO, leveraged buy-out	rachat de société par un emprunt
• locked up capital	capital immobilisé
• majority owner / shareholder	actionnaire majoritaire
• NDA / non-disclosure agreement	accord de confidentialité
• outlay	mise de fonds
• patent, to patent	brevet, breveter
• profitable / lucrative	rentable
• to raise capital	lever des capitaux

• to register a business	immatriculer au registre du commerce
• registered capital	capital social
• round of financing	tour d'investissement / de table
• to run out of cash	être à court de liquidités
• scheme	plan, projet
• stake	enjeu, participation
• start-up capital	capital initial
• start-up costs	frais de lancement
• subscribed capital	capital souscrit
• to sustain a loss	subir une perte
• to trade	travailler, fonctionner, commercer
• venture	petite entreprise à risque
• working capital	fonds de roulement

USE THE LIST

1 Fill in the gaps with words from the list, making the necessary changes. Then translate the sentences into French.

a. This scheme will require an initial o… of $4.5 million.
b. When will your firm start to t… ?
c. You must work out the projected c… f… of your first 12 months' trading.
d. She has not d… her losses to her investors yet.
e. He has h… s… in the company for seven years now.
f. Let us hope that this dynamic entrepreneur will not f… in his new v… .
g. He made a fortune thanks to an l… .
h. Because of the current bad economic outlook, we will have difficulty r… c… .
i. When entrepreneurs are good managers, their f… rate is much lower.
j. This business angel has got a huge s… in his nephew's start-up.

2 Choose five words in the list that seem important to you and write sentences with them, using the dictionary or the Internet if necessary. Mind the context.

GRAMMAR WORK

Le prétérit et le *present perfect*

▶ Aide-mémoire grammatical, p. 256.

Analysez et traduisez les exemples suivants :

1. Winmark was born 24 years ago.
2. Mr Simmons has just launched a new business.
3. He recently purchased a bigger head office.
4. Since 2006, his situation has been pretty good.
5. He has been holding shares in this company for five years now.
6. In 2008, he was already developing his Web site.
7. He worked hard for years before becoming rich.

1 **Mettez les verbes entre parenthèses au temps correct : prétérit ou *present perfect* simple ou progressif, puis traduisez les phrases. Vous avez parfois le choix, mais vos phrases auront des nuances différentes !**

a. Mr Simmons just *(view)* his company's latest advertisements on his laptop.
b. The ad for a pre-paid bank card *(feature)* only young people, but he *(not like)* it.
c. He immediately *(telephone)* the man who *(commission)* it.
d. The recent credit crunch *(drive)* a lot of poor people out of normal financial services.
e. Mr Simmons *(do)* well enough to *(earn)* a lot of money for himself.
f. His success *(bring)* him a fabulous way of life and several luxurious homes.
g. Lately, he increasingly *(focus)* on other aspects of life.
h. He *(set up)* his first company 20 years ago and he *(be)* rich by 1999.
i. He *(run)* his second one since 2005.
j. He *(be)* an example to many poor would-be entrepreneurs for years now.

2 **Traduisez en anglais.**

a. M. Simmons fait du yoga depuis quelque temps.
b. L'an dernier, il a investi de l'argent dans une nouvelle société.
c. Rita a récemment acheté une boutique en franchise qui achète et vend des vêtements d'occasion.
d. Pour cela, elle a vendu des actions qu'elle possédait en Bourse.

e. J'ai créé ma société il y a 35 ans, et elle est devenue une énorme multinationale depuis.

f. Nous avons fait des affaires ensemble pendant des années.

Équivalents de « comme » : *as* ou *like* ?

▶ Aide-mémoire grammatical, p. 229.

Analysez et traduisez les exemples suivants :

1. As the customer walked into the shop, he was greeted by a charming shop-assistant.
2. It works like the other franchises.
3. He is best known as the godfather of hip-hop.
4. Artists such as DMC have set up their own music company.

■ Remarques

– *As* et *like* ne sont pas interchangeables.
– « Comme » n'est pas toujours la traduction la plus élégante.

3 Complétez les phrases suivantes avec *as* ou *like*, selon le cas, puis traduisez-les.

a. … a businesswoman, Rita is very successful.
b. She, … other entrepreneurs, has to work very hard.
c. In a sector … this one, competition is extremely tough.
d. This is not an isolated request for subsidies, … he receives many … this one.
e. This boss is … a father to his employees.
f. … usual, sales drop when times are hard.
g. His profits were low, … he feared they would be.
h. I sincerely admire Russell, or Rush … he is called.
i. … I see it, the situation is just … it was a few years ago.
j. In this country, competition is becoming tougher, … in America.
k. Not many entrepreneurs are … Bill Gates.

EXAM WORK

DOCUMENT 1

Thrift shops[1] on Easy Street[2]

Winmark's used-goods empire is outperforming[3] other retailers.

Hard times have been pretty[4] good to Rita Cortese. Since 2006, she has owned a Plato's Closet used clothing store in Deptford, N.J.[5]. In recent months, Cortese says, business has exploded as people descend on her store to buy or sell castoff[6] shirts, dresses, and jeans. Cortese is so busy she recently built a shed out back[7] to contain her overflowing[8] inventory.

Winmark, the Nasdaq-listed[9] company that sold Cortese her Plato's Closet franchise, is a rarity in a scorched[10] retail landscape: it's growing rapidly and making money. Sales at Plato's Closet outlets open for more than a year were up 19.6% in August, vs. 1.7% for the industry as a whole. "I don't wish this economy on[11] anyone," says John Morgan, Winmark's chief executive. "But we're going to make hay while the sun shines[12]."

The company that would become Winmark was born 25 years ago as Play It Again Sports, which sold used hockey sticks, baseball mitts, and so forth. Ten years later the company went public as Grow Biz. But by 2000, it was suffering the usual ills of overexpansion. Enter Morgan, who renamed it Winmark and focused on four franchises: Play It Again Sports, Once Upon A Child (kids' apparel), Music Go Round (used musical instruments), and Plato's Closet (which, like the other franchises, also sells some new items). Today, Winmark has 861 stores nationwide.

Franchisees pay a $20,000 one-time fee[13], plus 3% to 5% of weekly sales. In return, Winmark provides the business model, training[14], and marketing. "All the risk falls on the franchisee," says Graeme Rein, research analyst for Bares Capital Management, which owns 14% of the company. "It's on their shoulders to create a profit." Because franchisees pay cash on the spot[15], they have powerful bargaining leverage[16]. For example, Cortese pays $6.80 for a pair of Hollister jeans and resells them for $18.

Since consumers are going to be hurting[17] for a while, it's a fair bet[18] that Winmark [...] will continue to outperform the retail sector. Not that Morgan, who owns a quarter of the company, is standing pat[19]. He's plowing[20] Winmark profits into another franchise operation he expects to do well in hard times – leasing office equipment to credit-parched[21] small businesses. And guess who he's recruiting to run the franchises: managers who've lost their jobs.

Jane Porter, *Business Week*,
October 20th, 2008.

---

1. *Thrift shop:* boutique de vêtements d'occasion. **2.** *Easy Street:* rue de la Misère (d'après un film de Charlie Chaplin). **3.** *To outperform:* mieux réussir que. **4.** *Pretty:* plutôt. **5.** *N.J.:* New Jersey. **6.** *Castoff:* dont on ne veut plus. **7.** *Out back:* derrière. **8.** *Overflowing:* débordant. **9.** *Nasdaq-listed:* coté au Nasdaq. **10.** *Scorched:* brûlé, dévasté. **11.** *To wish on:* souhaiter à. **12.** *"Make hay while the sun shines":* « battre le fer tant qu'il est chaud ». **13.** *One-time fee:* commission forfaitaire. **14.** *Training:* formation. **15.** *On the spot:* sur-le-champ. **16.** *Bargaining leverage:* pouvoir de négociation. **17.** *To hurt:* avoir mal. **18.** *It's a fair bet:* on peut parier. **19.** *To stand pat:* rester sans rien faire. **20.** *To plow:* investir. **21.** *Credit-parched:* financièrement à sec.

1 Answer the following questions in English.

a. Give as many details as you can about Rita Cortese.

b. What is Plato's Closet, and what does it sell?

c. What is Winmark?

d. What sort of a business is it, and how does it work?

e. How was it set up?

f. Who is Morgan and what does he do?

2 Traduisez en français le titre, le sous-titre et le premier paragraphe.

Voir Méthodes, p. 285.

3 Rédigez une note en français sur ce document, destinée à un entrepreneur français souhaitant créer en France un système comparable à celui de Winmark.

Vous lui donnez les détails les plus utiles pour la création d'un tel réseau. *(200 mots environ.)*

DOCUMENT 2

Hip-hope

Can Russell Simmons promote entrepreneurship as well as he sells music, fashion and finance?

[...] Mr Simmons is not your typical financier, which may be why his business is growing [...]. Best known as the "godfather of hip-hop", he made his first fortune as co-founder of Def Jam records, guiding the careers of artists such as Run DMC, the Beastie Boys, Public Enemy and Jay-Z. The company was sold to Universal Music for $100m. He made a second fortune in fashion, ultimately selling his Phat Farm "urban apparel[1]" business [...] for $140m in 2004. His sprawling[2] Rush conglomerate, headquartered on the 43rd floor of a Manhattan skyscraper and guarded by a huge but seemingly amiable bodyguard, also features[3] jewellery (big diamonds a specialty), running shoes and energy drinks. Mr Simmons has just launched a new range of Argyle clothing, for "those guys who are not young men anymore, but who want to still be part of that urban lifestyle." [...]

Phat and happy

Mr Simmons is increasingly presenting himself as a role model for young entrepreneurs, especially African-Americans. Last year he published a bestselling book, "Do You! 12 Laws to Access the Power in You to Achieve Happiness and Success." [...] He recently visited the New York Stock Exchange to launch Race to BE, a prize for young entrepreneurs in fashion, film and music which will be presented during the first Global Entrepreneurship Week (November 17th-23rd).

Entrepreneurship, according to Mr Simmons, is consistent[4] with hip-hop, which is "all about believing in your vision". It is much more a part of the African-American culture than when he started out as a promoter of rappers, he recalls. Back then[5] there were few role models. Those, like him, who succeeded were "all hustlers[6], who learnt their entrepreneurship on the street." Now he gives speeches about entrepreneurship at colleges.

Mr Simmons did not complete[7] college[8], in which respect[9], he notes, "I am just like Bill Gates". Yet he urges[10] today's youngsters to get educated. This is excellent advice, probably far more useful to most of his fans than encouraging them to be entrepreneurs, desirable though that is[11]. Dropping out of school[12] seems to be a common feature of many an entrepreneur's life story, yet the truth is that succeeding as an entrepreneur is a lot harder than making a decent living[13] with a college education. Admirably, Mr Simmons urges aspiring entrepreneurs to be authentic ("Do You"). But few of his fans are likely to have the instinctive gift for creating successful brands that has made Doing Him so lucrative.

The Economist, October 18th, 2008.

1. *Apparel:* habillement. 2. *Sprawling:* tentaculaire. 3. *To feature:* comporter. 4. *Consistent:* cohérent. 5. *Back then:* à ce moment-là. 6. *Hustler:* arnaqueur. 7. *To complete:* terminer. 8. *College (US):* études supérieures. 9. *In which respect:* ce en quoi. 10. *To urge:* pousser. 11. *Desirable though that is:* si tentant que cela soit. 12. *To drop out of school:* abandonner ses études. 13. *To make a decent living:* bien gagner sa vie.

4 Répondez aux questions suivantes en français.

a. Qui est Russell Simmons ?

b. En quoi le titre de l'article introduit-il son histoire ? Expliquez le jeu de mot en résumant celle-ci.

c. Que fait Russell Simmons maintenant ?

d. Quel est son slogan, et que signifie-t-il ?

e. Selon lui, quelles qualités faut-il pour réussir à devenir un bon créateur d'entreprise?

5 Match the following words or expressions from the text with their synonyms below.

Words form the text:

a. headquartered – **b.** lifestyle – **c.** increasingly – **d.** to achieve – **e.** consistent – **f.** to recall – **g.** youngster – **h.** to succeed – **i.** to have a gift for.

Synonyms:

1. to remember – **2.** more and more – **3.** way of life – **4.** to have a talent for – **5.** to manage – **6.** based – **7.** young person – **8.** compatible – **9.** to get.

6 Mr Simmons vient parler à des étudiants en France. Rédigez un court discours en français *(150 mots environ)* pour le présenter, en faisant bien ressortir l'histoire de sa réussite et ses principaux conseils.

7 EXPRESSION. Write a teaser[1] for a would-be investor, such as a business angel, in England.

You want to start a project consisting in delivering French organic food[2] (like fruit and vegetables, dairy produce, gourmet snacks and chocolate) to customers' homes or office staff in London. Specify your market and competitive advantage. You have an experienced partner. You need £50,000 as an initial outlay, and will send your business plan on request with a non-disclosure agreement. Imagine necessary details about your partner and yourself. Present it in an attractive way.

DOCUMENT 3

Start-ups in Silicon Valley today: boom, bubble[1], or bust?

Now, the worry is that all the turmoil[2] on Wall Street will spread to the West Coast. Can Silicon Valley really prosper if the U.S. economy tips back into a recession? Can you make a fortune on your initial public offering if the market is falling? Probably not. But then, people should not work in Silicon Valley unless they are prepared to be lucky. Even in worrisome[3] moments like this one, the essential optimism of this place endures.

"There's a greater-fool theory," said Lise Buyer, who was a technology stock analyst during the dot-com bubble[4] and is with Class V Group, a consulting firm that advises on initial public offerings. "In Silicon Valley, we are, as a species, wildly optimistic. But if we weren't, we wouldn't have so many entrepreneurs, because no one who's being rational would ever found a company."

And so start-ups are multiplying. Engineers are deciding that this is the right time to create would-be Groupons[5] or Facebooks "me-too companies," Valley-speak[6] for start-ups that are basically copycats[7] of a winning formula — or yet another local, social mobile app.

[...] Backing another start-up is a status symbol, the no. 1 splurge[8], and it captures the technology industry's belief in the future and its fear of missing the next big thing.

Even before the fragility of the stock market became apparent, people in the Silicon Valley had been asking: are we in a new technology bubble?

The optimists — or, some would say, the self-interested who stand to profit from the hype[9] note that the amounts being invested are nowhere near what they were in 2000 and that the companies this time are generally profitable and mature. The pessimists say yes, a bubble has been inflating, yet even they are not fleeing. They hope to be the smart[10] ones who get lucky and get out before it pops...

Twenty-two American technology companies went public in the second quarter, for a total of $5.5 billion, the highest dollar amount since 2000, according to the National Venture Capital Association. Only six went public in 2008.

[...]

Ms Moah and Mr Moore had come to the Valley to raise money for Baydin, their e-mail start-up, but their meetings had not gone well... The other day, Mr Moore went to a start-up event to learn about "quick exits" — Valley talk for cashing out[11] of your company while you still can, with executives from large technology companies coaching young entrepreneurs on how to sell their nascent[12] start-ups.

Just in case.

Abridged from *The International Herald Tribune*, August 22, 2011.

---

1. *Bubble:* bulle. **2.** *Turmoil:* folles fluctuations. **3.** *Worrisome:* préoccupant. **4.** *Dot-com bubble:* bulle de jeunes sociétés sur le Web qui se forma puis éclata très vite entre 1995 et 2000. **5.** *Groupon:* site Internet américain offrant des coupons de réduction, qui a grandi exponentiellement en 2 ans. **6.** *Valley-speak:* jargon de la (Silicon) Valley. **7.** *Copycat:* copieur. **8.** *Splurge:* folie dépensière. **9.** *Hype:* battage. **10.** *Smart:* malin (US). **11.** *To cash out:* revendre en faisant du bénéfice. **12.** *Nascent:* naissant.

8 **Find the words or expressions in the text that mean:**

a. faire faillite – **b.** s'étendre – **c.** rebasculer – **d.** sauf si – **e.** avoir de la chance – **f.** conseiller (vb) – **g.** symbole de statut social – **h.** faire du bénéfice – **i.** être mûr – **j.** lever de l'argent – **k.** soutenir financièrement – **l.** bulle qui éclate – **m.** potentiel.

9 **Explain: "There's a greater-fool theory".**

10 **Résumez cet article en *100 mots environ*, en faisant ressortir le scepticisme de l'auteur sur le sujet.**

DOCUMENT 4

The Economist, October 18th, 2008.

11 **EXPRESSION. Explain and comment on this cartoon. Why is the date when it was published important? To what extent does it illustrate the Americans' entrepreneurial spirit? *(About 150 words.)***

12 **COMPRÉHENSION. Rédigez une note de synthèse en français, de 250 *mots environ*, sur l'ensemble des documents proposés pour mettre en évidence les secrets de la réussite des créateurs d'entreprise (points communs et différences) qui y sont présentés.**

CHAPITRE

16

Corporate strategy

La stratégie de l'entreprise

BACKGROUND

General definition

The word "strategy" comes from the Greek word meaning "generalship" or "commanding an army". And just as a general wants to lead his army to victory, so a company manager wants to get his firm to make a profit[1], keep making it and grow.

Many definitions have been given of corporate or company strategy. This essential, if ambiguous, notion can be broadly[2] summed up as a bridge between the firm's long term aims and its tactics or concrete actions to attain them. The best definition of a successful strategy may have been given by Steve Jobs, the founder of Apple: "Think different".

A company's strategy is the responsibility of the Board of Directors[3] and of top management, who set its objectives.

The objectives

They can be anything, in addition to[4] making a profit. They have to be legitimate and ethical, and benefit the firm and those who work for and with it: first the clients, then the employees, and the investors. Indeed the primary requirement[5] is to attract clients and develop their loyalty, and diversify the markets: a good strategy is customer-oriented. A good leader must also bring imagination, a vision and a perspective that should be both long term and fairly realistic. He needs a clear and wide understanding of what his company is and can do, and of the environment in which they operate. The ends to be attained are defined after a SWOT analysis (Strengths, Weaknesses, Opportunities and Threats).

In other words, strategy answers the following questions: "How big are we and how big can we become? What can we do differently from, and better than, our competitors? What innovations can we launch to prepare the future?" The objectives are usually discussed at various levels of the company: how far down and to what extent[6] is part of the strategy itself, and of the management style. They may also have to evolve[7] in order to adjust to changes in the political and economic situations. Determining these ends is a matter of governance, which also ensures that the rules are respected. Management consists in achieving[8] these ends.

How to attain the objectives

Strategy also controls the concrete actions when defining the tactics to be employed by those who manage. Strategy is long term thinking, whereas tactics is short term acting. Those who govern and those who manage are jointly responsible for utilizing the company's human and financial resources. They answer the questions: "What will we make? What will we buy, from whom? To whom will we sell our products or services? How will we distribute and price them? What technologies and resources will we use and how? What capacities will we employ? What are our options? How will we compete with[9] others? How much should we spend on R&D (research and development)?"

Management policy

It is also essential to communicate well, clearly and frequently with all the parties concerned: customers, staff and investors. Listening to them, convincing them, establishing trust, keeping them satisfied, making the right decision at the right moment and informing people clearly about it are part of the strategy. The morale of all those concerned will be kept high and they will be motivated by a strategy meeting their demands and promising rosy perspectives.

There are different management styles, depending on the managers' philosophy, the current fashions, and the type and size of the firm, with their advantages and drawbacks. They shape[10] the company's culture, *i.e.*[11] its values and traditions.

1. *To make a profit:* faire des bénéfices.
2. *Broadly:* en gros.
3. *Board of Directors:* conseil d'administration.
4. *In addition to:* en plus de.
5. *Requirement:* besoin, exigence, condition requise.
6. *To what extent:* dans quelle mesure.
7. *To evolve:* évoluer.
8. *To achieve:* réaliser.
9. *To compete with:* faire concurrence à.
10. *To shape:* façonner.
11. *i.e.:* c'est-à-dire.

Repérer les notions essentielles

Les propositions suivantes sont-elles conformes au texte ?

a. Le mot stratégie est un terme d'origine militaire.

b. Il veut dire à peu près la même chose que « tactique ».

c. Le conseil d'administration décide de la stratégie conjointement avec les dirigeants.

d. Le premier objectif de toute stratégie est de créer des emplois.

e. Le client est au cœur de la stratégie d'une entreprise.

f. L'utilisation de technologies ultramodernes est le pilier de la stratégie.

g. La gouvernance d'entreprise est une notion différente de celle de management.

h. Toute stratégie doit savoir s'adapter au changement.

i. Il n'y a qu'une façon de bien diriger une entreprise.

j. La culture d'entreprise est une sorte de philosophie managériale.

Résumer le texte en français

Résumez ce texte *(100 mots environ)*, en faisant bien ressortir les objectifs, la méthode et les conditions d'une bonne stratégie.

Approfondir

"The most important people for a company are its clients."

Do you agree? Why or why not? What about the managers, the employees and the investors? How can a company's strategy be adapted to that objective?

LEXICAL WORK

• to appoint	nommer
• appointment	nomination / rendez-vous
• balance sheet	bilan
• CEO / Chief Executive Officer	directeur général
• to chart a strategy	planifier une stratégie
• to close down	fermer ses portes
• competitive advantage	avantage compétitif / concurrentiel
• competitiveness	compétitivité
• corporate / company manager	chef d'entreprise
• cost-effectiveness	rentabilité
• costing	estimation du prix de revient
• to cut / cut back	supprimer / réduire
• cut / cutback	compression / réduction / suppression
• decision making	prise de décision
• to display managerial skills	montrer des qualités de manager
• to downsize	réduire les effectifs
• efficient	efficace / performant
• empowerment	responsabilisation
• to encourage	inciter
• facilities	installations / infrastructures
• flourishing / thriving	florissant / prospère
• to foresee	prévoir
• foresight	vision (de l'avenir)
• governance	gouvernance
• to grow / develop	se développer
• to hire / recruit / take on sb	embaucher qqn
• in charge of / responsible for	responsable / en charge de
• incentive	stimulation, encouragement
• internal / external growth	croissance interne / externe
• job cut	suppression d'emplois
• joint management	cogestion
• to launch	lancer
• lay-off, redundancy	licenciement
• to lay off / dismiss / make redundant	licencier
• location	implantation

• management by objectives	management par objectifs
• market segment / dynamics	segment / dynamique de marché
• output	rendement / productivité
• to outsource / subcontract	externaliser / sous-traiter
• performance	résultats
• to plan	prévoir / organiser / planifier
• to promote	promouvoir
• to provide for / foresee	prévoir
• to relocate	délocaliser
• to rely on	compter sur
• schedule / plan / agenda	plan / programme
• to run / operate a business	diriger / faire marcher une affaire
• turnover / revenue	chiffre d'affaires

USE THE LIST

1 Fill in the gaps with words from the list, making the necessary changes, then translate.

a. Let us hope that this new plan will raise our company's r... .

b. Yes, but don't forget that the t... is not the same as the profit.

c. If you want to r... your own business, you will have to work very hard.

d. In order to c... the production costs, the CEO has decided to o... the manufacturing of this line of products in China.

e. Why doesn't he at least s... this task to a factory in Eastern Europe?

f. The boss is both very humane and incredibly e... .

g. This CEO is very good at p... ahead and f... all the possible difficulties.

h. I wonder if m... by o... can really improve the workers' o... .

i. L... this new product very early on will give us a tremendous c... a... .

j. Assessing the c... e... of all its products is an essential aspect of a company's strategy.

k. E... consists in giving more power and responsibility to employees so as to motivate them.

2 Choose five other words from the list which you think are important and make sentences with them, with the help of a dictionary or of the Internet if necessary.

GRAMMAR WORK

Expression de l'obligation avec *must*, *have to*, *need to*, *should*

▶ Aide-mémoire grammatical, p. 232.

Analysez puis traduisez les exemples suivants :

1. They <u>have to</u> be legitimate.

2. A good leader <u>must</u> bring imagination.

3. How much <u>should</u> we spend?

4. The employees <u>need to</u> work harder.

5. We will <u>have to</u> charge higher prices.

1 **Traduisez en anglais.**

a. Une entreprise doit d'abord et avant tout faire du bénéfice.

b. Il faut aussi qu'elle investisse puis réinvestisse l'argent qu'elle gagne.

c. Il faudrait que le P-DG communique mieux avec ses subordonnés.

d. Nous avons besoin de recruter davantage de cadres pour améliorer notre productivité.

e. La société a été obligée de réduire ses effectifs car elle a moins de commandes.

f. Les règles devraient être moins strictes, à mon avis.

g. Serons-nous obligés de sous-traiter ce travail pour avoir des prix plus compétitifs ?

h. Il pense que la société va devoir se délocaliser à l'étranger.

i. La bonne gouvernance d'entreprise doit maintenant intégrer la notion de développement durable.

j. Il va nous falloir analyser la concurrence et la demande du marché.

Les différentes traductions de « faire + verbe »

▶ Aide-mémoire grammatical, p. 241.

Analysez puis traduisez les exemples suivants en utilisant la construction « faire + verbe ».

1. The CEO wants to <u>get his firm to</u> make a profit.

2. He <u>had the factory renovated</u> last year.

3. We must have them improve their bottom line.
4. The boss's jokes don't make me laugh at all.
5. Our new manager makes us work much harder.

2 Complétez les phrases avec *make, have,* ou *get* + *to* au temps approprié, et traduisez-les.

a. I do not know what ... her do it, but she did it!
b. The boss ... me believe I would get a pay rise, but I did not get one, in the end.
c. I will ... him call you back as soon as possible.
d. The CEO ... the investors put more money in his project.
e. The idea ... them smile.
f. The traffic was so bad it ... me arrive late at the office.
g. They want to ... the buildings refurbished next year.
h. Before launching this product, they should have ... more market research carried out.

3 Traduisez en anglais.

a. Il faudrait que l'on fasse faire le travail par une autre société, c'est-à-dire qu'on le sous-traite.
b. Ce patron fait venir ses subordonnés très tôt au bureau le matin.
c. Elle a fait transformer complètement son bureau l'an dernier.
d. Vous devriez vous faire payer un nouvel ordinateur par l'entreprise.
e. Une bonne stratégie doit faire augmenter les bénéfices.
f. Il faut que nous fassions changer l'implantation de notre siège social.
g. Il sera obligé de faire vérifier ce rapport par le directeur adjoint.
h. Nous devrions faire faire une analyse de la rentabilité de ce produit par notre service financier.

EXAM WORK

DOCUMENT 1

Hyundai Motor Zooms[1] ahead

The Korean auto-maker pulled off some feats[2] that many rivals haven't been able to accomplish or dared to try. How?

[...] Mr Yang[3] is now dealing with how to move Hyundai forward. He acknowledges Hyundai has been a "fast follower," essentially mimicking Toyota's strategy. [...]

Instilling creative thinking is a work in progress. A few times a week, video screens around Hyundai's headquarters in Seoul show a one-minute clip that has become a favorite among staffers. It shows an open office where workers wearing the same shirt and haircut are beavering away[4]. Then a new person arrives with a different hair cut. Each time he voices an idea, the others shout him down[5]. Eventually[6] he gets the same haircut and everybody likes him. Then a question appears: "Aren't we stuck[7] in conventional thinking?"

Hyundai also faces the prospect of limited production in the next few years because its plants are maxed out[8] and the next new factories, located in China and Brazil, won't start churning out[9] cars until next year. Mr Yang said he was content for the company to "walk for the time being" and that productivity increases should help.

Several years ago, Hyundai made no secret that it hoped to become the world's largest auto maker some day. Mr Yang says that thinking has changed. GM and Toyota became the world's largest and then stumbled[10], he noted, adding that making 10 million cars a year would require running 50 factories—more, in his view, than a company can run effectively. "Should there be a certain range, maybe 6 million or 7 million, that is best?" Mr Yang said. "We don't know what size is optimum. But bigger, bigger, biggest is always good? We don't think so."

In New Port Richey, Fla., Scott Fink, owner of the Hyundai dealership, can't stock enough Sonatas and Elantras. His dealership[11] sold 610 cars last month—an average of 20 a day. The Toyota dealership across the street sold 170 in the same period. Earlier this spring, Mr Fink's sales manager, David Frazier, was scanning shipping[12] data, hoping to find an available new Elantra in a batch headed to the U.S. but as Mr Fink read off[13] vehicle identification numbers, Mr Frazier ticked off[14] their status. "Sold. Sold. Sold. Sold," he said. "The sky is the limit for Hyundai," Mr Fink shrugged[15], "if we have the cars."

Mike Ramsey and Evan Ramstad;
Sharon Terlep contributed to this article.

1. *To zoom ahead:* filer de l'avant. **2.** *To pull off a feat:* réussir un exploit. **3.** *Mr Yang:* the co-CEO and President of Hyundai. **4.** *To beaver away:* travailler comme des fous. **5.** *To shout sb down:* huer qqn. **6.** *Eventually:* finalement. **7.** *To be stuck:* être coincé. **8.** *To be maxed out:* être exploité au maximum. **9.** *To churn out:* produire à la chaîne. **10.** *To stumble:* avoir des ratés. **11.** *Dealership:* concession. **12.** *Shipping:* expédition. **13.** *To read off:* lire à la chaîne. **14.** *To tick off:* cocher. **15.** *To shrug:* hausser les épaules.

1 **Complete the following sentences with words or expressions from the text:**

a. A small company should not m... a big one.

b. All our factories are l... abroad.

c. Where do you s... your products when they arrive?

d. We are making only a small profit for ... ... but we hope it will grow.

e. They are waiting for the last b... of goods to arrive.

2 **COMPRÉHENSION. Résumez ce texte *(150 mots maximum)*, en dégageant clairement la stratégie de Mr Yang. Quelle est l'opinion probable de l'auteur de l'article ?**

DOCUMENT 2

Lessons from a skinflint[1] CEO

Amerisource chief Dave Yost's frugal ways have kept the drug distributor thriving in a tight[2] market.

David Yost is acutely[3] aware of tougher times ahead for his customers. Consumers are cutting back on prescription drugs to save money and retailers are struggling[4] with less demand. But the Amerisource Bergen chief isn't worried. The balance sheet of the drug distributor, which acts as a middleman[5] between drugmakers and retailers[6], is strong. Besides, Yost has been tightening his belt[7] for years.

Even in an industry known for its razor-thin margins, Yost is remarkably cheap. He answers his own phone, flies economy class, and rarely strays [from his] headquarters in Valley Forge, Pa. Yost, 61, admits that his $66.1 billion company could absorb the cost of getting him extra secretarial help and a more comfortable seat on planes, but that's not the point[8]. "The leader is very important in controlling business costs," says Yost, whose headquarters lobby[9] is decorated with plastic plants to save on watering.

While Yost's zeal to cut costs may strike some as absurd, his efforts have helped Amerisource thrive. And he thinks the current credit crisis won't swing the company off course[10]. Not only has Amerisource held its own[11] against rivals McKesson and Cardinal Health, but leaner operations have helped it grow revenues 8% this year while the broader industry is growing half as fast. In the last quarter, Amerisource profits increased by 30%, [...] McKesson's and Cardinal's were up 8% and 13%, respectively. Yost's total paycheck last year (including stock options) was $4.8 million, less than half that of Cardinal's CEO and barely a sixth of McKesson's chief. "He is not flamboyant or flashy," says Bank of America Securities analyst Robert Willoughby of Yost [...]. Adds John W. Ransom of Raymond James & Associates: "At 1% margins, you have to be."

Now he's under even more pressure to watch the bottom line[12] as his customers struggle to stay competitive. Amerisource relies heavily on smaller, independent chains that are fast being gobbled by big players, who may have contracts with the distributor's rivals. But Yost predicts volume will pick up over the long term. "The older we get, the more drugs we take," says Yost, settling comfortably into a 1970s-era chair [...]

George Barrett, the CEO of Cardinal's drug distribution arm, says that what matters in a leader isn't frugality but foresight. "I don't want our people to see me as cheap but instead very efficient and cognizant of the environment in which we compete," says Barrett. But Yost insists he can be all those things. While he pays competitive salaries to attract talent, he allows employees to fly business class only if they pay for an upgrade themselves. And they must book 30 days in advance to get the best price. Yost is also investing more than $100 million over the next three to five years to improve customer service technology, and he paid $400 million to spruce up company distribution centers and consolidate operations. [...] While the Amerisource chief may not be eager to spend a buck[13], he certainly knows the value a dollar holds for others. Amerisource has returned more than a third of its free cash flow to shareholders for the last two years and used the rest for core acquisitions. "The landscape is littered[14] with companies that think they can do a lot of businesses well," says Yost [...].

Aili McConnon, *Business Week*, October 6th, 2008.

1. *Skinflint:* radin. 2. *Tight:* tendu, serré. 3. *Acutely:* extrêmement. 4. *To struggle:* rencontrer des difficultés. 5. *Middleman:* intermédiaire. 6. *Retailer:* détaillant. 7. *To tighten one's belt:* se serrer la ceinture. 8. *The point:* la question, l'objet. 9. *Lobby:* hall d'entrée. 10. *To swing off course:* faire dévier. 11. *To hold one's own:* bien se débrouiller. 12. *Bottom line:* résultat financier (final). 13. *To spend a buck:* dépenser un dollar. 14. *To litter:* encombrer d'ordures.

3 Write a summary of this document *(about 150 words)* answering the following questions:

What "lessons" can be learnt about and from this CEO's strategy? To what extent is it customer-oriented? What competitive advantage does it bring the company? Compare Dave Yost's strategy with George Barrett's. What may account for their differences? Could they be interchangeable?

DOCUMENT 3

Scott Adams, *The Dilbert Principle*, Harper Business, 1996.

4 EXPRESSION. Comment upon the cartoon, answering the following questions:

Who does the man at the top represent?
What happens when there is no strategy, and what happens when there is one?
Which is better, in your opinion?
What is satirized here?

DOCUMENT 4

Steve Jobs's Vision and Leadership: Models for US Businesses

Departing Apple Inc. chief executive Steve Jobs is being celebrated as the tech magician who brought you the iPod, but his tenure[1] with the company is just as notable for the alternative vision it offers for American businesses. His embrace of elegantly designed, high-price, high-value products looks like a radical statement in a bottom-line[2]-oriented world.... His leadership at Apple is the stuff[3] of legend. After co-founding the company out of a garage in Silicon Valley and popularizing the idea of the personal computer, Jobs was pushed out of the company in 1985. As computers became mere commodities[4] in the ensuing years, Apple's pricy Macintosh machines struggled to maintain their niche. But in its darkest hour in 1997, Apple brought Jobs back. A long string of hit[5] products soon followed: first the iMac, a candy-hued[6] machine that daringly lacked a floppy disk drive, and later the iPod, iPhone, and iPad.

In each case, Jobs's key insights[7] were that people were living more and more of their lives through computers and other electronic devices, and that glitch-prone[8], lowest-common-denominator products wouldn't meet their needs. As competitors sold PCs made to order over the Internet, Apple built high-end[9] retail stores, deployed an army of fresh-faced salespeople, and offered free customer support on-site. Jobs proved that the option that cuts costs the most, or does the most to juice this quarter's profits[10], isn't always the best for a company.

None of this means that Jobs has been gentle. Apple, like many other consumer-electronics firms, has its products manufactured in China. It owes its enviable profit margins in part to its power to negotiate deep discounts for crucial components—and buy up so much supply that competitors can't get at them. Indeed, this ruthlessly efficient[11] approach to logistics is the calling card[12] of Jobs's chief operating officer and handpicked[13] successor, Tim Cook. And despite all its advertising rhetoric about thinking different, and its enthusiastic customer base in art studios and in free-speech bastions like Cambridge and Berkeley, Jobs's company is infamous[14] for its penchant for secrecy. [...]

It's easy to connect Jobs's personality and decision-making to Apple's success. And as US companies confront competitors around the world, Jobs offers a useful lesson—a focus on short-term matters is much less important than a vision for the future and the confidence to bet big[15] on it.

Boston.com, August 26, 2011.

1. *Tenure:* fonction occupée. 2. *Bottom-line:* résultat financier. 3. *Stuff:* trame. 4. *Mere commodity:* simple produit de base. 5. *Hit:* succès. 6. *Candy-hued:* couleur bonbon. 7. *Insight:* intuition. 8. *Glitch-prone:* sujet à des pannes. 9. *High-end:* haut de gamme. 10. *To juice profits:* extraire le maximum de bénéfice. 11. *Ruthlessly efficient:* d'une efficacité redoutable. 12. *Calling card:* carte de visite. 13. *Handpicked:* choisi soigneusement. 14. *Infamous:* renommé (pour un défaut). 15. *To bet big:* parier gros.

5 Résumez ce texte en français, en dégageant les aspects emblématiques de la stratégie de Steve Jobs, à la source de son succès *(150 mots environ).*

6 EXPRESSION. Write a letter of application to one of the company CEOs described in these documents, choosing the one that appeals to you most. Explain that you would like to work as an intern or trainee in his firm for three months, give your motivations, and say why you think you are suited for the company. Date, usual greetings and salutation. *(About 150 words.)*

7 Rédigez une synthèse en anglais des quatre documents *(150 mots environ).* Vous montrerez dans quelle mesure la caricature s'applique aux articles. Cette caricature est-elle justifiée ?

CHAPITRE

17

Analysis of business performance

L'analyse des performances de l'entreprise

BACKGROUND

Work that is not measured cannot be managed

Without an analysis of its performance an organization might not identify faults and not enhance competitiveness[1]. In a context where large numbers of companies have had to face bankruptcy[2], the study of their performance or even viability is a daily concern for managers.

The bottom line is not all

The process of evaluating a business requires recognizing its strong and weak points as well as improvement opportunities; hence the necessity of defining criteria for company operations at all levels. Not only is the balance sheet[3] a strong indicator of company value and performance, but so are a host of other "softer" indicators such as environmental policies, employee satisfaction, work safety regulations, or investor attraction, to name a few.

Auditing methods

Large corporations have their own internal audit committees which release[4] annual audits at the end of every fiscal year, with transparent accounting statements.

In order to do their job properly[5], auditors ought to be given access to all company emails, archives, current documents or to question any employee. Of course, they use different methods such as sampling[6], the reliability level[7] of which is sometimes questioned as it is not comprehensive[8] enough. This is why they perform more complete reviews of company operations over a given period. Nowadays audit software[9] which is specialized for any given specific purpose, like statistical analyses[10], cross tabulations, special data queries[11], fraud detection and so on, is increasingly reliable. Continuous monitoring is also used and is effective, provided the company has all of its computer systems supervised continuously.

Moreover, companies may exceptionally resort to the services of exterior auditing firms which provide expertise that may be useful not only for improving company performance but for rooting out[12] fraud, or even pre-empting[13] scandals such as the ones that engulfed two big American companies, WorldCom and Enron in 2002. Paradoxically, in the latter case, the auditing company, Arthur Andersen, was accused of covering up Enron's accounting books. That is why auditing companies need to remain independent from any possible source of influence to avoid any conflicts of interest.

Security audits

Because the computing power of systems and the speed of Internet exchanges are difficult to control, it is worth[14] making sure that rogue[15] employees or rogue traders will not manipulate the numbers and secret codes, or that insider trading[16] will not illegally benefit those who are in the know.

Corporate governance

In British and American companies, the separation between ownership (shareholders' interests) and management often leads to a conflict of interest. Shareholders have no control over the managers' qualifications, management methods and financial compensations. Scandals of blue-chip companies[17] fiddling[18] accounts, of managers speculating on the price of stocks in order to draw out bigger sums from stock-options instead of running the company properly in the shareholders' and employees' interest, of other managers leaving failed companies with golden parachutes have hit the headlines[19]. In the US, the Sarbanes-Oxley Act in 2002 was passed to prevent corporate fraud by implementing better accounting accuracy[20].

Whistleblowers[21]

The American whistleblower statute enables employees to reveal to authorities the misdeeds[22] of a corporation which are a violation of law.

1. *To enhance competitiveness:* améliorer la compétitivité.
2. *Bankruptcy:* faillite.
3. *Balance sheet:* bilan comptable.
4. *To release:* publier.
5. *Properly:* correctement.
6. *Sampling:* échantillonnage.
7. *Reliability level:* niveau de fiabilité.
8. *Comprehensive:* complet.
9. *Software* (nom indénombrable): logiciel(s).
10. *Analyses:* pluriel de *analysis*.
11. *Query:* requête.
12. *To root out:* dénicher.
13. *To pre-empt:* empêcher, prévenir.
14. *It is worth:* cela vaut la peine.
15. *Rogue:* malhonnête.
16. *Insider trading:* délit d'initié.
17. *Blue chip company:* société phare de la cote.
18. *To fiddle:* truquer.
19. *To hit the headlines:* faire la une.
20. *Accuracy:* exactitude.
21. *Whistleblower:* informateur.
22. *Misdeed:* méfait.

Repérer les notions essentielles

Answer the following questions.

a. Why are financial statements and balance sheets so important for companies?

b. Why isn't the balance sheet the only indicator to assess a firm's performance?

c. How do auditors work?

d. Why should auditors remain independent from a firm's interests?

e. Why have computers made company safety all the more risky?

Résumer le texte en français

Résumez le texte en *150 mots environ*.

Approfondir

Browse the Internet and find information to answer the following questions.

a. Find out about a famous whistleblower's case in the USA and write a note about it.

b. Find out about rogue employees who ruined their company's performance and write a note about their story.

c. What should the ten commandments of the perfect accountant be?

d. What skills does management expect from an external auditor before hiring him/her?

LEXICAL WORK

• accountant / bookkeeper	comptable
• accounts book	registre de comptabilité
• to amortize a debt / machine	amortir une dette / un équipement
• assets and liabilities	actif et passif
• to audit an account	vérifier un compte
• auditor	contrôleur, commissaire aux comptes
• bad debt	créance irrécouvrable
• to balance the accounts	équilibrer les comptes
• to balance the books	dresser le bilan, arrêter les comptes
• balance sheet	bilan comptable
• to be in surplus	être excédentaire
• benchmarking	étalonnage concurrentiel, benchmarking
• book value	valeur comptable
• bookkeeper	comptable
• bookkeeping, accountancy, accounting	comptabilité
• to borrow money from sb	emprunter de l'argent à qqn
• bottom line	résultat financier
• capital, funds	capitaux
• to carry out an audit	faire un audit
• cash	trésorerie
• CFO (Chief Financial Officer)	directeur financier
• chartered accountant	expert-comptable
• cooking the books, window dressing	truquage de comptes
• creative accounting	comptabilité falsifiée
• current assets	actifs circulants / de roulement / réalisables
• current financial year	exercice financier en cours
• current liabilities	passif exigible, dettes
• debt	endettement, créance
• draft	traite, effet
• embezzlement	détournement de fonds
• to evade taxation, tax evasion	frauder le fisc, fraude fiscale
• false billing	fausse facturation
• to file for bankruptcy	déposer le bilan
• financial statement	état de la situation financière
• fiscal year	exercice budgétaire, année fiscale
• fixed assets	immobilisations, actifs immobilisés
• fraudster	fraudeur/euse

• funding	financement, provisionnement
• to go bust / bankrupt	faire faillite
• goodwill	survaleur
• intangible asset (copyright / patent)	immobilisation incorporelle
• loan	emprunt, prêt
• overbilling	surfacturation
• overheads	frais généraux
• to owe sb money	devoir de l'argent à qqn
• to own	posséder
• to pay off a debt	rembourser une dette
• performance assessment	évaluation des performances
• profit	bénéfice (financier)
• profit and loss account (GB), income statement (US)	compte de résultat
• retained earnings	bénéfices non distribués
• to run into / show a deficit	être déficitaire
• SEC (Securities and Exchanges Commission)	COB (Commission des opérations boursières)
• shareholder equity (US), share capital (GB)	capitaux propres, capital propre
• short / long-term liabilities	dettes à long / court terme
• statutory auditor	commissaire aux comptes
• stock (GB), inventory (US)	inventaire
• (to do) stock taking	(faire l') inventaire
• turnover, revenue	chiffre d'affaires
• working capital	fonds de roulement

USE THE LIST

Find the missing word from the list above (put it into the plural when necessary), then translate.

a. At the end of every f... y..., the accounting department has to review the financial situation of the company and state what its a... and l... are. O..., which are its regular expenses, have to be taken into account as well. Thanks to all these indicators, it will establish the b... s..., which is one of the most important f... s... for any company.

b. Internal a... usually perform this job but a... from outside the company can be hired for checking the process. They certify that all transactions have been honest and legal and state whether the company is running into a deficit or not.

c. B... have a duty to provide transparent numbers on corporations – an impossible task if they o... stock in the companies whose b... they are supposed to oversee independently. To guarantee independent audits, the a... profession needs to follow clear lines against possible c... of i... .

GRAMMAR WORK

Les noms composés

Aide-mémoire grammatical, p. 246.

Analysez et traduisez les exemples suivants :

1. Auditing professions are quite popular among business students today.
2. Irregular accounting procedures may be detected thanks to efficient software.
3. Companies need accurate performance assessment.
4. Safety regulations are compulsory.
5. Accountants can play the role of business advisers.
6. He works in the accounts department.
7. She is examining the financial accounts of a mail order company.

■ Remarque

Attention à l'ordre des termes dans les noms composés soulignés !

1 Voici des noms composés. Placez-les dans les énoncés suivants, que vous traduirez.

Exchange rate – brand image – employment agency – job opportunities – working hours – balance sheets – computer network – savings accounts – pie chart.

a. Long ... increase the workers' chances of illness and injury.

b. A technician had to be called to repair our ... .

c. Young workers know that there are many ... in accountancy.

d. It is not always easy to understand what is written on ... .

e. The ... of the dollar fluctuates every day.

f. With the financial crisis, consumers feared for their ... .

g. A ... is a circle divided into sections to show the proportions of a set of things.

h. If you are jobless, go to your local ... .

i. The ... of a company determines the way consumers perceive its products.

Les prépositions

Analysez et traduisez les exemples suivants :

1. Production has increased <u>by</u> 5% this year.
2. Prices have dropped <u>by</u> half.
3. An increase <u>in</u> exports would help us out.
4. This policy has led <u>to</u> a fall <u>in</u> unemployment.
5. We expect an increase <u>of</u> <u>about</u> 2% <u>for</u> next year.
6. Our sales figures have risen <u>to</u> £4m.
7. A loss <u>of between</u> 6,000 <u>and</u> 7,000 pounds.

2 **Les chiffres suivants sont extraits d'un bilan financier. Complétez les phrases par des prépositions pour commenter ce bilan.**

Overheads – 2008: £10,010 - 2007: £10,000.

UK sales – 2008: £3m - 2007: £1.4m.

Orders (Europe) – forecast for 2009: £6.2-6.3m - 2008: £5m - 2007: £4.2m.

Over the past few months, figures have been worrying. Our sales in the UK fell ... about half this year. This sharp drop ... sales is quite alarming. A decrease ... 50% is the worst thing that could have happened to us. However, orders from the whole of Europe have increased ... £5m and we expect another rise ... £1m and £1.5m, especially as we expect the exchange rate of the euro to drop ... 0.5%. Concerning overheads, there has only been a slight increase ... spending.

3 **Traduisez en anglais.**

a. Les coûts de main-d'œuvre ont augmenté de 10 % depuis l'an dernier.

b. Il y a eu une baisse de production dans toutes les usines de voitures.

c. On s'attend à une augmentation du taux de chômage d'environ 2 %.

d. De graves problèmes de trésorerie peuvent conduire une entreprise à la faillite.

e. Pour les directeurs d'entreprise, une perte de 2 à 3 % serait acceptable.

EXAM WORK

DOCUMENT 1

Metrics: Overmeasuring Our Way to Management

Business has caught a terrible case of the measurement flu[1]. Companies seem more focused on performance indicators than on the actual health of what they are trying to measure. Beyond this confusion of measurement, there are side effects: depersonalization, a decrease in trust, and a false sense that costs and risks are actually being managed.

If you overmeasure a relationship, you alter[2] the nature of the relationship itself—the very thing you're trying to measure. When the concept of customer loyalty was first popularized in the late 1980s, the term had deep emotional connotations: it conjured up such phrases as "*semper fi*,"[3] or "till death do us part."[4] After two decades of overmeasurement, the term is effectively synonymous with price-based promotions to encourage repeat business[5]. Corporate customer-loyalty programs have become all about the metrics. The net result? Loyalty itself has declined, the victim of degradation by over-measurement.

How did we get this way? Technology has been seductive; think of the power of the spreadsheet[6]. Consider also the recent celebration of the "hard" sciences over those such as psychology or economics. Too often this thinking has implied that lack of measurement implies irrelevance. Both measurement and management will be improved if we can rediscover how to think about each of them independently. Financial performance will improve, too. Another plus is the reintroduction of the human element into business. You can't measure it, but you can't deny its impact.

By Charles H. Green, abridged from Gigaom, February 2, 2010.

1. *Flu:* grippe. **2.** *To alter:* transformer. **3.** *Semper fi:* toujours fidèle. **4.** *Till death do us part:* jusqu'à ce que la mort nous sépare. **5.** *Repeat business:* fidélisation du client. **6.** *Spreadsheet:* tableur.

1 **What problem is raised by this article? What are the causes and consequences? *(About 100 words.)***

DOCUMENT 2

Who Benefits More From an Accurate Financial Statement?

Most people who tune in to[1] business shows on television or radio have a keen interest in corporate profitability, governance and productivity. Besides the public, other groups of financial-statement readers—most of whom are sophisticated financiers—delve into[2] accounting reports to find the next economic jewel with attractive potential. These include traders, portfolio managers and financial analysts. A financial statement tells various groups important information about a business, as well as how it fares[3] in the competitive landscape. Investors glean[4] valuable data from the reports and determine whether they should include stocks or bonds in their investment bets. Going through corporate performance data also enables financiers to identify firms that are making money and pinpoint[5] businesses that are lying low[6], competitively speaking. Government watchdogs have a pointed interest in the way businesses prepare and report financial statements. Regulatory agencies appreciate firms that consistently[7] generate well-prepared and accurate financial reports. In a modern economy replete with[8] round-the-clock business news, the public may want to know how a specific company fares, especially if the business is a stalwart[9] multinational organization employing several thousand people. This interest comes from the fact that inaccurate financial reporting and regulatory inquiries adversely[10] impact a company and could ultimately affect an entire economic sector. Rivals review corporate financial statements to understand specific routes that a company takes to reach its economic zenith. Financial-statement accuracy at the corporate level increases transparency in an entire industry.

By Marquis Codjia, abridged from eHow.com, 8 April 2011.

1. *To tune in to:* écouter. 2. *To delve into:* se plonger dans. 3. *To fare:* réussir. 4. *To glean:* glâner. 5. *To pinpoint:* repérer. 6. *To lie low:* ne pas faire des étincelles. 7. *Consistently:* invariablement. 8. *Replete with:* rempli de. 9. *Stalwart:* exemplaire. 10. *Adversely:* défavorablement.

2 Qui s'intéresse aux rapports financiers des entreprises et pourquoi ? *(150 mots environ.)*

3 Traduisez ces groupes nominaux tirés du document :

a. business shows – **b.** competitive landscape – **c.** corporate performance data – **d.** regulatory agencies – **e.** financial-statement accuracy.

DOCUMENT 3

True and fair[1]

The collapse[2] of companies such as Enron and WorldCom in the aftermath of[3] the Internet bubble demonstrated the central role of accounting in good corporate governance. Both companies manipulated their figures[4] and then persuaded their auditors (Arthur Andersen in both cases) to sign off[5] on accounts that were at best misleading[6], at worst downright criminal[7].

The cases highlighted a contrast between the modern American approach to accounting and the more old-fashioned British approach. America's accounting rules have developed in the context of the increasingly litigious nature of that country's corporate life. This has put pressure on American accountants to be very precise about what is and what is not permissible in company accounts.

In the UK, by contrast, accountants have tried to stick more closely to the old idea of "true and fair", of accepting that precision in accounting is a chimera, that the best you can hope for is that the figures appear (to an honest, independent expert of goodwill[8]) to be as true and fair a reflection[9] of the corporate reality as it is possible to achieve. In the UK, auditors are required to state whether[10] the accounts they are signing show a "true and fair view" of the organisation's affairs.

Although this principle can overrule specific legal requirements, there is no precise legal definition of what true and fair means. Despite its vagueness, however, the Sarbanes-Oxley Act (American legislation passed in the wake of[11] the Enron and WorldCom accounting scandals that is applicable to all companies quoted[12] on an American stock exchange) reinstated the principle into American accounting.

For most of the 20th century, in the UK and the many countries that follow British accounting principles, the true and fair view held the upper hand[13] [...] but was not helped by a general debasement[14] of the accounting profession itself. It was common to denigrate "bean counters[15]". What's more, whereas three decades[16] ago accountancy training was essential for a young manager aiming for the top, the MBA replaced it for aspiring young executives. Even chief financial officers have largely abandoned accountancy qualifications.

Two things in particular have compromised the accountants' vision of what is true and fair. One is their desire to do (more glamorous) things than accounting and auditing – in particular, consulting. The other distortion comes from the excessively familiar relationships that grow up in cases where an auditor remains with the same client for many years. At Enron, many of the employees in the company's accounts department had previously worked for Arthur Andersen, and vice versa.

Abridged from *The Economist*, September 22nd, 2008.

---

1. *Fair:* juste et équitable. **2.** *Collapse:* effondrement. **3.** *In the aftermath of:* à la suite de. **4.** *Figure:* chiffre. **5.** *To sign off:* valider. **6.** *Misleading:* trompeur. **7.** *Downright criminal:* carrément délictueux. **8.** *Goodwill:* bonne volonté. **9.** *Reflection:* reflet. **10.** *To state whether:* déclarer si. **11.** *In the wake of:* dans le sillage de. **12.** *To quote:* coter. **13.** *To hold the upper hand:* dominer. **14.** *Debasement:* dévalorisation. **15.** *Bean counter* (péj.): petit comptable. **16.** *Decade:* décennie.

4 Drawing information from the whole text, answer the following questions.

a. Why is auditing central to the good corporate governance of firms?

b. What are the main differences between the British and the American conceptions of auditing?

c. Why is auditing not considered by many as a glamorous profession?

d. What has undermined the quality of fair accountancy?

DOCUMENT 4

1. *A gimmick:* une combine. **2.** *A record:* un document. **3.** *Confusing:* déroutant.

1. *Assignment:* mission.

Scott Adams, http://search.dilbert.com, 17 and 20 June 2002.

5 EXPRESSION. Using both cartoons and any knowledge you have about the topic, explain what makes accounting fraud possible. *(About 200 words.)*

6 COMPRÉHENSION. En vous appuyant sur les documents 1, 2, 3 et 4 expliquez quels sont les avantages et les limites de la mesure chiffrée des performances de l'entreprise. *(250 mots environ.)*

7 EXPRESSION. À partir du scénario suivant, vous rédigerez un courrier en anglais.

Vous êtes M. Robin Legard, contrôleur de la société AudiPerfect (96 Marylebone Road, London, NW1 5LA), recruté par l'entreprise ToolBox 3000 (130 Tottenham Court Road, London W1 9HP) pour effectuer son audit financier de l'année. Vous écrivez à la directrice de cette entreprise (Mme Amanda Holmes) pour lui présenter votre rapport et le bilan financier lui-même, soit deux pièces jointes.

Indiquez que votre travail a été effectué dans de bonnes conditions et dans les temps requis car vous avez eu accès à des sources claires ; que vous avez apprécié les efforts de collaboration du comité d'audit de l'entreprise, ainsi que de tous les membres du personnel. Vous espérez avoir donné toute satisfaction et que l'entreprise aura de nouveau recours à votre société.

Date et formules d'usage. Copie de ce courrier au directeur financier, M. Hawkins.

▶ Méthodes, p. 274.

DOCUMENT 5

Balance Sheet Sample

Assets			Liabilities		
Current Assets :			**Current Liabilities :**		
Cash	$	50,000	Short-term debt	$	30,000
Accounts Receivable	$	40,000	Accounts Payable	$	50,000
Merchandise Inventory	$	100,000	Salaries	$	110,000
Total Current Assets	$	190,000	Total Current Liabilities	$	190,000
Plant & Equipment			Long-term debt	$	20,000
Equipment	$	30,000	Total Liabilities	$	210,000
Less : Accumulated Depreciation	$	(2,000)	Owner's Equity	$	8,000
Total Assets	**$**	**218,000**	**Total Liabilities & Owner's Equity**	**$**	**218,000**

www.beechmontcrest.com

8 Write out your answers in English and then read them out loud.

a. How much cash on hand or in the bank has the company left, according to this table?

b. How much is due from customers who have made purchases from the business on credit? What name is given to that sum of money?

c. How much is the merchandise owned by the company worth?

d. What name is given to the portion of equipment cost used in the process of operating the business? What does it mean? What is the equipment valued at?

e. How much does the company owe vendors and / or suppliers for purchases made on credit?

f. How much is owed to employees in terms of salary?

g. How does one calculate the shareholders' equity?

9 What can you say about this balance sheet and the state of the company? *(About 50 words.)*

CHAPITRE

18 Internal and external company communication

La communication interne et externe de l'entreprise

BACKGROUND

Internal communication

Effective company internal communications are of great importance. Employees who are better informed are more satisfied, feel more involved[1] in the future of the company and therefore contribute more to its success. The employees' motivation and sense of belonging play a big part in achieving the objectives of the company, namely[2] attracting more customers, increasing sales, making a profit. Their motivation will also enable them to deal with company or management changes.

Advantages and methods of internal communication

To be successful, companies have to create a workforce that understands the goals[3], values and procedures of the organization. The employees must have a set of common goals on which they can act every day. If they are encouraged to make certain decisions at the production line level, then they will feel more confident and be more efficient. A coherent, shared organizational culture can reduce day-to-day conflict, which is good for the employees' morale and for the running of the company. Most importantly, perhaps, management behaviour and decisions must be consistent with the messages sent out[4] to the workforce. An inconsistent approach to communication causes resentment and cynicism.

Companies use various methods to create a common culture as a strategic advantage, first in their written communication: memos[5], brochures, newsletters, billboards[6], slogans, e-mails, performance appraisal[7] documents. They also develop oral communication through meetings, periodic speeches by the CEO, open house[8] sessions, etc. When possible, some form of informal communication is also very effective because it can encourage two-way communication which gives management a good idea about how the company is perceived among employees.

Employees who leave a company sometimes do so because they do not feel that they are part of a team, or that anybody cares what they do or say. They do not leave the company, they leave the people, be it[9] managers or colleagues.

External communication: its different forms

In order to achieve that, the company communicates with the public by means of advertising, marketing, public relations and publicity.

Advertising consists of informing customers about a product or service and is usually done by means of billboards, leaflets[10], brochures, ads (advertisements) in newspapers and magazines, television and radio commercials[11], direct mailings or e-mail messages, web banners, personal contact, buzzing, etc.

Marketing is composed of a number of activities, one of which is to ensure that the company is still meeting the needs of its customers. Market research enables the company to find out what groups of potential customers exist, what their needs are, which of those needs can be met and how. It is also important to analyse the competition, to position and price a new product or service according to market demand. Direct marketing includes promoting a product through continued advertising, promotions and public relations.

Public relations uses ongoing[12] activities to make sure that the company has a strong public image and to help the public understand the company and its products. Public relations are often carried out through the media, namely newspapers, magazines, television, radio, etc.

Another form of communication is **publicity** which means that reporters and writers will mention or discuss the company and/or its products in the media. It is they and not the company that will decide what is said, hence[13] the importance of a good public image.

Nowadays, **vaunting its ethical and ecological commitments**[14] has become an important element of the company's public image. More and more companies publicly acknowledge their responsibility to their workforce, to society and to the environment. Pressure groups have played an important part in making the business world aware of social problems in their own communities and worldwide. In newspapers, companies sometimes take up a whole page to explain their ethical and environmental policy. This can only have a very positive effect upon the general public and future customers.

1. *To involve:* impliquer.
2. *Namely:* à savoir.
3. *Goal:* but, objectif.
4. *To send out:* transmettre.
5. *Memo:* note de service.
6. *Billboard:* panneau d'affichage.
7. *Appraisal:* évaluation.
8. *Open house:* portes ouvertes.
9. *Be it:* que ce soit.
10. *Leaflet:* dépliant.
11. *Commercial:* annonce, pub, spot publicitaire à la radio et à la télévision.
12. *On going:* en cours.
13. *Hence:* d'où.
14. *Commitment:* engagement.

Repérer les notions essentielles

Answer the following questions.

a. Why is good internal communication very important?
b. What negative feelings may be produced among employees, and why?
c. Why is informal communication recommended?
d. Why is external communication absolutely essential?
e. What are the various methods used?

Résumer le texte en français

Résumez le texte en *100 mots environ*.

Approfondir

What techniques are used by advertisers to catch the attention of the public?

Are you for or against banning advertisements during children's TV programmes? *(About 100 words.)*

LEXICAL WORK

• advertisement (ad)	annonce publicitaire, publicité
• to advertise a product	faire de la publicité pour un produit
• advertiser	annonceur
• advertising	publicité commerciale
• advertising blurb	texte publicitaire
• to be a market leader	dominer un marché
• to be worth	valoir
• boardroom	(salle du) conseil d'administration
• brand image / name	image / nom de marque
• brand, trademark (mark)	marque
• buzzing / word-of-mouth advertising	publicité par le bouche-à-oreille
• to convey	faire comprendre, transmettre
• corporate behavior	comportement de l'entreprise
• to crack / break into a market	pénétrer un marché
• to damage	endommager, nuire à
• to emphasize / highlight / underline	souligner
• to entail	entraîner, comporter
• to escalate	s'intensifier
• fashionable, trendy	à la mode
• friendly	amical, sympathique
• to gain a foothold	se faire connaître sur un marché
• to get in touch with	contacter
• greenwashing	blanchiment écologique
• to implement	mettre en pratique
• to lobby	faire du lobbying
• to market	commercialiser
• market share	part de marché
• market survey / study	étude de marché
• niche, opportunity	créneau
• to open up a market	créer un marché
• opinion survey / poll	sondage
• personnel / staff turnover	rotation du personnel
• pressure group / lobby	groupe de pression
• promotional strategy	plan de promotion
• publicity	publicité (par journalistes, etc.)
• to reinforce / enhance	renforcer
• relationship	relations, rapport
• sale / sales	vente / soldes
• sales forecast	prévision des ventes
• sales patter / talk	boniment

• spin doctor	expert en relations publiques
• target	cible
• to target	cibler
• to upgrade / downgrade a product	améliorer / diminuer la qualité d'un produit
• training scheme	plan de formation
• upmarket / downmarket	haut / bas de gamme
• ways and means	moyens, ressources
• web banner, banner ad	bannière publicitaire (sur le Net)
• workplace	lieu de travail
• worthwhile	valable, digne d'intérêt

USE THE LIST

1 Match and translate the following words

a. staff	**1.** a market
b. web	**2.** image
c. market	**3.** behaviour
d. spin	**4.** turnover
e. brand	**5.** forecast
f. corporate	**6.** scheme
g. training	**7.** a foothold
h. to gain	**8.** doctor
i. sales	**9.** banner
j. to open up	**10.** survey

MORE VOCABULARY

2 Fill in the gaps of the following text with one of the words below, making the necessary changes, and then translate the whole text:
team – prosper – improve – achieve – ensure

To ... that the company survives and ... , it is necessary to have a public relations ... which adds value to a company by helping it ... employees' understanding of what has to be ... .

GRAMMAR WORK

Le cas possessif

Aide-mémoire grammatical, p. 234.

Analysez et traduisez les exemples suivants :

1. Where is Ann's file? – I think this one is hers. – No, it is mine.
2. My colleagues' documents are over there with the manager's.
3. The company's communication policy has changed.
4. Wednesday's meeting will be held in room 8.
5. Whose speech was that? It was Mr Hadley's.

■ **Quelles formes d'expression de la possession apparaissent ici ?**

1 **Écrivez une nouvelle phrase en mettant les mots soulignés au cas possessif.**

Ex.: The talks last week were very useful. → Last week's talks were very useful.

a. The meeting next month has been postponed.
b. The economic policy of the government has been criticised.
c. The success of both firms is the result of good advertising.
d. The books written for children can be a means of advertising.
e. The dresses worn by the models were very trendy.
f. The needs and complaints of customers should be taken into consideration.
g. The queries sent in by Mr James must be answered at once.
h. For the conference of this year, we have chosen a fashionable theme.

Expression de l'interdiction et de l'absence d'obligation

Aide-mémoire grammatical, p. 231.

Analysez et traduisez les exemples suivants :

1. Put the van in the garage, as you need not deliver the appliance until tomorrow.
2. The manager and his assistant need not have gone to Vienna, since the meeting had been cancelled.
3. They did not have to go to Edinburgh for the Annual Conference, because it was held in Paris.
4. Advertisements must not tell lies about the products they advertise.

2 **Mettez les verbes à une forme exprimant l'interdiction ou l'absence d'obligation, puis traduisez les phrases.**

a. We have an efficient delivery system, so we ... (to update) it.

b. Last year, the company ... (to change) its strategy, because business was brisk.

c. You ... *(to criticize)* our managers as it might damage our image.

d. The staff ... *(to come)* to the office on Saturday, but they were told too late about it.

e. We ... *(to rush)* to Oslo yet. In fact, the fair does not start until next Wednesday.

f. We ... *(to take)* lots of notes, since the lecture is being recorded.

g. They ... *(to worry)* about the financial results: they were too pessimistic, all is well.

3 **Traduisez les phrases suivantes.**

a. Tous les magazines de mode nous ont déjà contactés, donc vous n'êtes pas obligé de leur téléphoner.

b. Il faut tenir compte des remarques des clients si on veut les garder.

c. Vendre de bons produits à un prix raisonnable est dans l'intérêt de tout le monde.

d. L'engagement du directeur général en faveur de l'amélioration de la communication interne plaît beaucoup au personnel.

e. Elsie Smith n'est pas encore obligée de prendre sa retraite car l'âge officiel de départ à la retraite vient d'être repoussé.

f. Je vous ai déjà dit hier que vous n'êtes pas obligé de prendre vos congés le mois prochain.

g. Vous ne devez pas poser toutes ces questions : ces informations sont confidentielles.

h. Il ne faut pas lancer cette campagne de publicité trop tôt : elle risque de nuire à notre image.

i. Vous n'avez pas besoin de parler du dernier projet en date du directeur commercial.

j. Nous n'étions pas obligés de faire autant de concessions au client : il était déjà convaincu.

k. Les brochures de l'an dernier n'auront pas besoin d'être réimprimées : il en reste beaucoup.

EXAM WORK

DOCUMENT 1

Say hello to the virtual boardroom

Video-conferencing

The process has become far more cost-effective[1] – and often free. Skype has just released version 4.0 of its popular Internet-communications software and this promises greatly enhanced video quality for conference calls[2].

Though video-conferencing has been around[3] for a while, it has been slow to take off[4] because of the outlay[5] required on cumbersome equipment. Jerky[6] pictures, dropped connections and annoying time-delays made things worse. Talking to a contact on the other side of the Atlantic resembled watching a badly lip-synched[7] film.

Now as the global recession sinks its teeth into so many firms' bottom lines[8], it is an idea whose day has come. Whether you need to keep in touch[9] with partners and clients based in other countries or people stranded[10] by bad weather, it is now cheap and easy to make a conference call using not expensive specialist equipment but a standard broadband-enabled computer and webcam.

These days you can negotiate on your laptop's screen as you sup a latte[11] in a café that has wi-fi. Thanks to new software, you can even project a fake backdrop[12] onto the image so your contact sees you in a bustling[13] office or against a city skyline.

Tech-savvy[14] firms are employing video-conferencing tools not only to slash back[15] on their travel needs but to create an entirely virtual office. If you want to go the whole hog[16], Cisco, the telecommunications giant, offers Telepresence – a life-size video-conferencing suite that can accommodate up to 16 people in each location and makes it look as if they are sitting opposite you in the room. Fitting this deluxe service will set your firm back[17] a sobering[18] £125,000 a year, but many services are equipped with it.

The video element is only one aspect of the evolution in the way business is conducted in today's virtual office. It is easy to find business partners in countries you have never been to and then collaborate on documents that are stored online, no matter[19] where your new colleagues are based. Indeed, you can set up and run a successful international firm with your virtual colleagues without any of you leaving your own postcodes.

By Alex Petit, *The Sunday Times*, February 15th, 2009.

1. *Cost-effective:* rentable. **2.** *Conference call:* téléconference. **3.** *To be around:* exister. **4.** *To take off:* décoller. **5.** *Outlay:* mise de fonds. **6.** *Jerky:* saccadé. **7.** *To lip-synch:* doubler. **8.** *Bottom line:* résultat financier. **9.** *To keep in touch:* garder le contact. **10.** *Stranded:* en rade. **11.** *To sup a latte:* déguster un café au lait. **12.** *Fake background:* fausse toile de fond. **13.** *Bustling:* animé, où l'on s'affaire. **14.** *Tech-savvy:* calé en technologie. **15.** *To slash back:* tailler dans les dépenses. **16.** *To go the whole hog:* aller jusqu'au bout. **17.** *To set back:* coûter. **18.** *Sobering:* qui donne à réfléchir. **19.** *No matter:* peu importe.

1 **Answer the following questions.**

a. How can you get to a meeting without travelling?

b. Why has video-conferencing taken so long to become popular?

c. Why has it become popular now?

d. What does it enable you to do technically and how?

2 **Sum up the text, analyzing the advantages and disadvantages of using video-conferencing as an important part of a company's external communication.** ***(About 150 words.)***

3 **Translate the following passage.**

It is well-known that the cause of most internal problems being faced by a company often stems from ineffective communication. A recent survey revealed that 95% of American CEOs considered that "effective internal communication" was of great importance to the success of the organization. The person in charge of human relations should be highly qualified in understanding the communication process.

▶ Méthodes, p. 285.

DOCUMENT 2

Corporate Communication Tips

At the root of a successful corporation is effective communication. Without it, misunderstandings can be rampant, resulting in loss of employee morale and valuable clients. By applying the necessary communication strategies, you can improve the overall operation of your business.

Perhaps the most frequently used form of corporate communication is email. Before typing an email remember that your reader has other tasks to attend to. Therefore, try to keep it brief, while maintaining his interest. A confusing email makes for difficult reading, so make yours concise, clear and interesting. Know what you want to convey, how you want the reader to perceive your message, and use plain English to relay it. Although email is a worthy communication tool, it should not be used for every message you want to send. Many executives rely on sending emails, even when the person is only a few feet away. This can create a certain emotional distance between you and the employee.

If there are no communication policies or rules in place, employees will communicate however they feel they should; the business may crumble as a result. Take control of the standards you want to set for your employees to follow. Outline, document and relay to your employees all the specifics regarding your company's brand and target audience; be very clear in how you want them to represent the company. As the business owner or CEO, you should sign this document, then ensure it reaches Human Resources, managers, supervisors and employees, all of whom need to sign. When employees sign documentation, it has a much more impacting effect than if you had simply told them.

Work stress may cause you to become agitated. Try to remain calm in such situations, so your employees can emulate your positive behavior. Barking at them one day, then smiling at them the next will result in them losing respect for you and them projecting your actions upon each other.

By Natalie Grace, eHow Contributor, adapted from: www.ehow.com.

4 **Présentez les idées principales du texte. *(100 mots environ.)***

DOCUMENT 3

Why your company needs fat-free[1] communication

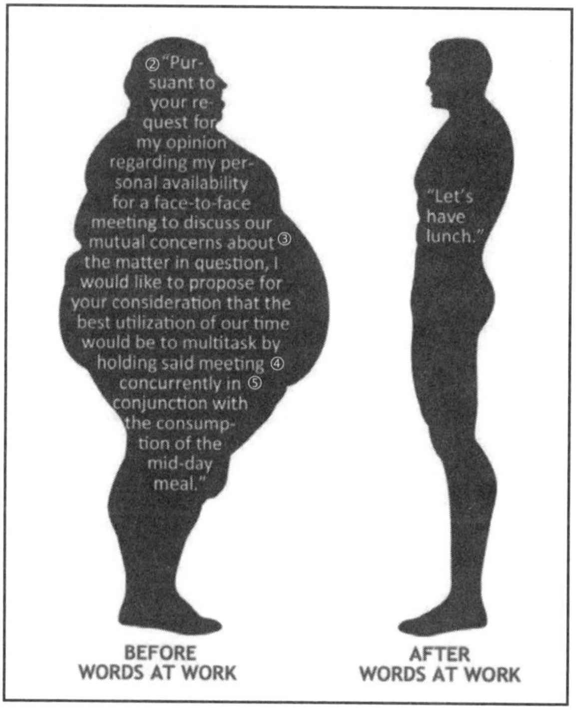

http://words-at-work.net

1. *Fat-free:* allégé. 2. *Pursuant:* suite à. 3. *Concern:* soucis. 4. *Said meeting:* ladite réunion. 5. *Concurrently:* simultanément.

5 **EXPRESSION. What is the message conveyed by this poster? Can you imagine why companies might want to use it? *(About 150 words.)***

DOCUMENT 4

The Greenwash guide

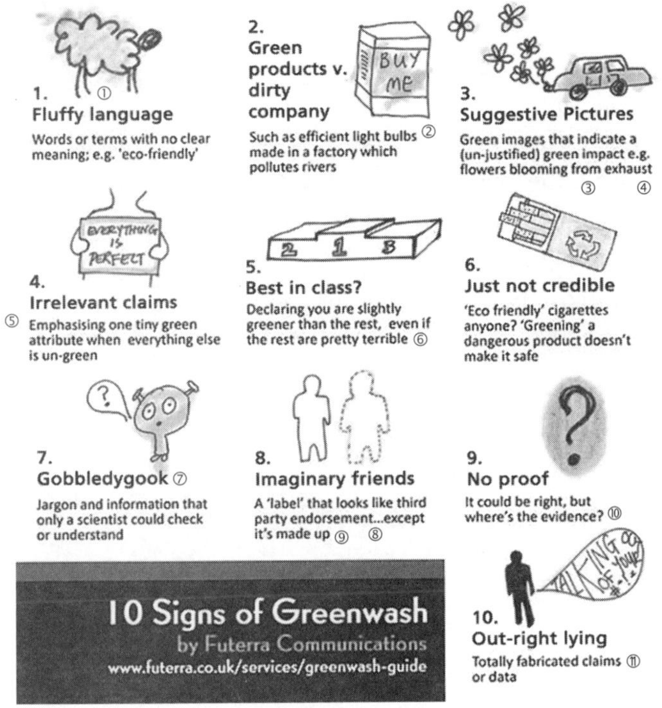

"The Greenwash guide", www.futerra.co.uk

1. *Fluffy:* séduisant et creux. 2. *Light bulb:* ampoule électrique. 3. *To bloom:* fleurir. 4. *Exhaust:* pot d'échappement. 5. *To emphasize:* insister sur. 6. *Pretty terrible:* plutôt affreux. 7. *Gobbledygook:* charabia. 8. *Endorsement:* soutien. 9. *Made up:* inventé. 10. *Evidence:* preuves. 11. *Claim:* déclaration.

6 **D'après ce document, à quoi reconnaît-on qu'une entreprise se livre à un éco-blanchiment de sa marque ou de ses activités ? *(Environ 200 mots.)***

7 **COMPRÉHENSION. Rédigez une note de synthèse *(de 200 mots environ)* sur les documents 1, 2, 3 et 4, en dégageant et analysant les moyens et l'importance d'une bonne communication entre l'entreprise, ses employés et ses clients, tels qu'ils y sont présentés.**

8 **EXPRESSION. Le Directeur des Ressources humaines de votre entreprise veut améliorer la communication entre les employés et la direction. Il vous demande de préparer une note de service à transmettre par mél à tous les employés.**

À partir du mois prochain, une réunion hebdomadaire d'une heure sera organisée dans chaque service avec les employés pour discuter des problèmes qu'ils auront constatés, des conditions de travail, des solutions et améliorations possibles, des avancées réalisées, etc. Chaque chef de service remettra un compte rendu au Directeur.

Une fois par mois, le Directeur organisera une réunion avec les personnes concernées.

Dans l'intervalle, un employé pourra solliciter un rendez-vous avec le Directeur qui l'accueillera le plus rapidement possible en fonction de ses disponibilités. *(100 mots environ, en anglais.)*

AIDE-MÉMOIRE GRAMMATICAL

FICHE 1 Articles

1. L'article défini : *THE*

▸ L'article *THE* a une valeur déterminante, voire démonstrative et s'emploie devant des noms dans un **sens déterminé**.

• Sens déterminé explicitement **par le contexte** :

The oil crisis of 1973 triggered inflation.
Le choc pétrolier de 1973 a provoqué de l'inflation.

The articles which are on sale in this shop are out of fashion.
Les articles qui sont en vente dans ce magasin sont démodés.

• Sens déterminé implicitement **par le contexte** :

The manager wants to know where you have stored the files.
Le directeur veut savoir où vous avez rangé les dossiers.

▸ Certains **noms** sont **toujours précédés de *THE***.

• C'est le cas de certains **noms de pays** déterminés par un nom commun :

the United States of America – the United Kingdom – the Netherlands.

• Les **adjectifs substantivés** permettent de désigner des catégories de personnes déterminées. Ils ne prennent pas la marque du pluriel :

the poor – the rich – the unemployed – the British.

• Les **inventions** et des lieux d'activités :

the Internet – the radio – the cinema – the theatre – the train – the plane – the office
sauf ∅ *television* (*the television* désigne le poste de télévision).

• D'autres **noms courants précédés de *THE*** :

the environment – the economy – the consumer society – the world – the sun.

2. L'article ∅

▸ L'**article défini français** (le / la / les) permet de désigner les choses de manière déterminée, mais aussi générale. Dans ce dernier cas, l'anglais a recours à ∅.

• Les **indénombrables** :

∅ *Business is ∅ business.*
Les affaires sont les affaires.

∅ *Unemployment is an economic and social issue.*
Le chômage est un problème économique et social.

Everyone has to adapt to ∅ modern society.
Tout le monde doit s'adapter à la société moderne.

• Les **dénombrables au pluriel** :

∅ *Employees should be well paid.*
Les employés devraient être bien payés.

∅ *Companies have to make a profit.*
Les entreprises doivent faire du bénéfice.

▸ Un **groupe nominal incluant un nom propre de personne** :

∅ *President Obama was elected in 2008.*
Le président Obama a été élu en 2008.

∅ *Mr Smith's order has been sent.*
On a envoyé la commande de Monsieur Smith.

▸ **Les expressions de lieux familiers** suivants : *home, church, hospital*

Many people now work from home.
Beaucoup de gens travaillent depuis leur domicile maintenant.

3. L'article indéfini : *A / AN*

A / AN est toujours suivi d'un nom **dénombrable au singulier**.

• Il permet de désigner **les choses de manière générale** (au singulier) :

A merger consists in joining several companies.
Une fusion consiste à regrouper plusieurs entreprises.

• Il a une **fonction numérique** (= *one*) :

We spent a week, not two, on the report.
Nous avons passé une semaine et non deux sur le rapport.

• On le trouve **après une préposition** (+ nom dénombrable au singulier) :

It is difficult to invest without a loan.
Sans prêt, il est difficile d'investir.

• On le trouve **devant les noms de profession** :

She is an accountant.
Elle est comptable.

REMARQUE

Si la fonction est unique et introduite dans un attribut, on omet l'article :

He was appointed ∅ sales manager.
Il a été nommé directeur des ventes.

- On le trouve dans les **exclamatives** (+ nom dénombrable au singulier) :

  What a relief when we heard the delivery had arrived in time!
  Quel soulagement quand nous avons appris que la livraison avait été faite à temps !

- On le trouve dans les **expressions de fréquence** :

  He checks the price of our shares twice a day.
  Il vérifie le prix de nos actions deux fois par jour.

REMARQUE

L'article ∅ + dénombrable au pluriel peut correspondre à « les » ou « des » selon le contexte.

∅ People came to visit the factory yesterday.
Des personnes sont venues visiter l'usine hier.

∅ People usually want ∅ lower prices.
Les gens veulent généralement des prix plus bas.

4. SOME / ANY / NO

SOME, ANY et NO permettent de **traduire l'article partitif français.**

We sent some brochures to our customers.
Nous avons envoyé des brochures à nos clients.

They did not lend us any money.
Ils ne nous ont pas prêté d'argent.

There is no social policy in this company.
Il n'y a pas de politique sociale dans cette entreprise.

FICHE 2 AS OU LIKE

AS et *LIKE* sont souvent des équivalents de « comme », mais il ne faut pas les confondre car en principe ils se construisent différemment, et *AS* a bien d'autres emplois que LIKE.

1. AS

AS a de nombreuses constructions.

- ***AS* conjonction (+ sujet) + verbe**

  As you know, he is an accountant.
  Comme vous savez, il est comptable.

  We can organise our work as we like.
  Nous pouvons organiser notre travail comme il nous plaît.

  He paid the bill immediately, as required.
  Il a payé la facture immédiatement, comme c'est demandé.

  She received a phone call just as she was leaving.
  Elle a reçu un appel téléphonique comme / au moment précis où elle partait.

As the company developed, so they needed more capital.
Comme / À mesure que la société se développait, ils ont eu besoin de plus de capitaux.

Things are not organised here as (they were) in my previous company.
L'organisation ici n'est pas comme dans mon ancienne société.

- ***AS* préposition + nom**

As an accountant, he is very efficient.
Comme / en tant que comptable, il est très efficace. (avec l'article indéfini en anglais)

Accountancy is considered as a complex job.
La comptabilité est considérée comme un travail complexe.

REMARQUE

On trouve aussi *AS* exprimant la comparaison après *THE SAME* et pour former les comparatifs d'égalité :

Working hours in France are not the same as in the UK.
Les horaires de travail en France ne sont pas les mêmes qu'au Royaume-Uni.

Their products are not as good as ours.
Leurs produits ne sont pas aussi bons que les nôtres.

2. *LIKE*

En principe, *LIKE*, toujours préposition, **ne peut être suivi que d'un nom ou d'un pronom.**

- *LIKE* peut introduire une **comparaison** :

He is a bookkeeper, like her.
Il est comptable, comme elle.

There are going to be job cuts, like last year.
Il va y avoir des suppressions d'emplois, comme l'an dernier.

Working hours in France are not like those in the UK.
Les horaires de travail en France ne sont pas comme ceux du Royaume-Uni.

- *LIKE* peut introduire un **exemple** :

A bank like HSBC would never have done that.
Une banque comme HSBC n'aurait jamais fait cela.

REMARQUES

1. On peut aussi dire *SUCH AS* pour introduire un exemple :

A bank such as / like Citibank...

2. Dans la langue parlée (américaine surtout), on entend souvent *LIKE* à la place de *AS* ; cette construction est à éviter dans la langue soignée, surtout à l'écrit.

Like I said, he is very successful.
Comme je l'ai dit, il réussit très bien.

As I said est nettement préférable.

FICHE 3 Auxiliaires modaux *CAN, COULD, MUST, NEED, OUGHT TO, MAY, MIGHT, SHOULD, HAD BETTER, USED TO*

1. Généralités

• Les auxiliaires modaux, très fréquents en anglais, indiquent des modalités de la pensée, des sentiments ou des opinions du locuteur.

• Ils ne prennent pas de *s* à la 3e personne du singulier.

• Ils s'utilisent sans *do*, *does*, *did*, à la forme négative ou interrogative.

• Ils sont suivis de l'infinitif sans *to*.

• Ils sont parfois remplacés par d'autres formes verbales.

2. CAN, COULD

CAN et *COULD* s'emploient pour indiquer :

• la **possibilité**

I can / could finish drawing up the estimate by Thursday.
Je peux / pourrais finir d'établir le devis pour / d'ici jeudi.

• la **capacité**

My assistant, who can speak four languages, could already speak three when she was a child.
Mon assistante, qui sait parler quatre langues, savait déjà en parler trois lorsqu'elle était petite.

• la **permission**

The employees can / could clock in at 7am or 8am.
Les employés peuvent / pouvaient pointer / arriver à 7 heures ou 8 heures du matin.

• la **déduction** à la forme négative avec *CANNOT / CANNOT HAVE*

They cannot be very pleased at the moment: they cannot have been expecting their firm to go bankrupt!
Ils ne doivent pas être très contents en ce moment. Ils ne devaient pas s'attendre à ce que leur entreprise fasse faillite !

• l'**éventualité** avec *COULD (HAVE)*

If it was not for the airline strike, I could be in Copenhagen now.
Sans la grève de la compagnie aérienne, je pourrais être à Copenhague maintenant.

They could have missed the train.
Ils ont peut-être raté le train (car ils sont en retard).

Ils auraient pu rater le train (s'ils n'avaient pas couru).

• une forme de **regret** ou de reproche avec *COULD HAVE* :

They could have told us that the meeting had been postponed!
Ils auraient pu nous dire que la réunion avait été remise à plus tard !

REMARQUE

COULD est remplacé par ***was able to / managed to*** pour exprimer une action que l'on a pu accomplir malgré des difficultés.

We were able to / managed to send the order on time.
Nous avons pu / avons réussi à envoyer la commande à la date prévue.

3. *May, might*

MAY et *MIGHT* s'emploient pour indiquer :

• l'**incertitude**, l'**éventualité**, le **risque**

– au présent :

We may / might deliver the articles this afternoon.
Il se peut / pourrait que nous livrions les articles cet après-midi.

– au futur :

The company may / might lay off two hundred workers next month.
L'entreprise va peut-être / risque de licencier deux cents ouvriers le mois prochain.

– au passé

The company may / might have changed its policy last year.
Peut-être que l'entreprise a changé de politique l'an dernier.

The company might have changed its policy if its shareholders had asked for it.
La société aurait pu changer de politique si ses actionnaires l'avaient demandé.

• la **permission** (emploi moins fréquent que ***CAN***)

May I have a day off, please?
Puis-je prendre un jour de congé, s'il vous plaît ?

4. *Must* et *have got to*

MUST et *HAVE GOT TO* expriment des obligations légèrement différentes :

• une **obligation que le locuteur s'impose ou une recommandation :** ***MUST***

I must remember to call him back.
Il faut que je pense à le rappeler.

You must go on this communication training course.
Il faut absolument que vous vous inscriviez à ce cours de formation à la communication.

• une **obligation imposée de l'extérieur :** ***HAVE GOT TO***

We have got to move: this building is too small now.
Nous sommes obligés de déménager : ce bâtiment est trop petit maintenant.

• une **obligation au futur :** ***MUST / WILL HAVE TO***

You must / will have to start working on the project next week.
Il faudra que vous commenciez à travailler sur le projet la semaine prochaine.

5. MUST / MUST HAVE

MUST et *MUST HAVE* s'emploient pour indiquer :

- une **déduction faite par le locuteur** selon des faits ou indices

  That company has developed very quickly: the CEO must be very efficient; he must have been very lucky too!
  Cette entreprise s'est développée très rapidement. Le PDG doit être très efficace. Il a dû avoir aussi beaucoup de chance !

- l'**interdiction** avec ***MUST NOT***

  You must not borrow too much money.
  Il ne faut pas emprunter trop d'argent

6. DO / DID NOT HAVE TO / DO NOT NEED TO / NEED NOT

DO / DID NOT HAVE TO, DO NOT NEED TO et *NEED NOT* s'emploient pour indiquer l'**absence d'obligation**.

- Au présent

  The customers do not have to / do not need to / need not pay when they place an order.
  Les clients ne sont pas obligés de payer lorsqu'ils passent une commande.

- Au passé : deux cas différents

  They did not have to go as far as the shopping centre.
  Ils n'ont pas été obligés d'aller jusqu'au centre commercial (et ils n'y sont pas allés).

  They need not have gone as far as the shopping centre.
  Ils n'étaient pas obligés d'aller jusqu'au centre commercial (mais ils y sont allés !).

7. SHOULD / OUGHT TO

SHOULD et *OUGHT TO* s'emploient pour exprimer :

- un **conseil** au présent

  They should / ought to do more management research.
  Ils devraient faire plus de recherche sur le management.

- une **probabilité** au présent

  The file should be in the top drawer.
  Le dossier devrait être dans le tiroir du haut.

8. SHOULD HAVE / OUGHT TO HAVE

SHOULD HAVE et *OUGHT TO HAVE* s'utilisent pour exprimer :

- un **conseil** au passé

  You should have explained that the job entailed long hours.
  Vous auriez dû expliquer que le poste imposait de longues journées.

• une **probabilité** au passé qui peut être déjà réalisée

You should have received the report by now.
Vous devriez avoir reçu le rapport maintenant. (Vous l'avez peut-être reçu.)
Vous auriez dû recevoir le rapport maintenant (mais vous ne l'avez pas reçu).

9. *HAD BETTER*

HAD BETTER s'emploie pour souligner l'importance d'agir :

They had better take more interest in their workers' health.
Ils feraient bien de s'intéresser davantage à la santé de leurs salariés.

10. *USED TO*

USED TO s'emploie pour indiquer des **faits** ou des **actions d'un passé révolu** :

This building is now a supermarket. It used to be a furniture shop.
Ce bâtiment est maintenant un supermarché. C'était autrefois un magasin de meubles.

People used to do their shopping locally. They used not / did not use to drive to a supermarket.
Autrefois, les gens faisaient leurs courses dans leur quartier. Ils ne prenaient pas leur voiture pour aller au supermarché.

REMARQUE

Il ne faut pas confondre *USED TO DO* (infinitif) avec to *BE / GET USED TO DOING* (gérondif).

He used to work in a warehouse.
Il travaillait autrefois dans un entrepôt.

He was used to working in a warehouse.
Il était habitué à travailler dans un entrepôt

Now he is used to working in an office. He got used to that very quickly.
Maintenant, il a l'habitude de travailler dans un bureau. Il s'y est habitué très rapidement.

FICHE 4 Cas possessif et expression de la possession

1. L'emploi

▸ On emploie le cas possessif surtout avec les **êtres vivants**, **groupes** et **collectivités** :

my assistant's office	*the firm's policy*	*London's architecture*
le bureau de mon assistant	la politique de la firme	l'architecture de Londres

▸ On utilise le cas possessif aussi avec des indications de **date** ou **durée** :

today's newspaper	*last month's results*	*a three hour's wait*
le journal d'aujourd'hui	les résultats du mois dernier	une attente de trois heures

REMARQUE

Il ne faut pas abuser de l'utilisation du cas possessif.

2. La formation

▸ **+ 's après un nom singulier, un pluriel irrégulier, un nom de famille au pluriel :**

John's book – the women's bags – the traders' money – the Jones's car

▸ **+ '*(s)* après un nom singulier en -s :**

James'(s) camera

▸ **+ 's après une expression comportant plusieurs mots :**

the Prime Minister's speech

▸ **+ 's lorsqu'il y a plusieurs possesseurs d'un seul objet :**

Bill and Mary's telephone
le téléphone de Bill et Mary

▸ **+ 's + 's lorsqu'il y a plusieurs possesseurs et plusieurs objets :**

Bill's and Mary's mobiles
les portables de Bill et Mary

▸ **+ ' (sans *s*) après un pluriel en -*s***

Our employees' salaries
Les salaires de nos employés

3. Les adjectifs possessifs

my – your – his / her / its – our – your – their

Le choix entre *his*, *her*, *its* dépend du possesseur :

He has lost his job, and she has lost her job too.
Il a perdu son emploi et elle a perdu son emploi aussi.

This building is very modern – its windows are round.
Ce bâtiment est très moderne – ses fenêtres sont rondes.

4. Les pronoms possessifs

mine – yours – his / hers / its – ours – yours – theirs

His salary is higher than hers. Mine is even higher!
Son salaire (à lui) est plus élevé que le sien (à elle). Le mien est encore plus élevé.

a friend of mine — un de mes amis
a colleague of hers — un(e) de ses collègues (à elle)
a colleague of Peter's — un collègue de Peter

5. *WHOSE*

WHOSE indique ou demande à qui appartient un objet, ou quelle est la relation entre deux personnes :

Whose colleague is he? He is Jane's (colleague).
De qui est-il le collègue ? Il est le collègue de Jane. / C'est celui de Jane.

Whose papers are these? They are hers / theirs.
À qui sont ces papiers ? Ils sont à elle / eux / elles. / Ce sont les siens / leurs.

The employee whose report has disappeared is angry.
L'employé dont le rapport a disparu est en colère.

REMARQUE

Notez l'absence d'article après un cas possessif, et après *WHOSE* :

Jane's papers... – The employee whose report...

FICHE 5 Comparatifs et superlatifs

1. Les comparatifs et superlatifs de supériorité

Adjectifs ou **adverbes courts** (une, parfois deux syllabes)

adjectif + *(E)R* + *THAN* (comparatif), ou *THE* + adjectif + *(E)ST* (superlatif) :

B&A is a smaller firm than C&D, but it is better for us because it is closer.
B&A est une entreprise plus petite que C&D, mais elle est mieux pour nous car elle est plus proche.

Mr Abbott is the oldest employee in / of the company.
M. Abbott est le salarié le plus ancien de la société.

We have fewer branches than them / they do.
Nous avons moins de succursales qu'eux.

Flying is faster than sailing.
L'avion est plus rapide que le bateau.

Adjectifs ou **adverbes longs** (deux syllabes et plus)

MORE + adjectif / adverbe + *THAN* (comparatif), ou *THE MOST* (superlatif) + adjectif / adverbe :

His mobile is more expensive than mine.
Son téléphone portable vaut plus cher que le mien.

This laptop is the most efficient of all, in my opinion.
Cet ordinateur portable est le plus efficace de tous, à mon avis.

REMARQUES

1. Le second élément d'un comparatif de supériorité est toujours *THAN*.

2. Court ou long ? Les adjectifs / adverbes de deux syllabes sont longs, sauf s'ils se terminent en *-e*, *-y*, *-er*, *-ow* :

close / closer – friendly / friendlier – clever / cleverer – narrow / narrower.

Adjectifs irréguliers

- *Good / Well* → *better, the best.*
- *Bad / Ill* → *worse, the worst.*
- *Far* → *farther, the farthest* (loin), ou *further / the furthest* (employé dans un sens figuré).

I shall not go any further into the matter. *Do you need any further details?*
Je n'irai pas plus loin sur ce sujet. Avez-vous besoin d'autres détails ?

- *Many → more, the most*

He has many customers / more customers than her / the most customers.
Il a beaucoup de clients / plus de clients qu'elle / le plus de clients.

- *Little → less, the least*

It is Sylvia who earns the least money.
C'est Sylvia qui gagne le moins d'argent.

▸ Ces règles de formation s'appliquent au **comparatif progressif** :

Prices are getting higher and higher.
Les prix sont de plus en plus élevés.

Cars are more and more expensive.
Les voitures coûtent de plus en plus cher.

The situation is changing more and more rapidly / faster and faster.
La situation change de plus en plus rapidement.

▸ Le **double comparatif**

The harder they work, the more money they earn.
Plus ils travaillent, plus ils gagnent d'argent.

2. Les comparatifs d'égalité

▸ Le **comparatif d'égalité positif** se forme avec *AS* + adjectif / adverbe + *AS*. *AS* s'emploie aussi après *THE SAME*.

My new office is as pleasant as my old one.
Mon nouveau bureau est aussi agréable que l'ancien.

She gets the same salary as he does / him.
Elle a le même salaire que lui.

REMARQUE

Le pronom complément *him* est plus familier qu'une proposition sujet + auxiliaire.

▸ Le **comparatif d'égalité négatif** se forme avec *NOT AS / SO ... AS* :

I do not earn as much money as (I did) before.
Je ne gagne pas autant d'argent qu'avant.

3. Les comparatifs d'infériorité

▸ Les **comparatifs d'infériorité** se forment avec *LESS / FEWER ... THAN* :

I have less work to do and fewer responsibilities than before.
J'ai moins de travail, et moins de responsabilités qu'avant.

REMARQUES

1. *LESS / LEAST* s'emploie avec un indénombrable ou avec un verbe, et *FEWER / FEWEST* avec un dénombrable au pluriel.

We use the machine less than we used to.
Nous utilisons moins la machine qu'autrefois.

It takes less time to warm up.
Elle met moins de temps à chauffer.

We now have fewer people at the office.
Nous avons maintenant moins de gens au bureau.

2. Le comparatif d'égalité négatif *NOT AS ... AS* est beaucoup plus courant que *LESS ... THAN* :

The new accountant is not as / so competent as the previous one (plus courant que *less competent than*).
Le nouveau comptable n'est pas aussi compétent que l'ancien.

FICHE 6 Discours direct et discours indirect

1. Définitions

▸ Le **discours direct** désigne des paroles dites ou écrites « en direct ».

"This report is inaccurate. John will have to do it all over again."
« Ce rapport est inexact. John devra entièrement le refaire. »

▸ Le **discours indirect** consiste à rapporter des paroles après coup. L'action est perçue du point de vue de celui qui rapporte les paroles.

• On peut rapporter ces paroles avec un **verbe au présent**.

He says (that) this report is inaccurate and (that) John will have to do it all over again.
Il dit que ce rapport est inexact et que John devra le refaire entièrement.

Dans ce cas, le temps des verbes n'est pas modifié.

• On peut rapporter ces paroles avec un **verbe au passé**.

He said (that) the report was inaccurate and (that) John would have to do it all over again.
Il a dit que ce rapport était inexact et que John devrait entièrement le refaire.

Dans ce cas, les verbes sont modifiés en fonction des règles suivantes :

Discours direct	Discours indirect
Présent	Prétérit
Prétérit	Plus-que-parfait
Present perfect	Plus-que-parfait
will / can / may	*would / could / might*
would / could / might / should	*would / could / might / should*
must / need (modal)	*must / need*
Impératif	Infinitif

• Une action considérée comme étant toujours valide quand on la rapporte peut rester au même temps :

"We want to merge with some competitors."
→ *They declared that they want to merge with some competitors.*

• Avec le prétérit modal ou le plus-que-parfait modal, il est obligatoire de conserver le temps :

"If the company had more customers, it would make more profit."
→ *He said that if the company had more customers, it would make more profit.*

• D'autres modifications interviennent, dues aux changements de repères spatiaux et temporels :

Discours direct	Discours indirect
"here"	*there*
"this / these"	*that / those*
"today"	*that (same) day*
"yesterday"	*the day before*
"next week"	*the next week / the following week*
"last week"	*the week before / the previous week*
"now"	*then*

"These documents can be filed here until next week."
→ *He said that those documents could be filed there until the following week.*

• Des **changements de pronoms personnels et de possessifs** interviennent en fonction du point de vue de celui qui rapporte les paroles :

"I'll give you my point of view," he (=Mr Jones) said to her (=Helen).
→ *Mr Jones said he would give her his point of view.*

Le choix des pronoms se fait en fonction de la ou des personnes désignées dans le contexte précis.

▸ *SAY* ou *TELL* ?

• *SAY* est employé pour rapporter les paroles d'un locuteur, sans mention de l'interlocuteur :

He said it would be done by the next day.
Il a dit que ce serait fait dès le lendemain.

• *TELL* est utilisé quand un interlocuteur est mentionné :

He told us it would be done by the next day.
Il nous a dit que ce serait fait dès le lendemain.

• *SAY (TO SOMEBODY)* sert plutôt en fin d'énoncé au discours direct :

"Well done", he said (to me).
« Bon travail », (m')a-t-il dit.

• Autres verbes utilisés pour rapporter des déclaratives : *declare (to sb) / announce (to sb) / explain (to sb) / suggest (to sb) / propose (to sb).*

He has announced (to his team) (that) he is going to resign.
Il a annoncé (à son équipe) qu'il va démissionner.

• La conjonction *THAT* peut être omise après des verbes déclaratifs.

▸ **L'ordre des termes dans une interrogative directe et dans une interrogative indirecte** en anglais est différent.

"Where are all the files?"→ He asked where all the files were.
Où sont tous les dossiers ? → Il a demandé où étaient tous les dossiers.

▸ **Les formes contractées**

Elles sont réservées à l'oral ; à l'écrit, il faut utiliser les formes entières :

"I wouldn't have ordered so many samples if I'd known."
« Je n'aurais pas commandé autant d'échantillons si j'avais su. »

→ *He said he would not have ordered so many samples if he had known.*
Il a dit qu'il n'aurait pas commandé autant d'échantillons s'il avait su.

FICHE 7 *DURING, WHILE, FOR, SINCE* suivis d'une expression de durée ou de date

Quoique généralement (mais pas toujours) équivalents de « pendant » ou « depuis », il ne faut pas confondre *DURING*, *WHILE*, *FOR* et *SINCE*, et il faut faire attention aux temps des verbes qui les accompagnent.

1. *DURING*

DURING indique à quelle période de temps une action a, a eu ou aura lieu :

She works / worked / as a trainee during her holidays / the summer months.
Elle travaille / a travaillé comme stagiaire pendant ses vacances / les mois d'été.
(Remarquer l'emploi du prétérit au passé.)

2. *WHILE*

▸ *WHILE* s'emploie au début d'une proposition de temps :

It happened while Dave was travelling.
C'est arrivé pendant que Dave voyageait. (Remarquer l'emploi du prétérit au passé.)

▸ *WHILE* ne peut être suivi de *WILL* dans un contexte futur :

The goods will arrive while we are away.
Les marchandises arriveront pendant que nous serons partis.

3. *FOR*

▸ *FOR* équivalent de « pendant » est suivi d'une indication de durée :

We exported that product to Sweden for years.
Nous avons exporté ce produit en Suède pendant des années.
(Remarquer le prétérit au passé : l'action est maintenant terminée.)

▶ *FOR* équivalent de « depuis »

> *We have been importing gas from Norway for years.*
> Cela fait des années que / Depuis des années nous importons du gaz de Norvège.
> (Remarquer le *present perfect* en anglais, et le présent en français : l'action continue au moment où l'on parle.)

4. Since

Équivalent de « depuis », *SINCE* est suivi d'une date, même s'il introduit une idée de durée :

> *We have been waiting for that payment since February 1st / last month.*
> Nous attendons ce règlement depuis le 1er février / le mois dernier.
> (Remarquer le *present perfect* en anglais correspondant à un présent en français.)

REMARQUES

1. *SINCE* peut également avoir le sens de « comme », « étant donné que » et être alors suivi du présent :

> *Please ignore this letter since your account is closed.*
> Veuillez ne pas tenir compte de cette lettre étant donné que votre compte est fermé.

2. *AGO*, souvent présenté avec *FOR* et *SINCE*, est traité avec le prétérit, Fiche 17.

FICHE 8 Faire faire

1. Traductions de « faire faire quelque chose à quelqu'un »

▶ Dans le sens le plus courant, « faire faire » quelque chose à quelqu'un se traduit par *to get somebody to do something.*

> *We are going to get a supplier to come and change our equipment.*
> Nous allons faire venir un fournisseur pour qu'il change nos équipements.

▶ Construction un peu moins fréquente : *to have somebody do something*

> *Are you going to have Smith and Co install it for you?*
> Allez-vous les faire installer par Smith and Co ?

▶ Sens d'**obliger** : *to make somebody do*

> *The new manager made the employees work overtime.*
> Le nouveau directeur a fait faire des heures supplémentaires aux employés.

▶ Sens de **causer** : *to make somebody do*

> *His jokes do not make us laugh at all.*
> Ses plaisanteries ne nous font pas du tout rire.

▶ **Se faire faire** : *to make oneself +-ed*

> *Did I make myself understood?*
> Me suis-je bien fait comprendre ?

> *The connection was so bad she could not make herself heard.*
> La connection était si mauvaise qu'elle ne pouvait se faire entendre.

2. Traduction de « faire faire quelque chose » (par quelqu'un)

On utilise: *to have / get sth done (by sb)* :

We had / got the new machine installed yesterday (by a specialist).
Nous avons fait installer la nouvelle machine hier (par un spécialiste).

FICHE 9 Futur

1. Le futur simple avec *WILL* ou *SHALL*

- Lorsqu'on prédit une action au futur, on emploie *WILL* :

When will Mr Ferguson arrive?
Quand est-ce que M. Ferguson arrivera ?

REMARQUES

1. *WILL*, auxiliaire modal, peut aussi avoir un sens de volonté ou d'habitude ; il n'exprime donc pas nécessairement le futur :

Any bank will do it for us.
N'importe quelle banque le fera / acceptera de le faire pour nous.

The new boss will talk all the time.
Le nouveau patron ne peut s'empêcher de parler tout le temps.

2. La forme négative, *WILL NOT*, s'emploie souvent pour exprimer un refus :

I have told him to apply for that job but he won't (will not).
Je lui ai dit de poser sa candidature pour ce poste mais il refuse.

- La forme *SHALL* s'emploie surtout à la **forme interrogative** pour demander l'opinion ou l'autorisation de quelqu'un :

Shall I invite Richard to the meeting next Thursday?
Voulez-vous que j'invite Richard à la réunion de jeudi prochain ?

- Comparez :

Shall I change the date of the conference?
Voulez-vous que je change la date du colloque?

Will you cancel the conference, please?
Pourrez-vous annuler le colloque, s'il vous plaît ?

- On ne peut mettre *WILL* après les conjonctions de temps telles que *WHILE*, *WHEN*, *AS SOON AS*, *AS LONG AS*, même dans un contexte futur :

When the construction of the factory is finally completed next May, 300 people will be employed there.
Quand la construction de l'usine sera enfin terminée en mai prochain, 300 personnes y seront employées.

2. Le futur programmé avec le présent simple ou progressif, ou le futur progressif

Horaires et programmes

On emploie le présent simple :

Our plane leaves at 10.30 and arrives at 12.15. (Remarquer les différences d'écriture des horaires.)
Notre avion part à 10 h 30 et arrive à 12 h 15.

When do you start work on the international project?
Quand allez-vous commencer à travailler sur le projet international ?

Action future programmée

Le locuteur emploie le présent progressif ou le futur progressif :

I am going to Japan on business next week. I will be staying in the same hotel as last time.
Je vais au Japon pour affaires la semaine prochaine. Je descendrai dans le même hôtel que la dernière fois.

Action qui durera au futur

Le locuteur emploie le futur progressif :

We will be working twelve hours a day while you are away on holiday.
(Notez le present après *WHILE*.)
Nous travaillerons douze heures par jour pendant que vous serez parti en vacances.

3. Le futur d'intention avec TO BE GOING TO

Lorsque le locuteur annonce une **intention** ou un **événement à venir**, il emploie *BE GOING TO DO* :

We are going to invest in some top quality new office furniture.
Nous allons investir dans du nouveau mobilier de bureau haut de gamme.

The economic situation is not too good and it is going to get worse.
La situation économique n'est pas très bonne et va s'aggraver.

4. Le futur antérieur

Lorsque le locuteur annonce une action ou un événement antérieur à une autre action ou événement ou moment au futur, il emploie le futur antérieur *WILL HAVE DONE* :

On March 1, Tom will have worked for this company for 40 years.
Le 1er mars, Tom aura travaillé 40 ans pour cette entreprise.

FICHE 10 Infinitif ou gérondif ?

1. Certains verbes régissent toujours l'infinitif (TO + V)

Les principaux :

afford	*deserve*	*intend*	*promise*
agree	*enable*	*manage*	*refuse*
allow	*expect*	*offer*	*seem*
aim	*fail*	*plan*	*wish*
ask	*hesitate*	*prepare*	*would like*
decide	*hope*	*pretend*	*etc.*

They have decided to review this year's sales.
Ils ont décidé de faire le point sur les ventes de cette année.

2. Certains verbes régissent toujours le gérondif (V-ING)

Les principaux :

admit	*dislike*	*go on*	*practice*
avoid	*enjoy*	*can't help*	*recommend*
consider	*feel like*	*keep*	*risk*
delay	*finish*	*mind*	*can't stand*
deny	*give up*	*miss*	*etc.*

They considered outsourcing production.
Ils ont envisagé de délocaliser la production.

3. Autres cas

▸ Certains verbes sont suivis **soit de l'infinitif**, **soit du gérondif** en entraînant des **modifications de sens**. Il s'agit de : *regret*, *remember*, *try*.

I regret to announce such news.
J'ai le regret d'annoncer une telle nouvelle.

I regret sending the letter.
Je regrette d'avoir envoyé la lettre.

Remember to post the letter.
N'oubliez pas de poster la lettre.

I can't remember posting the parcel.
Je ne me rappelle pas avoir posté le paquet.

I'm trying to understand the message.
J'essaie (en faisant un effort) de comprendre le message.

Try phoning them at 6am.
Essaie (pour voir) de les appeler à 6 heures du matin.

▸ Certains verbes sont suivis **de l'infinitif ou du gérondif**, **sans** entraîner de **modifications de sens**. Il s'agit de : *start, begin, continue, like, hate, love.*

Have they started advertising / to advertise yet?
Ont-ils déjà commencé à faire de la publicité ?

▸ Certaines **expressions comportant un nom** entraînent un gérondif :

It is not worth sending the catalogues too early.
Cela ne vaut pas la peine d'envoyer les catalogues trop tôt.

They spend their time answering the phone.
Ils passent leur temps à répondre au téléphone.

It is no use typing that report all over again.
Cela ne sert à rien de taper tout ce rapport à nouveau.

They had trouble finding the address.
Ils ont eu du mal à trouver l'adresse.

▸ Quand **un verbe suit une préposition**, il est toujours au gérondif. Attention à la préposition *TO* dans : *look forward to* (avoir hâte de, se réjouir à l'idée de), *contribute to*, *when it comes to* (lorsqu'il s'agit de), *be / get used to* (être habitué à / s'habituer à), qu'il ne faut pas confondre avec la marque de l'infinitif.

The commission reproached him with cooking the books.
La commission lui a reproché de truquer les comptes.

CO_2 emissions contribute to warming up the atmosphere.
Les émissions de CO_2 contribuent à réchauffer l'atmosphère.

I look forward to hearing from you soon.
J'espère avoir bientôt de vos nouvelles.

You could photocopy the report instead of copying it out by hand.
Vous pourriez photocopier le rapport au lieu de le recopier à la main.

▸ L'**infinitif** correspond plutôt à des **actions qui vont avoir lieu ou qui commencent juste** :

Pleased to meet you.
Enchanté(e) (de vous rencontrer).

Le **gérondif** correspond plutôt à des **actions qui ont déjà eu lieu** :

It was a pleasure meeting you.
Ravi(e) d'avoir fait votre connaissance.

▸ ***NEED*** suivi du gérondif entraîne un sens passif :

The offices need repainting. (ou : The office needs to be repainted.)
Les bureaux ont besoin d'être repeints.

FICHE 11 Mots composés

N'inventez pas de mots composés ; apprenez-les au fur et à mesure que vous les rencontrez.

1. Les noms composés

▸ Les noms composés anglais sont bâtis « de droite à gauche » ; le mot le plus important est déterminé par tous ceux qui le précèdent :

a car race — une course de voitures
a race horse — un cheval de course

Plusieurs noms peuvent ainsi se suivre :

a mail order company — une société de vente par correspondance
an employment research organization — un organisme de recherche d'emploi

▸ Au pluriel, seul le nom le plus important (le plus à droite) se met au pluriel :

a car factory — une usine de voitures
car factories — des usines de voitures

▸ Tous les noms composés anglais ne se traduisent pas automatiquement par un nom composé en français :

a wage earner — un salarié
a phone call — un appel téléphonique

2. Les adjectifs composés

Ce type d'adjectif n'existe pas en français et requiert une traduction parfois analytique. Comme tous les adjectifs anglais, l'adjectif composé est invariable et placé à gauche du nom qu'il détermine :

a full-time position — un poste à plein temps
a London-based company — une entreprise située à Londres

capital-intensive activities — des activités à forte intensité capitalistique
ground-breaking innovations — des innovations révolutionnaires

a time-saving device — un appareil qui fait gagner du temps
a short-term contract — un contrat à durée déterminée

FICHE 12 Noms dénombrables et indénombrables

Les noms en anglais sont divisés en deux catégories :

– les **dénombrables *(countable)*** qui ont une forme au singulier et une au pluriel ;
– les **indénombrables *(uncountable)*** qui n'ont qu'une forme au singulier.

Certains noms peuvent appartenir aux **deux catégories** avec des sens plus ou moins différents.

1. Les noms dénombrables

Les noms dénombrables désignent des êtres, des objets, des événements, etc. que l'on peut dénombrer. Ils peuvent être précédés de l'article défini ***THE*** ou indéfini ***A / AN / SOME***, d'un quantificateur : ***(A) FEW, MANY, SOME*** ou nombre.

the / a / one / four / some lawyer(s)
l' / un / quatre / quelques avocat(s)

We have five offices, one on the ground floor and the others on the first floor.
Nous avons cinq bureaux, l'un au rez-de-chaussée et les autres au premier étage.

REMARQUE

Certains noms dénombrables s'emploient sans article quand l'accent est mis sur l'idée et non sur l'objet physique ; par exemple : *school, church, hospital, town, market, prison, college, cinema, television.*

In the USA, more young people go to college than in France.
Aux États-Unis, davantage de jeunes fréquentent un établissement d'enseignement supérieur / font des études supérieures qu'en France.

City College of San Francisco is one of the biggest colleges in the nation.
Le City College de San Francisco est l'un des plus gros établissements d'enseignement supérieur du pays.

2. Les noms indénombrables

Les noms indénombrables désignent des **substances**, des **concepts**, etc., qui ne peuvent pas se diviser en éléments séparés, donc qui n'ont pas de pluriel, ne sont jamais précédés d'un nombre, et s'emploient souvent sans article.

Ils peuvent être précédés de ***MUCH, A LOT OF, (A) LITTLE, SOME.*** Ils peuvent correspondre à un pluriel en français.

Par exemple : *milk, advice, information, furniture, luggage, work, equipment, transport, money.*

We are always pleased to get good advice; you gave us some very good advice yesterday.
Nous sommes toujours contents de recevoir un / de bons conseil(s) ; vous nous avez donné un / de très bon conseil(s) hier.

We have not got much money left.
Il ne nous reste pas beaucoup d'argent.

REMARQUE

Certains indénombrables peuvent être précédés de l'article indéfini dans certains cas, comme après ***to be***, dans les expressions ***WHAT A / SUCH A***, et dans certaines expressions idiomatiques :

He is in a hurry.
Il est pressé.

What a pity / shame you lost your post!
Quel dommage que vous ayez perdu votre poste !

It was such a relief to hear you have found another one!
Quel soulagement de savoir que vous en avez trouvé un autre !

Why are you are making such a fuss?
Pourquoi faites-vous tant d'histoires ?

3. Les noms tantôt dénombrables tantôt indénombrables

Certains noms sont **dénombrables** quand ils sont utilisés dans un **contexte précis** ou concret, et sont **indénombrables** quand ils sont utilisés dans un **contexte général** ou abstrait ; le nom change alors de sens :

business	*a business*
les affaires	une entreprise / affaire

Advertising plays a very important role in business.
La publicité joue un rôle très important dans les affaires.

The company was a family business.
L'entreprise était une affaire de famille.

Many people believe that work is the key to success.
Beaucoup de gens pensent que le travail est la clef du succès.

The book about globalization became a commercial success.
Le livre sur la mondialisation est devenu un succès commercial.

Our company made a big profit last year.
Notre société a fait de gros bénéfices l'an dernier.

There will not be much profit in doing that.
Nous ne gagnerons pas grand-chose à faire cela.

REMARQUE

Le dictionnaire indique généralement si le nom est dénombrable (C : *countable*) ou indénombrable (U : *uncountable*).

FICHE 13 *No* / *not any* + *more* / *longer* et *not either* / *neither* : équivalents de « ne plus »

Ces expressions indiquent qu'une action ou un état n'est pas ou plus vrai, mais elles ne sont pas toujours équivalentes.

1. *No* / *Not any more*

Cette expression s'emploie dans un **sens de quantité** ou **temporel** :

We have not got any more of these products.	*There is no more left.*
Nous n'avons plus ces produits.	Il n'en reste plus.

Mrs Colson does not live in Swindon any more.
Mrs Colson n'habite plus à Swindon.

2. No / Not any longer

Cette expression s'emploie dans un **sens temporel** uniquement :

David Ashton is no longer with us.
David Ashton n'est plus chez nous.

We cannot stay any longer.
Nous ne pouvons plus rester.

We no longer sell those products.
Nous ne vendons plus ces produits.

3. Not either / Neither

Cette expression s'emploie **après une phrase négative** :

I cannot wait any more / longer – Neither can I / I can't either.
Je ne peux plus attendre – Et moi non plus. (Attention à l'ordre des mots !)

FICHE 14 Ordre des mots

1. La place des adjectifs

Les adjectifs qualificatifs épithètes se placent tous devant le nom, dans l'ordre suivant :
appréciation + **taille** + **âge / température** + **forme** + **couleur** + **origine** + **matière (+ nom).**

This shop sells elegant trendy high-heeled red Italian leather shoes.
Cette boutique vend d'élégantes chaussures italiennes à talons hauts, en cuir rouge, très mode.

REMARQUE

L'adjectif ordinal (*first, second, third*, etc.), ainsi que *last, next, other*, se placent avant le chiffre ou le quantificateur :

the first two months — les deux premiers mois
the last few days — les derniers jours
the other two figures — les deux autres chiffres

2. La place des adverbes ou expressions adverbiales

En principe, l'adverbe ne doit pas séparer le verbe du complément d'objet direct.

He managed his company very well. — Il a très bien géré sa société.
He speaks German fluently. — Il parle couramment l'allemand.

L'adverbe se place généralement devant le mot sur lequel il porte (adjectif, verbe ou autre adverbe) :

He works very hard. — Il travaille très dur.
We hardly ever use this machine. — Nous n'utilisons pratiquement jamais cette machine.

S'il porte sur une phrase ou proposition, l'adverbe se place, selon les cas, au début, au milieu ou à la fin de la proposition ou de la phrase. On peut parfois avoir le choix.

Au début (forme d'insistance)

- Adverbes de **liaison**

  Our sales dropped; consequently we had to advertise.
  Nos ventes ont baissé ; par conséquent, nous avons dû faire de la publicité.

- Adverbes de **lieu** et/ou **temps**

  Afterwards, our turnover rose.
  Après, notre chiffre d'affaires a augmenté.
  Over there, business is exciting.
  Là-bas, travailler dans les affaires est passionnant.

- Adverbes indiquant un **jugement**

  Fortunately, his business improved.
  Heureusement, ses affaires se sont améliorées.

Au milieu

En principe, les adverbes suivants précèdent immédiatement le verbe à un temps simple, ou se mettent après l'auxiliaire ou après le premier verbe s'il y en a plusieurs.

- Adverbes **négatifs** ou **semi-négatifs**, de **temps imprécis**, de **fréquence**, ainsi que ***ALSO***. Attention à l'ordre des mots !

  We barely / hardly know them.
  Nous les connaissons à peine.

  We had rarely / never experienced such a serious situation.
  Nous avions rarement / Nous n'avions jamais connu une situation aussi grave.

  People often commute by public transport.
  Les gens vont souvent au travail par les transports en commun.

  Have you ever met them?
  Les avez-vous déjà rencontrés ?

  She will soon have finished typing her letter.
  Elle aura bientôt fini de taper sa lettre.

  Not all laws are fair.
  Toutes les lois ne sont pas équitables.

Your remittance still has not arrived.
Votre versement n'est toujours pas arrivé.

We also sell spare parts for German cars.
Nous vendons aussi des pièces détachées pour voitures allemandes.

- Adverbes de **manière** : placés après le dernier auxiliaire (ou après le verbe)

The report has been very carefully typed (very carefully).
Le rapport a été tapé très soigneusement.

REMARQUE

Avec *to be* à un temps simple, l'adverbe vient après :

The receptionist is seldom absent from the reception.
La réceptionniste est rarement absente de la réception.

The bill was still on my desk.
La facture était encore sur mon bureau.

À la fin

Les adverbes qui se mettent au début peuvent aussi souvent venir à la fin, selon l'intention du locuteur, le style, ou la construction du reste de la phrase :

Yesterday, I sent him an e-mail (yesterday).
Hier, je lui ai envoyé un mél (hier).

Unfortunately, the goods arrived late (unfortunately).
Malheureusement, les marchandises sont arrivées en retard (malheureusement).

REMARQUES

1. Les **adverbes se rapportant à un seul mot**, en particulier *ONLY / JUST*, se mettent immédiatement devant le mot :

We received the goods only yesterday.
Nous n'avons reçu les marchandises qu'hier.

They arrived just in time for the fair.
Ils sont arrivés juste à temps pour la foire.

2. Des adverbes tels que ***daily***, ***monthly***, ***yearly***, ***yet*** (après *not*), se placent seulement en fin de phrase, et ***too*** en fin de phrase ou après le mot auquel il se rapporte :

We send our bills monthly.
Nous envoyons nos factures tous les mois.

They have not finished it yet.
Ils ne l'ont pas encore terminé.

He too asked for a discount.
Lui aussi a demandé une réduction.

He asked for a discount too.
Il a demandé aussi une réduction.

FICHE 15 Passif et traductions de « on »

1. Formation

Un groupe verbal au passif est composé de *BE* conjugué au temps désiré ou mis à la forme désirée, suivi du participe passé du verbe choisi.

- Présent simple

  Offices are usually painted in pale colours.
  Les bureaux sont généralement peints en couleurs claires.

- Présent progressif

  Our office is being repainted.
  Notre bureau est en train d'être repeint.

- Prétérit

  My office was painted dark blue.
  Mon bureau était peint en bleu foncé.

- Prétérit progressif

  While my office was being repainted, I worked in another one.
  Pendant que l'on repeignait mon bureau, j'ai travaillé dans un autre.

REMARQUE

Au passif, la forme progressive n'existe pas au *present perfect* ni au plus-que-parfait.

- *Present perfect*

  My office has been renovated.
  Mon bureau a été rénové.

- Plus-que-parfait

  My office had been renovated when I arrived.
  Mon bureau avait été rénové quand je suis arrivé.

- Avec un modal

  Your office will be renovated next year.
  Votre bureau sera rénové l'an prochain.

- Avec un infinitif

  Your office needs to be renovated.
  Votre bureau a besoin d'être rénové.

- Avec un gérondif

  Your office needs renovating.
  Votre bureau a besoin d'être rénové.

2. Utilisation

▸ Comme en français, la voix passive permet de mettre en valeur **le sujet grammatical** et de mettre au second rang, voire de passer sous silence **l'agent de l'action** :

All these boxes have been sent back by angry customers.
Tous ces paquets ont été renvoyés par des clients mécontents.

A few shares will have to be sold.
Quelques actions devront être vendues. (Agent non mentionné car il va de soi que ce sera par un courtier.)

▸ Certains **verbes pronominaux français** sont rendus par un passif :

Our bottles of wine are sold by the dozen.
Nos bouteilles de vin se vendent à la douzaine.

Speaking about one's salary is not done in France.
Cela ne se fait pas de parler de son salaire en France.

▸ Certains **verbes d'opinion** (*say*, *report*, *consider*, *believe*, *think*) permettent d'exprimer ce qui se dit à propos du sujet grammatical (réputations, rumeurs) :

The new manager is said to be efficient.
On dit que le nouveau directeur est efficace.

It was reported that some members of the board were disappointed with the result.
On a dit que certains membres du conseil d'administration étaient déçus du résultat.

He is believed to have stolen money from the cash drawer.
On pense qu'il a volé de l'argent dans la caisse.

Ce dernier exemple est souvent traduit par un conditionnel en français :

« Il *aurait volé* de l'argent dans la caisse. »

▸ Quand le sujet grammatical « on » dans une phrase active en français correspond à un agent qui n'a pas besoin d'être précisé ou n'a pas d'utilité pour le sens, la langue anglaise utilise couramment **un passif**. C'est fréquent avec les verbes à double complément (*give, lend, send, tell, teach, ask, show*, etc.).

Our workers were given information about hazardous substances.
On a donné à nos ouvriers des informations sur les substances dangereuses.

The trainees are taught basic knowledge about the workings of our department.
On apprend aux stagiaires les bases du fonctionnement de notre service.

▸ Le choix du sujet grammatical détermine ce sur quoi on veut faire porter l'accent. Dans les deux exemples suivants, il s'agit de la même situation, mais à chaque fois l'accent porte sur le sujet grammatical.

A report of the meeting was sent to our shareholders.
Un compte rendu de la réunion a été envoyé à nos actionnaires. (C'est un compte rendu de la réunion – et non autre chose – qui a été envoyé à nos actionnaires.)

Our shareholders were sent a report of the meeting.
On a envoyé un compte rendu de la réunion à nos actionnaires. (Ce sont nos actionnaires – et non d'autres personnes – à qui on a envoyé un compte rendu.)

▸ Autres traductions de « on »

• Dans un **registre soutenu**, pour exprimer une **généralité** : *one*

One should never leave one's handbag in an empty office.
On ne devrait jamais laisser son sac à main dans un bureau vide.

• Dans un **registre plus courant**, pour exprimer une **généralité** : *you*

If you are laid-off, you will get unemployment benefits.
Si on est licencié, on reçoit des indemnités de chômage.

• Quand « on » signifie **« nous »** : *we*

In our company, we are not allowed to drink coffee near a computer.
Dans notre entreprise, on n'a pas le droit de boire un café à proximité d'un ordinateur.

• Quand « on » signifie **les autres** / les gens : *they / people*

In that department, they are allowed to have a short nap.
Dans ce service, on a le droit de faire une petite sieste.

People imagine accountancy is boring.
On croit que la comptabilité est ennuyeuse.

• Quand « on » correspond à **quelqu'un d'inconnu** ou de non identifié : *someone*

Someone called while you were out.
On a appelé pendant que vous étiez sorti.

• Des **tournures impersonnelles** permettent de traduire « on » quand il correspond à un peu tout le monde.

It is possible to find all the employees' names in this directory.
On peut trouver les noms de tous les employés dans ce répertoire.

FICHE 16 Présent simple ou progressif

1. Le présent simple

▸ Le présent simple sert à indiquer :

• une **action habituelle ou répétée**

He always reads his paper when he commutes on the train in the morning.
Il lit toujours son journal quand il va à son travail en train le matin.

• une **action non située dans le temps**, qui caractérise le sujet

That company produces generic medicines.
Cette société produit des médicaments génériques.

The document explains how the WTO works.
Le document explique la façon dont l'OMC fonctionne.

- une **action permanente**

This company operates in Australia.
Cette société opère en Australie.

- une **vérité générale**

Organization charts show the structure of companies.
Les organigrammes montrent la structure des sociétés.

- un **jugement**, une opinion, une perception située **hors du temps**

I think this bank is very reliable.
Je pense que cette banque est très solide.

Do you understand / see what I mean?
Est-ce que vous comprenez / voyez ce que je veux dire ?

He says that he does not trust that bank.
Il dit qu'il n'a pas confiance dans cette banque.

- un **programme officiel**

The meeting starts at 4pm.
La réunion commence à 4 heures de l'après-midi.

▸ C'est la seule forme possible pour les verbes d'état situés au présent :

The boss's strategy seems to be very efficient.
La stratégie du patron semble très efficace.

2. Le présent progressif

Formé avec la base verbale + *-ing*, il s'emploie pour indiquer :

- une **action en cours** au moment où l'on parle, et qui ne durera pas

Please be quiet: they are listening to the manager's speech.
Veuillez ne pas faire de bruit : en ce moment ils écoutent le discours du directeur.

We are selling this new product very well.
Pour l'instant, nous vendons très bien ce nouveau produit.

- une action en cours, mais pas nécessairement au moment où l'on parle

He is learning German as well as English.
Actuellement, il apprend l'allemand ainsi que l'anglais.

- une **action répétée** sur laquelle on insiste car elle agace

That customer is always complaining.
Ce client n'arrête pas de se plaindre.

• un programme personnel, une intention

Today, we are closing at 4pm.
Aujourd'hui, nous fermons à 16 h.

REMARQUE

To think, to say et d'autres verbes de perception s'emploient généralement au présent simple ; au présent progressif, ils ont des sens différents :

What is he saying? I can't believe it.
Qu'est-ce qu'il dit, là ? Je ne peux pas le croire.

I am thinking of changing jobs.
J'envisage de changer d'emploi.

FICHE 17 Prétérit et *PRESENT PERFECT*

1. Le prétérit

Le prétérit simple

• Il exprime un **passé révolu**, coupé du présent. Le contexte passé peut être précisé explicitement ou implicitement par une date ou un lieu :

We received the consignment yesterday (date).
Nous avons reçu cet envoi hier.

He phoned me two days ago (ago s'emploie avec une expression de durée, mais exprime une date*).*
Il m'a téléphoné il y a deux jours.

I bought this watch (when I was) in Geneva (lieu).
J'ai acheté cette montre (quand j'étais) à Genève.

When did you last go to Chicago?
Quand êtes-vous allé à Chicago pour la dernière fois ?

He worked in that company for years.
Il a travaillé dans cette société pendant des années.

• Le prétérit simple s'emploie aussi lorsqu'il s'agit d'une action répétée au passé :

He commuted to London every day.
Il se rendait à son travail à Londres tous les jours.

Le prétérit progressif

Il s'emploie pour exprimer une action qui a duré au passé, souvent interrompue par un événement soudain mis au prétérit simple :

She was telephoning on her mobile when her fixed line phone rang.
Elle téléphonait sur son portable quand son téléphone fixe a sonné.

2. Le PRESENT PERFECT

Il s'emploie pour un événement ou une action ayant eu lieu au passé et continuant au présent, directement ou indirectement. Ce n'est pas vraiment un temps, et il correspond parfois à un présent en français.

Le *present perfect* simple

On s'intéresse au résultat de l'action.

I have lost key data on my computer.
J'ai perdu des données essentielles sur mon ordinateur.

It has happened many times before.
C'est arrivé de nombreuses fois auparavant.

I have finally recovered them.
Je les ai enfin récupérées.

I have tried to understand why again and again – but I still can't.
J'ai essayé de comprendre pourquoi de nombreuses fois, mais je n'y arrive toujours pas.

He has not answered our e-mail so far / yet.
Il n'a pas répondu à notre mél jusqu'ici / encore.

We have just received an answer.
Nous venons de recevoir une réponse.

You have already met them.
Vous les avez déjà rencontrés.

We have had business dealings with them for years / since 2000 perhaps.
Nous sommes en affaires avec eux depuis des années / peut-être depuis 2000.

We have known them for years and years.
Cela fait des années et des années qu'on les connaît.

How often have you talked to them?
Combien de fois leur avez-vous parlé ?

Have they ever replied?
Ont-ils jamais répondu ?

REMARQUE

En américain, *EVER* et *NEVER* s'emploient toujours avec le prétérit :

They never replied.
Ils n'ont jamais répondu.

Le *present perfect* progressif

On insiste sur cette action commencée au passé et se prolongeant au présent, et sur sa durée :

Our company has been trading with China for 9 years (durée), *since 2000* (date).
Cela fait 9 ans que notre société a des relations commerciales avec la Chine, depuis 2000.

We have been negotiating for over a week now.
Cela fait plus d'une semaine que nous négocions.

How long have they been talking?
Cela fait combien de temps qu'ils discutent?

That customer has been complaining again!
Ce client s'est encore plaint !

FICHE 18 Pronoms relatifs et traductions de « dont »

1. Les pronoms relatifs

Ce sont : *who(m), which, that, ∅, whose, when, where, what*. On les choisit en fonction de deux facteurs.

▸ Le choix du pronom relatif dépend de la **nature de l'antécédent** :

– être humain ou personnifié (*workers, Mr Jones, secretary, my cat*) : *who, that, ∅, whose* ;

– non humain (*factory, job, advice, animals*) : *which, that, ∅, whose.*

▸ Le choix du pronom relatif dépend aussi de la **fonction grammaticale du pronom relatif** : sujet, complément d'objet ou complément de nom.

- Pronom relatif **sujet de la relative**

A man who / that works *too much can become ill.*
Un homme qui travaille trop peut tomber malade.

A job which / that pays well *would be my dream.*
Un travail qui paie bien serait mon rêve.

- Pronom relatif **complément d'objet du verbe de la relative**

The visitor *who(m) / that / ∅ you saw is Indian.*
Le visiteur que vous avez vu est indien.

The machine which / that / ∅ we bought works well.
La machine que nous avons achetée fonctionne bien.

REMARQUES

1. Le pronom relatif ∅ n'est possible que lorsqu'il est complément d'objet de la relative, surtout dans la langue parlée.

2. THAT et ∅ ne s'emploient guère dans une langue soignée (langue des affaires par exemple).

• Le pronom relatif qui permet **d'introduire un complément de nom** est *WHOSE*. Il n'est jamais suivi d'un article.

A manager whose assistant speaks several languages is more efficient.
Un directeur dont l'assistant(e) parle plusieurs langues est plus efficace.

2. Les traductions de « dont »

Le pronom français DONT ne se traduit pas toujours par *WHOSE* car tous les « dont » n'ont pas la même valeur.

▸ Si DONT a une **valeur de possessif**, il se traduit par *WHOSE* :

Companies whose workers are on strike lose money.
Les entreprises dont les ouvriers sont en grève perdent de l'argent.

REMARQUE

OF WHICH peut être utilisé au lieu de *WHOSE*, en particulier lorsque l'antécédent n'est pas une personne. Construction lourde et peu fréquente.

A balance sheet the figures of which are wrong is useless.
Un bilan comptable dont les chiffres sont faux ne sert à rien.

▸ Quand on traduit un verbe suivi de la préposition « de », tel que « parler de », ou « avoir besoin de », DONT se traduit par *WHICH, WHO, THAT* ou bien ∅, selon la nature et la fonction de l'antécédent :

The companies which / that / Ø we talked about are losing money.
Les entreprises dont nous avons parlé perdent de l'argent.

▸ Si DONT a une **valeur partitive,** c'est-à-dire qu'il permet de désigner un sous-groupe de l'antécédent, alors il sera traduit par : expression de quantité (*two / a few / some / several / many / most*) + *OF WHICH / OF WHO(M) / OF WHOSE* = dont deux / quelques / certains / plusieurs / beaucoup / la plupart.

REMARQUES

1. L'ordre des mots est différent en français et en anglais.

2. Ces relatives partitives sont toujours placées entre virgules.

These companies, several of which export to Japan, will face difficulties.
Ces entreprises, dont plusieurs exportent au Japon, auront des difficultés.

Our employees, several of whom do not speak English at all, have applied for a language course.
Nos employés, dont plusieurs ne parlent pas du tout l'anglais, se sont inscrits à un stage de langue.

Our branches, most of whose managers are fluent in Chinese, are performing well.
Nos filiales, dont la plupart des directeurs parlent chinois couramment, ont de bons résultats.

▸ En anglais, l'**antécédent et son relatif** sont **inséparables**, contrairement au français.

The manager whose report you have read is away.
Le directeur dont vous avez lu le rapport est absent.

▸ **CE QUE, CE QUI, CE DONT** se traduisent différemment selon le rôle qu'ils jouent.

• ***WHAT*** sert à introduire ou à annoncer quelque chose :

What we need is a new photocopying machine.
Ce dont nous avons besoin est une nouvelle photocopieuse.

I didn't understand what he was saying.
Je n'ai pas compris ce qu'il disait.

• ***WHICH***, après une virgule, sert à reprendre quelque chose :

They sent us a few samples, which was a good idea.
Ils nous ont envoyé quelques échantillons, ce qui était une bonne idée.

▸ Le pronom relatif ***THAT*** ne peut jamais être séparé de son antécédent par une virgule, car il permet d'introduire une proposition relative « définissante » :

The customers that / who were angry wrote a letter of complaint.
Les clients (qui étaient) mécontents ont écrit une lettre de réclamation.

Our customers, who are mainly in China, place large orders.
Nos clients, qui sont principalement en Chine, passent de grosses commandes.
(Le renseignement apporté par *who are mainly in China* n'est pas essentiel pour définir *our customers*. Dans ce dernier cas, *THAT* est impossible.)

▸ Après *SOMETHING, EVERYTHING, ANYTHING, THE LAST, THE FIRST, THE ONLY*, les superlatifs et les quantificateurs, le pronom relatif est *THAT*. Il peut bien sûr être omis s'il est complément d'objet (voir plus haut).

The only banks that will survive the crisis are those which receive aid.
Les seules banques qui survivront à la crise sont celles qui reçoivent des aides.

It is by far the best proposal (that) we have had.
C'est de loin la meilleure offre que nous ayons eue.

All the parcels that arrived had red labels.
Tous les paquets qui sont arrivés avaient une étiquette rouge.

There is not much that can be done.
Il n'y a pas grand-chose à faire.

FICHE 19 Propositions infinitives

1. La proposition infinitive verbe + nom ou pronom complément + *TO* + infinitif

Elle s'emploie après des verbes qui expriment :

• une **volonté**, un **ordre**, un **désir**, une **interdiction**, une **intention** ou une **préférence** :

want	*prefer*	*intend*	
like	*force*	*mean*	
love	*compel*	*order*	
hate	*forbid*	*urge*	etc.

The manager wants his employees to work every other Saturday.
Le directeur veut que ses employés travaillent un samedi sur deux.

He would also like them to arrive very early in the morning.
Il voudrait aussi qu'ils arrivent très tôt le matin.

The chief accountant ordered the bank to refund the sum at once.
Le chef comptable a donné l'ordre à la banque de rembourser la somme tout de suite.

• une **invitation à agir** :

ask	*advise*	*require*	*remind*
beg	*warn*	*teach*	*help*
request	*tell*	*allow*	*dare*
persuade	*invite*	*enable*	*challenge*
etc.			

The disabled man asked the job centre to help him to find a job.
L'handicapé a demandé au pôle emploi de l'aider à trouver un emploi.

The company lawyer has advised the manager to revise their equal opportunities policy.
L'avocat de l'entreprise a conseillé au directeur de revoir leur politique d'égalité des chances.

• une **attente** :

wait for	*depend on*	*trust*	*call on*
expect	*rely on*	*count on*	etc.

He has always counted on his personal assistant to remind him to go to a meeting.
Il a toujours compté sur son assistant personnel pour lui rappeler d'aller à une réunion.

They expected the manager to show his appreciation of their work.
Ils s'attendaient à ce que le directeur leur montre comme il appréciait leur travail.

They waited for him to congratulate them, in vain!
Ils ont attendu qu'il les félicite, en vain !

2. La proposition infinitive *FOR* + nom / pronom + *TO* + infinitif

Elle s'emploie :

• lorsque la phrase exprime un **but** et que les **deux sujets sont différents** :

He organised the meeting on Tuesday for them all to be able to be present.
Il a organisé la réunion pour mardi afin qu'ils puissent tous être présents.

I have brought this report for you to read.
J'ai apporté ce rapport pour que vous le lisiez.

• **après certains adjectifs** ou **adverbes** précédés de *it is / was : important, necessary, easy, difficult, impossible, time, unusual*

It is necessary for you to have a plan of action if you want to win the competition.
Il faut que vous ayez un plan d'action si vous voulez gagner le concours.

It was impossible for me to agree with their marketing policy.
Il m'était impossible d'être d'accord avec leur politique marketing.

It is time for you to improve your ethical commitments.
Il est temps que vous amélioriez vos engagements éthiques.

FICHE 20 Quantificateurs : expression de la quantité

1. *SOME, ANY, NOT ANY, NO*

▸ ***SOME*** s'emploie dans des phrases affirmatives ou interrogatives pour exprimer une quantité peu précise :

We have had some staff problems recently.
Nous avons eu quelques problèmes de personnel récemment.

They have bought some wine.
Ils ont acheté du vin.

Would you like some papers to read?
Voulez-vous des journaux à lire ? (C'est une proposition.)

▸ **ANY** s'emploie dans des phrases négatives ou interrogatives :

We have not had any news of the construction plan.
Nous n'avons pas reçu de nouvelles du projet de construction.

Have you got any books to read?
Avez-vous des livres à lire ? (C'est une question.)

I have not brought any books.
Je n'ai pas apporté de livres.

No shops are open on Sundays here.
Il n'y a aucune boutique ouverte le dimanche ici. (*No* s'emploie surtout avec un sujet.)

REMARQUES

1. *ANY* par lui-même n'est pas négatif mais a le sens de « quelque / n'importe » :

Any date will do.
N'importe quelle date conviendra.

2. Les composés *SOMETHING, SOMEBODY, NOTHING, NOBODY, ANYTHING* et *ANYBODY* s'emploient de la même façon.

2. *Much*

MUCH + nom indénombrable s'emploie surtout dans les phrases négatives ou interrogatives :

We have not got much mail to do.
Nous n'avons pas beaucoup de courrier à faire.

How much time have we got?
Combien de temps avons-nous ?

3. *Many*

MANY + nom au pluriel peut s'employer dans tout type de phrase :

We have had / have not had many opportunities to travel – have you had many?
Nous avons eu / n'avons pas eu beaucoup d'occasions de voyager – et vous ?

How many times has he called us?
Combien de fois nous a-t-il appelés ?

4. *A lot of / lots of / plenty of*

Ils peuvent s'utiliser avec un nom indénombrable ou un nom au pluriel :

The manager has a lot / lots of / plenty of time / help / employees to prepare the exhibition.
Le directeur a beaucoup de temps / d'aide / d'employés pour préparer l'exposition.

5. *Too much* + indénombrable, *too many* + pluriel, *too* + adjectif

Some people have too much work, others have too many days off, some firms are too big.
Certaines personnes ont trop de travail, d'autres ont trop de journées de congé, certaines entreprises sont trop grosses.

6. MOST + nom

Idée générale : ***MOST*** + **nom**.

Idée spécifique : ***MOST OF*** + ***THE*** + **nom** ou ***MOST OF*** + **pronom**

Most workers look forward to going on holiday.
La plupart des travailleurs attendent impatiemment le moment de partir en vacances.

Most of the employees in my firm also look forward to the weekend.
La plupart des employés dans mon entreprise attendent impatiemment le week-end aussi.

Most of them get along well with the management
La plupart d'entre eux s'entendent bien avec la direction.

7. (A) LITTLE + nom indénombrable

(Un) peu de

We have very little time for sporting activities.
Nous avons très peu de temps à consacrer aux activités sportives.

We have a little time to spend on golf.
Nous avons un peu de temps pour le golf.

8. (A) FEW + nom pluriel

Quelques / peu de

They have very few skilled technicians.
Ils ont très peu de techniciens qualifiés.

They have a few skilled workers.
Ils ont quelques ouvriers qualifiés.

REMARQUE

LITTLE et *FEW* sont souvent précédés de *VERY*.

9. Les nombres

Seuls les nombres cardinaux sont des quantificateurs.

Hundred, ***thousand***, ***million*** et ***billion*** ne prennent jamais de *-s* s'ils sont précédés d'un nombre et de *a few*, et ils sont suivis immédiatement du nom sur lequel ils portent (sauf pour les sommes d'argent). Attention aux différences entre ce qui se dit et ce qui s'écrit !

That project cost us over £3m ("three million pounds") / $2bn ("two billion dollars").
Ce projet nous a coûté plus de 3 millions de livres / 2 milliards de dollars.

He is in charge of <u>135 people</u> (one hundred and thirty-five).
Il a la responsabilité de 135 personnes.

REMARQUE

On dira ***hundreds / thousands / millions / billions of*** s'ils ne sont pas précédés d'un nombre car ils sont alors substantivés :

Renovating the building will probably cost <u>hundreds of thousands of</u> euros.
La renovation de ce bâtiment s'élèvera probablement à des centaines de milliers d'euros.

FICHE 21 Subordonnées de but

1. *To* + infinitif

C'est la construction la plus courante lorsque **le sujet des deux verbes est le même :**

The two firms merged <u>to make</u> economies of scale.
Les deux entreprises ont fusionné pour faire des économies d'échelle.

2. *In order to / so as to*

Forme d'insistance, ou plus formelle, ou que l'on trouve souvent en début de phrase :

<u>In order to get</u> compensation for their losses, they filed a lawsuit.
Afin d'obtenir un dédommagement pour leurs pertes, ils ont déposé une plainte.

3. *In order not to / so as not to*

Ces deux constructions sont plus courantes que la simple forme *NOT TO :*

The department has been completely reorganized <u>so as not to</u> become less competitive.
Le service a été totalement restructuré pour ne pas devenir moins performant.

4. *So that* + auxiliaire modal

SO THAT + auxiliaire modal (*CAN / WILL / MAY / SHOULD / WOULD / MIGHT*, etc.) est employé lorsque les deux sujets sont différents :

We have patented the new device <u>so that it will not</u> be copied.
Nous avons breveté le nouveau procédé afin qu'il ne soit pas copié.

REMARQUE

Lorsque les **deux sujets** sont **différents,** on peut aussi avoir un infinitif avec la construction suivante (voir Fiche 19) :

I e-mailed Jane the information right away <u>for her to</u> make a rapid decision.
J'ai ai envoyé les renseignements à Jane par mél immédiatement pour qu'elle prenne une décision rapide.

FICHE 22 Verbes d'état

1. Les verbes qui se rapportent surtout aux activités mentales, croyances, préférences, sentiments, ou à l'aspect

Ils ne s'emploient généralement pas à la forme progressive. Les plus courants :

think	*dislike*	*mean*	*remember*
admire	*doubt*	*owe*	*respect*
agree	*expect*	*own*	*seem*
appreciate	*feel*	*perceive*	*sound*
assume	*forget*	*possess*	*suppose*
be	*have*	*prefer*	*understand*
believe	*involve*	*realise*	*want*
consist	*know*	*recall*	*etc.*
contain	*like*	*recognise*	
disagree	*look*	*regret*	

I think he agrees with our new strategy.
Je pense qu'il est d'accord avec notre nouvelle stratégie.

He is telling me how to use this new machine, and I understand everything!
Il est en train de m'expliquer comment me servir de cette nouvelle machine, et je comprends tout !

I doubt that he means what he says.
Je doute qu'il pense vraiment ce qu'il dit.

The new project sounds appealing.
Le nouveau projet semble séduisant.

The manager looks very pleased with the results.
Le directeur semble / a l'air très content des résultats.

2. Les verbes de perception involontaire

Ils ne s'emploient généralement pas à la forme progressive, mais sont souvent précédés de *CAN / COULD*. Ce sont, par exemple : *see*, *hear*, *smell*, *taste*.

We can hear that dreadful noise in the whole building.
Nous entendons cet horrible bruit dans tout le bâtiment.

Can you see our new head office from here?
Apercevez-vous notre nouveau siège social d'ici ?

3. Les verbes d'état qui peuvent s'employer à la forme progressive

Employés à la forme progressive, ces verbes changent de sens. Ce sont surtout : *think, be, have, see, feel.*

I think we should reduce our expenses.
Je pense que nous devrions réduire nos frais.

We are thinking of extending our range of products.
Nous envisageons d'étendre notre gamme de produits.

He is very helpful.
Il est très gentil / serviable.

She is being very unpleasant.
En ce moment elle se comporte d'une manière très désagréable.

She has business contacts all over the world.
Elle a des relations d'affaires partout dans le monde.

She is having problems with her accountant.
En ce moment, elle a des problèmes avec son comptable.

I can see all your new equipment: well done!
Je vois tout votre nouveau matériel : bravo !

We are seeing the CEO tomorrow to discuss the project.
Nous voyons le P-DG demain pour discuter du projet.

He feels that a change in policy is a good thing.
À son avis, un changement de politique est une bonne chose.

He feels / is feeling depressed – business is bad.
Il se sent déprimé en ce moment – les affaires ne marchent pas.

FICHE 23 Verbes pronominaux : équivalents en anglais

1. L'utilisation de verbes simples

Il n'y a pas de verbes pronominaux en anglais. Là où la langue française utilise des verbes pronominaux, le plus souvent l'anglais utilise des verbes simples : *get up* (se lever), *hurry* (se dépêcher), *hide* (se cacher), *wonder* (se demander), *remember* (se rappeler), *apologize* (s'excuser), *meet* (se rencontrer), *agree* (se mettre d'accord), *sell well* (bien se vendre).

Je me demande quand la réunion va commencer.
I wonder when the meeting will begin.

Nous nous sommes mis à travailler à 8 h du matin.
We started to work at 8am.

2. L'utilisation du pronom réfléchi

Quand le sujet fait l'action sur ou pour lui-même, on peut utiliser un pronom réfléchi, qui est toujours accordé avec le sujet grammatical.

Le candidat s'est regardé dans le miroir avant l'entretien.
The applicant looked at himself in the mirror before the interview.

Mettez-vous à l'aise en attendant notre directeur.
Make yourselves comfortable while you are waiting for our manager.

Le client coréen ne parvenait pas à se faire comprendre.
The Korean customer could not make himself understood.

3. ONE ANOTHER / EACH OTHER

Quand il y a un sens réciproque (mutuel) on a recours à *ONE ANOTHER ou EACH OTHER.*

Ils travaillent en équipe en s'envoyant des méls.
They work in teams by sending e-mails to one another.

Nous nous téléphonons tous les lundi matins.
We call each other every Monday morning.

FICHE 24 *To wish* : expression du souhait et du regret

1. L'expression du souhait

Pour exprimer un souhait très vif mais quasiment irréalisable, *to wish* s'emploie suivi de ***WOULD, COULD :***

I wish the manager would stop asking me to do all those tedious tasks!
Je voudrais vraiment que le directeur cesse de me demander de faire toutes ces tâches ennuyeuses !

I wish I could find a well-paid, interesting job.
J'aimerais bien / Je rêve de pouvoir trouver un emploi bien rémunéré et intéressant.

2. L'expression du regret

Pour exprimer un sentiment de regret, *to wish* s'emploie suivi du **passé simple** ou du **plus-que-parfait :**

He wishes he had more time for sport, but his job occupies him 14 hours a day.
Il regrette de ne pas avoir plus de temps pour faire du sport, mais son travail l'occupe 14 heures par jour.

I wish I were really wealthy now: I could retire from business.
Je regrette de ne pas être vraiment riche maintenant: je pourrais me retirer des affaires.

I wish I had studied economics – it has become such an important subject.
Je regrette de ne pas avoir étudié l'économie – c'est devenu une matière si importante.

I wish you could have come to the party to celebrate my promotion.
J'aurais vraiment aimé que tu puisses venir à la soirée pour fêter ma promotion.

REMARQUE

Noter les expressions :

"I wish you a Happy Birthday", "I wish you a Merry Christmas and a Happy New Year."
Je vous souhaite un bon anniversaire, un joyeux Noël et une heureuse nouvelle année.

MÉTHODES

Describing charts[1] and tables[2]

Detailed information, and especially figures, can be presented visually in diagrams, charts, pie-charts[3], bar-charts[4], tables or graphs[5]. They help to compare elements in time or space. If you have to describe one of them, start by indicating the origin and date of the document, its subject, and the most important aspects. You may omit the details. What counts is highlighting the general trends or the contrasts. Pay attention to the verb tenses and the prepositions (which are sometimes omitted in the American press).

1 Beginnings

– This table was published in (name of source) dated ... / in the year 20— (the year is usually enough).
Ce tableau a été publié dans (nom de la source) en date du... / en 20—.
– This chart shows the situation of ... in...
Ce graphique montre la situation de ... en...
– According to the World Trade Organisation, ...
D'après l'Organisation mondiale du commerce...
– These findings come from a study by the European Union.
Ces conclusions proviennent d'une étude de l'Union européenne.

2 Time indications

– As from January 20— to / until December 20—...
À partir de janvier 20— jusqu'en / à décembre 20—...
– From / Starting from 20—...
Depuis 20— ...
– Between 20— and 20—, the situation improved noticeably.
Entre 20— et 20—, la situation s'est nettement améliorée.
– Since the beginning of last year, investors have had a hard time.
Depuis le début de l'année dernière, les investisseurs traversent une période difficile.
– This table highlights the most important figures year by year.
Ce tableau fait ressortir les principaux chiffres année par année.

1. Chart: *diagramme*. 2. Table: *tableau*. 3. Pie-chart: *camembert*. 4. Bar-chart: *histogramme*. 5. Graph: *graphique*.

– Mortgage lending has slumped by 30% year-on-year, to just £1.1 billion.
Les prêts immobiliers ont plongé de 30 % sur un an pour atteindre juste 1,1 milliard de livres.
– In February, industrial investment fell by about 20% from a year ago.
En février, les investissements industriels ont baissé de 20 % environ depuis l'an dernier.

3 Upward trends

– China's textile exports went up / grew / increased by 5.3% last year to CNY 6.5b.
Les exportations chinoises de textiles ont augmenté de 5,3 % l'an dernier, atteignant 6,5 milliards de yuans.
– Shares shot up /soared on the stock markets in 20—.
Les actions ont monté en flèche sur les marchés boursiers en 20—.
– American producers raised their prices significantly.
Les producteurs américains ont augmenté leurs prix de façon significative.
– Production rose by less / more than 3% in Brazil.
La production a augmenté de moins / plus de 3 % au Brésil.
– There was a big rise in commodity prices in 20—.
Il y a eu une forte augmentation /hausse des prix des matières premières en 20—.
– Taxes began to spiral upwards in the USA last month.
Les impôts se sont mis à monter en flèche au États-Unis le mois dernier.
– They peaked / reached a peak in...
Ils ont atteint un sommet / pic en...
– Last year, trade volumes grew by a sluggish 0.5%.
L'an dernier, le volume des échanges commerciaux a connu une croissance limitée à 0,5 %.
– Consumer-price inflation in the euro area edged up from 1.3% to 1.5% in June.
Le taux d'inflation des prix à la consommation dans la zone euro est passé de 1,3 % à 1,5 % en juin.

4 Downward trends

– Imports slowly dropped / fell / went down / decreased slightly by 2.4% afterwards.
Les importations ont lentement diminué / connu une légère baisse de 2,4 % ensuite.
– Oil prices suddenly spiralled downwards / plummeted / collapsed at the end of the year.
Les prix du pétrole ont soudain dégringolé / se sont effondrés / écroulés à la fin de l'année dernière.
– They reached their lowest level / point in...
Ils ont atteint leur plus bas niveau / leur point bas en / au...
– There has been a 4% drop / fall / decrease of 4% in oil consumption.
Il y a eu une baisse de 4 % de la consommation de pétrole.
– It is the biggest one-year decline in trade since the Second World War.
C'est la plus forte baisse d'échanges commerciaux sur une année depuis la Seconde Guerre mondiale.
– Australia's GDP shrank at an annualised rate of 1.2% in the last quarter.
Le PIB de l'Australie est tombé à un taux annualisé de 1,2 % au cours du dernier trimestre.

5 Stable trends

– House prices have remained stable / unchanged /steady since...
Les prix de l'immobilier sont restés stables / inchangés depuis...
– The recession has bottomed out...
La récession est à son plus bas niveau...

– There has been no change in this trend since...
La tendance n'a pas changé depuis...
– Germany maintained its position as the world's number-one exporter in the first quarter.
L'Allemagne a préservé sa position de premier exportateur mondial / de numéro un mondial pour les exportations au premier trimestre.

6 Comparisons

– The situation in the USA is better / worse than in the EU.
La situation aux États-Unis est meilleure / pire que dans l'Union européenne.
– There are more / fewer company failures now than in...
On observe davantage / moins de fermetures d'entreprises aujourd'hui qu'en...
– Dublin's population, compared to / with London's, is much smaller.
La population de Dublin, comparée / par rapport à celle de Londres, est bien plus petite.
– Unlike Indians, few Chinese people speak English.
À la différence des Indiens, peu de Chinois parlent anglais.
– Things are much the same as they were last year.
La situation est très semblable à ce qu'elle était l'an dernier.
– This product is twice /three times as expensive in ... as in...
Cet produit coûte deux fois plus / trois fois plus cher en ... qu'en...
– Office rents in New York are now half as high as in Tokyo.
Les loyers de bureaux à New York sont maintenant 50 % moins chers qu'à Tokyo.

7 Forecasts

– If present trends continue, the top three exporters may / will soon account for 25% of world trade.
Si les tendances actuelles continuent, les trois premiers exportateurs représenteront (peut-être) bientôt 25 % des échanges mondiaux.
– Banks are not likely to change their policy for a long time yet.
Les banques ne sont pas susceptibles de changer de politique avant longtemps.
– Some drastic changes are bound to occur soon.
Des changements drastiques ne manqueront pas de se produire bientôt.

8 Conclusion

Draw up a clear conclusion about the main aspects of the table or chart:
– To conclude / In conclusion / In short, this chart shows clearly that...
En conclusion/ En bref, ce graphique montre clairement que...

Layout of a professional letter

The presentation

The simplest form is the fully-blocked display with open punctuation. This means that all the lines, except the printed name of the company, start on the left, and only the body of the letter is punctuated.

1 The date

It is often put first, just above or below the reference ("Our ref/Your ref"). There must be no ambiguity concerning the date: the day in figures is followed by the month in letters, followed by the year.

▸ In American "9/4/20—" is "September 4, 20—".

▸ In British English, it is "9 April 20—."

To avoid confusion, it is better to write "September 4" (pronounced "September the fourth"), or "2 April 20—" (pronounced "the second of April").

2 The name of the addressee

The name is left out if you do not know it because it is the first time you have been writing to the firm. If you know it, use it with the title (unchanged) followed by the person's function or department:

▸ "Mr Pinkerton, General Manager"

▸ "Miss Farrow, Accounting Department"

When you do not know the marital status of the woman, write "Ms" (which is pronounced "Miz", and used more and more often).

3 The address and post code (zip code in the USA)

– In the United Kingdom the post code is placed after the name of the town, sometimes after the name of the country.

▸ "Marlborough SN81JA, Wiltshire, Great Britain"

– In the USA, the zip code is placed after the name of the state, which is abbreviated.

▸ "CA 94708-1544, USA"

4 The opening salutation

It will depend upon your level of contact:
– if you do not use the name of the addressee, the salutation is "Dear Sir / Madam";
– if you are answering a letter, you should use the name of the person who signed:

▸ "Dear Mr Hayley / Ms Fretter";

– if the relationship continues, you will soon receive a letter signed Joseph or Christine; then you do the same and address him or her as "Dear Joseph/ Christine". Most Anglophones will use your first name quickly, both in letters and on the phone.

5 The subject

If there is a subject heading, it can be placed straight after the salutation:

- "Request for information"
- "Application for a job offer"

6 The content

a Introduction

It is important to refer to the date whenever possible:

- "Thank you for your letter dated 7 August 20—."
- "We have received your letter / order / complaint dated June 3, 20—."
- "Following this morning's telephone conversation, we are pleased to confirm..."
- "I am interested in your job offer published in *The International Herald Tribune* of May 30."

b Facts

Put the relevant facts into a logical order, starting with the main one:

- "We wish to order 100 boxes of envelopes..."
- "Your product is exactly what we need, so we would like to meet you to discuss details..."
- "Your order will be dispatched today, so you should receive the articles in time...""

c Conclusion

You should end on a pleasant, polite note:

- "Thank you very much for your help / your offer."
- "May we apologize once more for this incident."
- "We look forward to your reply/ hearing from you / seeing you / working with you."

7 The closing salutation

It is always short and simple:

- "Yours faithfully"/ "Faithfully yours" (the most formal one, or if you do not use the person's name)
- "Yours sincerely" (the most common one)
- "Yours"/ "Best wishes" (if you know the person well)

8 The signature

Handwritten, it is followed by the full name typed like this: "Mary Smith / SMITH". A woman may indicate her marital status or gender: "Leslie Warren (Mrs)".

9 Enclosure

If there is one, it will be specified: "Enc/encs", followed by "Copy to" if necessary.

Remark

E-mails are often used nowadays to replace formal letters: their content, tone and presentation will be less formal, and will depend upon the context and, above all, on the people concerned.

LEWIS & JONES

INTERNATIONAL BUSINESS CONSULTANCY

Beecham Avenue
LONDON NE2 4ND
GREAT BRITAIN
Tel 0208 522 8358 – email bus@London.int

Our ref/your ref
10 June 20—

Mr Sebastien BAUTRAIN
Directeur des Ressources humaines
RELAIS MONDIAL
150 boulevard des Peupliers
75009 Paris
FRANCE

Dear Mr Bautrain

BUSINESS COURSE

Thank you for your letter dated 4 June 20— and for the interest shown in our intensive training course in English for Business and Communication. The next course will be held in Cardiff Castle 12-17 July.

As you will see from the brochure enclosed, the price includes classes and lectures, full board and lodging, plus evening entertainment on July 14, in honour of our French guests and such an important historical event.

You will also find enclosed the application form to be filled in and sent back to us with the payment by July 1.

Should you need any other information, please contact Emma Williams, ext 249, our public relations manager, who will be delighted to help you.

We look forward to hearing from you and to welcoming the course participants.

Yours sincerely

Edward Hayley
Manager

Encs

ACTION INTERNATIONALE
12 rue du Moulin Bleu
24000 Périgueux
FRANCE

18 March 20—

Mr Thomas TRIMMAN
QUALITY EQUIPMENT
10 Hewell Street
Bedford BE8 OPD
GREAT BRITAIN

Dear Mr Trimman

Request for information

Thank you for your letter dated 15 March 20— in which you ask for information about the French market. We are willing to offer you our services as sole agents for your products which, in our opinion, would sell very well in France. More and more people are joining walking clubs, walking further and further, and in need therefore of the right equipment. Your high-quality products would attract a wide range of walkers who would be happy to improve the conditions in which they pursue their leisure activities.

We suggest meeting as soon as possible to discuss the matter further. Over the next few weeks, our chief representative in Britain, Charles Leroger will be visiting several firms with whom we do business. He would be delighted to call on you, at your convenience, to give you all the information you need about the market and about our company, methods, terms and prices, etc.

You will find enclosed a document that will give you a good idea of the international activities of our company. We look forward to hearing from you and to doing business with you.

Yours sincerely

Pauline DUVAL
Marketing Manager

Enc: Brochure

▸ **Letter with invoice** facture

Institut Framotard
18 avenue Mariaud
69006 Lyon FRANCE

25 April 20__

Ms Lucy Llewellyn
Sales Manager
Rodell & Lewis
20 Somerset Road
Bristol BS9 4 UM
ANGLETERRE

Dear Ms Llewellyn

Order ref.55/LV

Thank you for your letter dated 17 April 20__. We enclose our pro forma invoice amounting to €15,450 for your order ref. 55/LV, together with the bill of exchange, no. 559. We will instruct our agent to forward your order as soon as we receive confirmation of credit transfer from your bank.

The invoice includes extra charge for air freight and special packing in insulated boxes. It also shows the 10% trade discount we have granted you as this is a trial order.

We hope these arrangements are satisfactory, and we look forward to doing further business with you.

Yours sincerely

Fabien Lebreton
Chief Accountant

Enc

▸ **Letter of apology**

STATIONERY SUPPLIES LTD
5 Whiteladies Road
Reading
ENGLAND RG3 5WW

12 February 20__

Mr Jean Thomas
Manager
TOUS CADEAUX
9 rue Sylvain Delaterre
14000 CAEN
FRANCE

Dear Mr Thomas

We thank you once again for your order n° 2003 which we had agreed to deliver by 1 April. Unfortunately, we have been informed that the manufacturer is unable to provide a certain number of the products in your order. He is confronted by a shortage of raw materials, particularly paper where there has been a cutback in supplies of imported pulp.

Thus, we will be unable to deliver the gift wrapping, gift boxes and paper bags in time, as we had promised, for the Stationery Fair. They will not be available until June.

We apologize profusely for this delay, and would ask you to let us know if you wish to maintain or cancel your order.

We look forward to hearing from you and to continuing our business activities.

Yours sincerely

Michael Ladley
Sales Manager

Reading and using a document or list of documents efficiently

1 Look at all the document(s) in a synthetic way to get a general idea:

- What *type* of document(s) is it / are they?
- *What* is it / what are they *about*?
- *Where* does it/ do they come from, and *when* was it / were they published?
- Is it / Are they British, American, or other?
- What do *you* already know about the theme?

2 Read the document(s) quickly once:

1. What do the title(s) and especially subtitle(s)[1] say? The subtitles often tell you more about the text, whereas the title may just be a catch phrase[2] or pun[3] which is difficult to understand.

▸ The title of the text page 186 "Thrift shops on Easy Street" will tell you less than the subtitle: "Winmark's used-goods empire is outperforming other retailers".

2. Try to get a general overview[4] by looking at the key (important) words, or by reading just the beginning and end of each paragraph, especially if it is a long document. It is important to go right to the end quickly, which often clarifies the whole text.

3. Avoid using the dictionary at first, even if there are words or passages which you do not understand. The context should help you, and in fact a few difficult words may not prevent you from understanding the whole document.

4. Avoid going back over words unconsciously and unnecessarily. Skip through[5] the long passages, especially if you are pressed for time.

3 Reread the document(s) for the detailed information given

You do so especially if you have to answer questions or learn about specific facts, or sum up the document(s).

1. Read the text again more slowly: you will find it easier to understand the second time, and you can focus[6] on what is important, or on finding the answers to the questions asked.

2. Read intelligently, which means trying to understand the *structure* of the text, and the organization of ideas, with the facts or examples, analysis of advantages and drawbacks, causes, consequences, and possibly solutions.
Underline[7] or highlight the key words if you can write on the text.

3. If you have to write a synthetic note about several documents answering a question about them, try to find what they have in common and where they differ in order to structure your note clearly.

4. Look up some (but not all) of the difficult words in the dictionary (if you can use one) especially those that seem important. Learn to understand words without using the dictionary if possible, with the help of the context, using logic and deduction.

You can analyse some words or expressions such as:
– compounds:

▸ petroleum exporting countries → the countries which export petroleum.

The last element is always the most important one, and often the first in French.

– verb particle constructions: there are many different types, and they are very common in English. It is almost impossible to generalize the meaning and construction of these expressions or words. You can try to guess or visualize their meanings.

▸ to take over a company → *racheter / reprendre une société.*

▸ to take over from somebody → *prendre la relève de quelqu'un, succéder à quelqu'un.*

▸ To overtake a competitor → *devancer un concurrent.*

– false friends: they can sometimes help you understand the text roughly[8], but cannot be translated literally.

▸ actually → *en fait.*

▸ to charge → *faire payer ou accuser.*

▸ delay → *retard.*

▸ Actually, the price they have charged us is outrageous, especially in view of the delay in the delivery.

▸ *En fait, le prix qu'ils nous font payer est exorbitant, surtout étant donné le retard dans la livraison.*

Make a list of them.

5. Try to remember what you have learnt (facts and vocabulary) by noting some key vocabulary and facts, and *revising* them thereafter[9].
Figures will be easier to remember if simplified:

▸ "395" can become "almost / nearly 400" or "about 400".

▸ "1,022" may be recalled as "over 1,000" or "about 1,000" – unless you have to quote[10] an exact amount, of course.

---

1. Subtitle: *sous-titre.* **2.** Catch phrase: *accroche.* **3.** Pun: *jeu de mots.* **4.** Overview: *vue d'ensemble.* **5.** To skip through: *négliger.* **6.** To focus: *se focaliser.* **7.** To underline: *souligner.* **8.** Roughly: *en gros.* **9.** Thereafter: *par la suite.* **10.** To quote: *citer.*

Writing a report or a note, or a memo

You should follow Winston Churchill's advice given in a memo sent to all Government departments in August 1940:
"To do our work, we all have to read a mass of papers. Nearly all of them are far too long. This wastes time, while energy has to be spent looking for essential points. I ask my colleagues and their staff to see to it that their reports are shorter. The saving of time will be great, while the discipline of setting out the real points concisely will prove an aid to clearer thinking".

Or to put it more simply: "KISS" = Keep It Short and Simple!

1 The title page/lines

It will include:
- the title of the report/ memo/note which announces the central theme;
- the names of the sender and receiver(s);
- the date and reference number.

2 The contents

They must be divided into paragraphs, except when they are short (100 words or less). If it is a long report, it contains the sections listed in sequence with page references and titles. Remember: one paragraph per idea, or idea per paragraph.

3 The summary

It is a statement of the contents of the report including the recommendations if there are any. It is very important because it may be the only part of the report that the busy businessman has time to read! Leave out details and examples.

4 The introduction

It will indicate the purpose or reason for the report, and outline the method of enquiry with sources.

5 The findings

They will indicate the data you have found, and what you have found out from this data. The findings will also be the basis of the conclusions and recommendations.

6 The conclusion

It will examine the evidence[1] in the main body of the report in order to come to conclusions, and recommendations if there are any.

1. Evidence: *faits*.

Réaliser une synthèse de documents

Un corpus est un ensemble de documents abordant une même thématique ou une même problématique sous des angles différents ou similaires. Il est suivi d'une question qui vous guidera dans la synthèse.

1 Repérer la thématique

Faites une lecture rapide de tous les documents pour repérer la thématique commune de l'ensemble du corpus.

2 Comprendre l'énoncé

Lisez l'énoncé avec attention pour garder à l'esprit ce qui est attendu au cours de la lecture détaillée de chaque document.
Les énoncés des exercices de synthèse sont souvent formulés avec des mots qui conceptualisent (notions abstraites) ce qui est parfois donné sous forme d'exemples concrets dans les documents : les problèmes, les solutions, les causes, les conséquences, les avantages, les inconvénients, les stratégies, les défis, etc. Ce sont ces mots ou notions qu'il faut repérer pour bien comprendre l'énoncé et souligner (ou surligner) de couleurs différentes.
Quand une question précise est posée, il faut veiller à y répondre non pas en vous appuyant sur des idées personnelles, mais uniquement à l'aide d'éléments tirés du corpus.

3 Comprendre un texte

Un texte inconnu peut être difficile à comprendre. Cherchez le sens global et les idées principales grâce au titre, au sous-titre le cas échéant (parfois plus éclairant), et aux connecteurs logiques.

▸ *so, but, however,* etc.

Ensuite, déduisez le sens des mots inconnus à l'aide du contexte, de votre bon sens et de vos connaissances.

4 Comprendre un document iconographique

Un document iconographique peut être ambigu ou polysémique (c'est-à-dire qu'il a plusieurs sens), c'est notamment le cas des dessins humoristiques. Il faut l'exploiter en fonction de la question posée dans l'énoncé, et trouver ses points communs avec le texte qu'il accompagne souvent.

5 Repérer les informations

Relisez en détail tous les documents en gardant l'énoncé à l'esprit et surlignez les éléments qui serviront à répondre à la ou aux question(s) donnée(s) dans l'énoncé. Utilisez des couleurs différentes pour repérer des éléments de catégories différentes.

6 Élaborer un plan

Organisez le plan de votre réponse en différentes parties, qui devraient correspondre aux différents points de vue apportés par les documents. Vérifiez que vous répondez à la question posée, ou que les éléments repérés correspondent bien à ce qui est demandé.

7 Rédiger un brouillon

Cette étape est indispensable : elle permet de bien structurer son plan, en faisant apparaître dans des paragraphes distincts les éléments de natures différentes. Chaque paragraphe a une autonomie de sens. Par exemple, si on vous demande de mettre en évidence les avantages et les inconvénients d'un phénomène, vous consacrerez un paragraphe aux avantages et un autre aux inconvénients.
Si votre synthèse est dans la même langue que le corpus (anglais), évitez de recopier le texte de départ, et ne reprenez surtout pas de phrases entières. Ne réutilisez que les termes essentiels, autant que possible.
Par ailleurs, le brouillon donne aussi la possibilité de corriger ses erreurs, de reformuler un premier jet un peu lourd, d'éviter des répétitions, d'ajuster le nombre de mots, etc. Il serait donc très risqué de ne pas en faire.

8 Recopier votre synthèse

Chaque fois qu'une idée provenant du corpus est utilisée, faites-la suivre de sa source entre parenthèses en fin de phrase pour ne pas gêner la lecture.

▸ La crise actuelle a suscité toute une série de critique vis-à-vis de la mondialisation (doc. 2 et 4).

Sautez une ligne entre les paragraphes pour la clarté de lecture, ou respectez un alinéa (un retrait) au début des paragraphes.

9 Relire votre travail

Il est important de prendre quelques minutes pour relire votre synthèse après l'avoir recopiée et ajuster les derniers détails. Indiquez le nombre de mots utilisés. Supprimez toute trace de comptage dans votre texte, qui gêne la lecture.

Conseils divers

– Une introduction n'est pas nécessaire, surtout pour une réponse courte (150 mots). Si vous en rédigez une, elle ne doit pas dépasser 8 % de l'ensemble (20 mots pour une synthèse de 250 mots).
– Ne puisez dans le corpus que les éléments concernant directement l'énoncé. N'utilisez pas d'éléments sans rapport avec la question posée sauf si on vous le demande.
– Une conclusion n'est pas obligatoire si vous considérez que l'ensemble des paragraphes couvre bien le champ à aborder. Si vous en faites une, elle doit être très brève (10 à 15 mots).
– Rendez une copie propre et lisible. Soignez votre style en proscrivant tournures familières et abréviations.

Traduction

Méthode générale

1 Comprendre

Lisez le texte à traduire entièrement, voire tout le texte d'où est tiré le passage à traduire, pour le comprendre globalement. Puis analysez chaque phrase pour repérer sa construction : sujet, verbe, complément(s), pronom(s), mot(s) de liaisons, subordonnée(s), etc.
Observez les phrases suivantes et leur traduction :

▸ *Most of the people found working in appalling conditions were underpaid.* (*found* est ici au passif, indiqué par le contexte)
→ La plupart des personnes qu'on a trouvées en train de travailler dans des conditions épouvantables étaient sous-payées.

▸ *Most of the people found the new product very easy to use.* (*found* est ici à la voix active, indiquée par le contexte)
→ La plupart des gens ont trouvé que le nouveau produit était très facile à utiliser.

2 Premier jet

Traduisez les phrases une à une sur un brouillon aéré afin de pouvoir y noter plusieurs solutions de traduction. Cherchez des synonymes, le mot juste, l'expression exacte dans la langue d'arrivée. Utilisez les techniques de traduction décrites ci-dessous.

3 Relecture critique

Reprenez votre brouillon et opérez des choix définitifs.
Tenez compte :
- du contexte ;
- du niveau de langue ;
- des règles de grammaire en vigueur dans la langue d'arrivée.

Prenez du recul pour ne pas écrire de phrases absurdes.

4 Rédaction finale

Mettez au propre en vérifiant l'orthographe et la ponctuation.
Relisez une dernière fois et complétez les éventuels blancs.

Remarque
Ne laissez jamais de blancs, toujours très pénalisés.

La version

On traduit un texte anglais en français.
Les difficultés sont de deux ordres : comprendre le texte anglais, puis rédiger en français correct et compréhensible, tout en restant fidèle au sens.

MÉTHODES

Face à des mots inconnus, ne restez pas bloqué(e) ; tenez compte du contexte, de la racine des mots, de l'analyse grammaticale de la phrase pour inférer le sens probable de ces mots.
Un texte anglais traduit en français est souvent plus long à l'arrivée car la langue française est analytique.

Le thème

On traduit un texte français en anglais.
Dans les examens, cet exercice est destiné à évaluer vos compétences en grammaire et vos connaissances lexicales. Il faut donc veiller à appliquer les règles apprises et à ne pas calquer des structures françaises, le plus souvent différentes.

▶ *When the new law is voted, restaurants will pay less VAT.*
→ Quand la nouvelle loi sera votée, les restaurants paieront moins de TVA.

Dans cet exemple, il faut appliquer la règle de grammaire sur le choix des temps dans les subordonnées de temps.

Un texte anglais est souvent plus court qu'un texte français car l'anglais est une langue synthétique qui ramasse le sens dans des formules courtes.

▶ *When questioned, debt-ridden consumers admitted they had several loans.* (9 mots)
→ Quand on les a questionnés, les consommateurs qui étaient criblés de dettes ont reconnu qu'ils avaient contracté plusieurs emprunts. (20 mots)

Les techniques

Le plus souvent, la traduction littérale ne suffit pas ; c'est pourquoi on a recours à des techniques éprouvées.

1 La transposition

On change de catégorie grammaticale.

▶ *The new manager speaks fluent Japanese.* (adjectif)
→ Le nouveau directeur parle couramment le japonais. (adverbe)

2 La modulation

On change de point de vue.

▶ *They were sent the invoice in time.* (passif)
→ On leur a envoyé la facture à temps. (actif)

3 L'équivalence

On recherche l'expression exacte.

▶ *I look forward to your reply.*
→ Dans l'attente de votre réponse. / Merci d'avance de votre réponse.

4 L'étoffement

On utilise plus de mots. Les prépositions anglaises font souvent l'objet d'un étoffement en français.

▸ *They spent money on training the workers.*
→ Ils ont dépensé de l'argent pour financer la formation des travailleurs.

5 L'effacement

On utilise moins de mots.

▸ Je suis allé à Bruxelles par avion.
→ *I flew to Brussels.*

Quelques difficultés classiques

1 Les faux amis

Ces mots faussement transparents sont nombreux. Voici les plus courants dans le lexique des affaires :

- *to achieve* : réaliser
- *actually* : en réalité
- *an agenda* : un programme / ordre du jour
- *an application* : une candidature
- *an appointment* : un rendez-vous
- *to attend* : assister à
- *a benefit* : un avantage, une allocation
- *to charge* : faire payer
- *a commodity* : une marchandise
- *a copy* : un exemplaire
- *currently* : actuellement
- *a delay* : un retard
- *to deliver* : livrer
- *to prevent* : empêcher
- *an issue* : une question, un problème
- *a location* : un emplacement / lieu
- *to rely on* : dépendre de
- *to survey* : examiner
- *to realize* : se rendre compte
- *to resign* : démissionner

2 Les relatives elliptiques

Le pronom relatif ∅ anglais n'est pas toujours facile à repérer pour un francophone (voir Fiche 18 de l'Aide-mémoire grammatical).

▸ *Ethical funds want the firms they invest in to put human rights in their corporate ethics.*
→ Les fonds éthiques veulent que les entreprises dans lesquelles ils investissent fassent figurer les droits de l'Homme dans leur éthique d'entreprise.

3 Les noms composés

Les noms composés anglais sont bâtis de droite à gauche. Pour les comprendre, on les déchiffre généralement en commençant par le nom le plus à droite (voir Fiche 11 de l'Aide-mémoire grammatical) :

▸ *a public awareness campaign* → une campagne de sensibilisation du public

4 La portée des mots

En anglais, un même mot peut déterminer plusieurs termes (séparés par *and* ou par une virgule).

▸ *The nation's air and rail links run mainly through London.*
→ Les liaisons aériennes et ferroviaires du pays passent essentiellement par Londres.

De même, les outils grammaticaux ne sont pas répétés en anglais quand ils portent sur plusieurs mots.

▸ *Auditors have to be given access to archives, e-mails and fiscal documents.*
→ Les contrôleurs doivent avoir accès aux archives, aux courriels et aux documents fiscaux.

Quelques règles

1 Les titres de civilité et noms propres

Les titres de civilité sont traduits pour les personnes réelles.

▸ *Mr and Mrs Smith, who live in London, are moving to Belgium.*
→ Monsieur et Madame (ou M. et Mme) Smith, qui vivent à Londres, vont déménager en Belgique.

Les noms propres ne sont pas traduits sauf s'il existe une traduction reconnue.

▸ *Doctor Stephen Jones works for the WHO (World Health Organization).*
→ Le docteur Stephen Jones travaille pour l'OMS (Organisation mondiale de la santé).
▸ *London is the capital of the United Kingdom.*
→ Londres est la capitale du Royaume-Uni.

2 Les devises ou monnaies

Elles ne sont pas traduites, mais sont écrites différemment.

▸ *It will cost a record $5m.* (Prononcer *five million dollars.*)
→ Cela va coûter la somme record de 5 millions de dollars.
▸ *It cost £50,000* (prononcer *fifty thousand pounds*), *not £50.50!* (prononcer *fifty pounds point fifty*).
→ Cela a coûté 50 000 livres, pas 50,50 livres !
▸ *This is worth €3bn.* (Prononcer *three billion euros.*)
→ Cela vaut trois milliards d'euros.

Remarque
Les chiffres ne s'écrivent pas de la même façon en français et en anglais. Attention aux différences de ponctuation.

3 Les emprunts à l'anglais en français

Ils sont à éviter lorsqu'il existe un équivalent.

▸ *a challenge* : un défi
▸ *fast food* : la restauration rapide
▸ *sponsoring* : le parrainage.

CPI
AUBIN IMPRIMEUR

Achevé d'imprimer en janvier 2013
N° de projet : 10194448 / N° d'impression 1212.0115
Dépôt légal février 2013 / Imprimé en France